OVER THE EDGE

OVER THE EDGE

The Growth
of Homelessness
in the 1980s

MARTHA R. BURT

RUSSELL SAGE FOUNDATION ■ NEW YORK

THE URBAN INSTITUTE PRESS ■ WASHINGTON, D.C.

The Russell Sage Foundation

The Russell Sage Foundation, one of the oldest of America's general purpose foundations, was established in 1907 by Mrs. Margaret Olivia Sage for "the improvement of social and living conditions in the United States." The Foundation seeks to fulfill this mandate by fostering the development and dissemination of knowledge about the political, social, and economic problems of America.

The Board of Trustees is responsible for oversight and the general policies of the Foundation, while administrative direction of the program and staff is vested in the President, assisted by the officers and staff. The President bears final responsibility for the decision to publish a manuscript as a Russell Sage Foundation book. In reaching a judgment on the competence, accuracy, and objectivity of each study, the President is advised by the staff and selected expert readers. The conclusions and interpretations in Russell Sage Foundation publications are those of the authors and not of the Foundation, its Trustees, or its staff. Publication by the Foundation, therefore, does not imply endorsement of the contents of the study.

Library of Congress Cataloging-in-Publication Data

HV
4505
.B88
1992

Burt, Martha R.
    Over the edge: the growth of homelessness in the 1980s / Martha
Burt.
        p.   cm.
    Includes bibliographical references and index.
    ISBN 0-87154-177-7
    1. Homelessness—United States.   2. United States—Social
conditions—1980-   I. Title.
    HV4505.B88   1992   91-18000
    362.5′0973—dc20

The paper used in this publication meets the minimum requirements of American National Standard for Information Sciences—Permanence of Paper for Printed Library Materials, ANSI 739.48-1984.

RUSSELL SAGE FOUNDATION
112 East 64th Street, New York, NY 10021

10 9 8 7 6 5 4 3 2 1

Contents

v

Preface

■ I began my research on homeless-related issues in 1984, long after the official end of the 1981–82 recession. I was asked to evaluate the new Emergency Food and Shelter Program (FEMA), which responded to the extraordinary increase in the numbers of people who found themselves homeless or hungry in those years. At that time, the recession and certain policies of the Reagan administration were seen as the main causes of this widespread hardship. The condition was seen as a temporary emergency, and the response reflected this assumption.

As the decade wore on, homelessness and hardship became repeated themes for many of the groups that I usually study. In several projects, I encountered evidence that the chronically mentally ill and other disabled adults were having a much harder time making ends meet in the 1980s than they had ever had before. Some faced the impossible dilemma of having to choose whether to spend their shrinking resources on housing, food, or medications; they could not afford all, and some ended up on the streets. Housing was, and remains, a major difficulty for teen parents, another population that I frequently study, and one contributing more than its share to the number of families who become homeless. Finally, physical and sexual violence in the present is clearly a precipitating cause of homelessness for many women, while childhood abuse and neglect figured prominently in the histories of many homeless people. At one point, it seemed as if any group I had ever studied was now on the streets.

I plunged deeply into homeless issues during the time that I directed the Urban Institute's 1987 national study of urban homeless shelter and soup kitchen users. During this time, debates raged about the correct numbers to use for the size of the homeless population and also about the true causes of homelessness. Our study and others provided clear evidence that many homeless people had certain problems or disadvantages—but were these the cause of their homelessness?

As I became more steeped in the research and reality of homelessness, I became increasingly dissatisfied with explanations that saw personal problems as the cause of homelessness. I knew that there had been no general population increase in the size of the many vulnerable groups who now made up the homeless, yet more of them were on the streets or in shelters. Clearly, conditions must have changed between the 1970s, when members of these vulnerable groups could maintain themselves in housing, and the 1980s, when they found it increasingly difficult or impossible to do so. But I distrusted many of the one-factor explanations invoking the societal causes that were popular with homeless advocates. I had seen homelessness in so many cities, produced under so many conditions, that I could only believe that many different configurations of circumstances could generate homelessness.

My year as a Scholar in Residence at the Russell Sage Foundation afforded me the opportunity to examine the causes of homelessness in the depth and complexity the subject deserves. My area of expertise is social services and vulnerable populations; in the normal course of my work I never have the time to develop a full understanding of housing, employment, and other conditions that impinge on the populations I study, or the specific federal policies that affect them. I know merely that these things matter. At Russell Sage I was able to devote the time necessary to think through the complex realities of housing issues and policies, unemployment, training and job structure issues and policies, mental health and chemical dependency policy and practice, and benefits policy. I appreciated that luxury at the time, and still appreciate it as a period of retreat and contemplation so necessary before one can begin to understand the intricate interactions of the many important potential causes of homelessness. Working on this book has been an intellectual treat. I hope the payoff is a more thorough understanding of the factors affecting homelessness, leading in turn to practical policies that address the important underlying causes rather than merely binding the obvious wounds.

Acknowledgments

■ Although only one person's name may appear as author on a book, such massive projects are rarely done alone. I could not have completed either the research on which this book is based or the final version of the book itself without the help, support, and encouragement of many friends and colleagues.

Small grants from the Rockefeller Foundation and the Federal National Mortgage Administration's Office of Housing Policy Research made it possible for me to hire research assistants to help with the massive task of assembling the data used in the analysis. An earlier version of portions of this book appeared as "Causes of the Growth of Homelessness During the 1980s," an article in *Housing Policy Debate* 2 (3) (1991), published by FannieMae. After returning to Washington and the Urban Institute, additional financial support from the Russell Sage Foundation and the Urban Institute made possible the final effort to turn the analysis into book form.

The Russell Sage Foundation deserves my heartfelt thanks for awarding me a Visiting Scholar position in its 1989–1990 "class." Many colleagues offered aid, comfort, and specific assistance as this project grew and developed. I thank Howard Chernick, Michael Katz, McKinley Blackburn, and Bob Plotnick, fellow Visiting Scholars at Russell Sage, for their willingness to listen to my speculations and strategies about how to do what I wanted to do, for their suggestions about specific data sources or techniques, and for their general enthusiasm and encouragement. To my other colleagues at Russell Sage and to Eric Wanner and the entire staff of the Foundation, I offer my appreciation for the warm and supportive atmosphere and sense of camaraderie and interest in each other's projects.

The task of constructing a data base as broad as the one used in this research was daunting because of the number of cities to be covered in addition to the range of factors for which variables had to be found. In this task I was greatly assisted by the generosity of many people. I specifically want to thank the following: Cushing Dolbeare of the Low Income Housing Information Service and the National Coalition for the Homeless, for providing several housing and income variables; Diane Canova of the National Association of State Alcohol and Drug Abuse Directors, for supplying data on state alcohol and drug expenditures and admissions from 1984 through 1988; Ted Lutterman of the National Association of State Mental Health Program Directors, for supplying data on state mental health program spending from 1981 through 1987; Fred Winkler of HUD's Office of Analysis and Evaluation, for making available CHAP progress reports on shelter bed counts and phone numbers for CHAP contacts in all the relevant cities; and Paul Jargowsky of the Center for Health and Human Resources Policy, John F. Kennedy School of Government, for supplying data on ghetto poverty and income means and standard deviations from which I could calculate a coefficient of variation as an index of inequality.

The first half of this book was conceived as a review of research done to date on changes during the 1980s in several structural factors that had been hypothesized to cause homelessness. The nature of this endeavor was such that no one person could be expected to be an expert on each of these factors. I was fortunate to have the help of many substantive experts in particular areas, each of whom reviewed a first draft of the chapter pertinent to his area of expertise. Chapters 3 through 6 benefited greatly from their assistance and insightfulness. Cushing Dolbeare of the Low Income Housing Information Service and the National Coalition for the Homeless, Michael Carliner of the National Association of Homebuilders, and Grace Milgram and Barbara Miles of the Congressional Research Service reviewed Chapter 3 on housing. McKinley Blackburn of the University of South Carolina, Robert Plotnick of the University of Washington, and Elaine Sorensen of the Urban Institute reviewed Chapter 4 on poverty, income, and employment. Robert Plotnick and Herbert Gans (of Columbia University) and Vee Burke and Joe Richardson of the Congressional Research Service reviewed Chapter 5 on benefit programs. Gary Bond of Indiana University, Barbara Dickey of Harvard University and the Massachusetts Mental Health Center, and Fred Osher of the National Institute of Mental Health reviewed Chapter 6 on mental health and chemical dependency policy and programs.

Peter Rossi reviewed the entire book in its draft form and a revised section of Chapter 9. His strong support as well as his trenchant comments and advice about the appropriate treatment of the analysis in the second half of the book contributed immeasurably to my thinking and to the final form of the analysis.

Research assistance was provided by Sangeetha Purushothaman, Christopher Vaz, Garth Green, and Laura Bonanomi. Sangeetha had the unenviable task of locating most of the data series that appear in the final data set, and transferring them from their original form onto my computer. Chris and Garth made thousands of phone calls to homeless coalitions, interagency councils, CHAP coordinators, shelters and General Assistance offices all over the country, to create the shelter bed counts and General Assistance program information incorporated into the analysis. Laura Bonanomi and Jennifer Parker assisted with these phone calls in the final push to complete the data set. Jennifer Parker of the Russell Sage Foundation and Mary Coombs of the Urban Institute suffered patiently, and cheerfully, through the typing and retyping of the many tables that appear throughout the book, as each went through several iterations. Nancy Jackson was my indefatigable copy editor.

Last, I want to thank my friends: my reading group in New York, Susan Gutwill, Juliet Ucelli, and Ann Liner, for providing stimulating talk and companionship on topics totally separate from homelessness; Barbara Donelan for proofreading post-editing changes; Connie Dunham and Freya Sonenstein for sympathetic listening, and Connie for suggesting graphs to display the impact of important variables. Most of all, I want to thank Betty-Carol Sellen, who helped a complete stranger find an affordable apartment in New York on two days' notice and has since become a fast friend, a fellow author who supplies appropriate sympathy and support for the work involved in producing a book *after* the final draft has been turned in, who proofread half the galleys, who owns more than 300 cookbooks (and uses them), and who loves jazz.

PART ONE

Changing Conditions

CHAPTER ONE

Introduction

■   During the recession of 1981–1982, emergency shelters and soup kitchens began reporting a greatly increased demand for their services, reflecting the effects of high unemployment, a rising cost of living, and a retrenchment in government programs that cushioned earlier economic downturns. Even when economic conditions improved after 1983, homelessness seemed to continue growing. The size of the homeless population was estimated at 250,000 to 350,000 for 1984 (Department of Housing and Urban Development, 1984) and 500,000 to 600,000 for 1987 (Burt and Cohen, 1989a). A comparison of these estimates yields an annual rate of increase of about 22 percent for these three years. As the decade progressed, the homeless population increasingly included new groups of people, such as mothers with children, and more of certain types of individuals, such as the severely mentally ill and drug abusers.

Homelessness is not an invention of the 1980s. During the Great Depression, a nationwide census conducted by the National Committee on Care of Transient and Homeless suggested that some 1.2 million persons were homeless in mid-January 1933—a figure regarded as conservative at the time despite considerable adjustment for unseen and uncounted individuals (Crouse, 1986). These 1.2 million homeless people represented 1 percent of the country's population at that time (122.8 million in 1930)—victims of the unemployment and social disruption of the Depression. As Crouse put it, "these people were not the vagrants and vagabonds, tramps and thieves that the laws had been written to guard against; these were the inheritors of optimistic America, its sons and daughters. . . . Many of these uprooted persons set out hopefully with the belief that in America all one needed to do when times got rough was to move on . . . but the dream was not working" (p. 48).

When advocates for the homeless estimate the size of today's homeless population at 2 to 3 million (about 1 percent of the U.S. population of 250 million), they are claiming that the current situation is as bad as it was at the depth of the Great Depression. Without minimizing the plight of today's homeless, it is clear that such estimates are exaggerated. Far more credible are the estimates derived from local and national studies with reasonably adequate methodologies (see, for example, Burt and Cohen, 1989a; City of Boston, 1983, 1986; General Accounting Office, 1988; Goplerud, 1987; Lee, 1989; Rossi et al., 1986; Vernez et al., 1988; Weigand, 1985). These studies suggest there are roughly 15 to 25 homeless persons for every 10,000 people living in the United States—a rate of about 0.2 percent.

Many explanations have been offered for the increase in homelessness during the 1980s. At first, blame fell on the 1981–1982 recession, unemployment, and certain Reagan administration policies. It was tempting to identify a single cause. To Robert Hayes, former director of the Coalition for the Homeless, that cause was "housing, housing, and housing." Others argued that plenty of housing was available but that homeless people had individual problems that kept them from maintaining housing (Butler, 1989). The most persistently discussed societal or structural explanations have been housing shortages and federal housing policy, changes in the structure of employment from manufacturing to services, reductions in the purchasing power of public benefits, and the policies of deinstitutionalization and severely restricted involuntary commitment of the mentally ill. The most persistently discussed personal problems have been mental illness, alcoholism, and drug abuse.

Research carried out during the 1980s shows clearly that homelessness cannot be attributed to a single factor, nor do its causes lie only with society or only within the individual. A few vignettes will illustrate the complexity of the problem. The following four "case histories" are fictitious composites, but they correspond in their basic outlines to the stories of many homeless people.

Joe is a white man in his forties, who does occasional day labor in the skid rows of several southern cities, among which he moves. He had many years of stable employment in a Midwestern factory job. During that time he married, had three children, supported his family, and drank a lot. He had no trouble maintaining his job until the factory closed. Other factories in his city also closed, leaving many out of work. His drinking increased, and after a futile search for work locally, he left town to look for work. He returned home every few months for the first year, but has not been home now for three years. He earns whatever money he spends, sleeps in cheap hotels when he can afford it and in shelters when he can't, eats at soup kitchens, and continues drinking.

Latoya is a woman in her late twenties, with three children. Her oldest child was left with relatives so he could attend school. Her two preschoolers live with her. She has never been married, and lived with her mother until she became pregnant with her third child. Thereafter she stayed with relatives or boyfriends, but has never had primary responsibility for paying her own rent, because she never had enough money to do so. She is a high school dropout and has never worked. She left her last boyfriend (the father of her third child) because he persistently abused her physically. She does not have enough money to pay rent for her own apartment although she receives welfare. She is psychologically depressed.

Sally is a middle-aged woman with a history of several mental hospitalizations. She is always neatly dressed and clean. Her family, in another part of the country, regularly sends her money. They would like her to live with them, but she doesn't want to be controlled or observed. Usually rational and civil, she bursts out with streams of obscenities and extremely angry pronouncements for five- to ten-minute periods two or three times a day. She has a "beat" of several blocks in a well-to-do urban neighborhood, where residents watch out for her to make sure she has what she needs. When she was released from her last hospital stay, the social worker helped her to enroll in Supplemental Security Income (SSI) and to locate an apartment. She was caught in the SSI accelerated review process that began in 1981, and her eligibility was disallowed. She lost her apartment, became extremely embittered, and left town. Since then she has refused contact with anyone who might help her get reinstated with SSI. She cannot be hospitalized against her will because she is not an immediate danger to herself or others.

Bart is in his early thirties. He is a veteran with some college training, who for several years worked steadily at a very visible, high-paying job. He maintained his own apartment in a fashionable part of town. He used cocaine and other drugs regularly, as he had done since his military service, but his life did not begin to come apart until he tried crack cocaine. He developed a heavy crack habit, became very unreliable at work, and was eventually fired. He wore out the patience and sympathy of his friends, and then of his family, since he stole from them whenever he could and failed to fulfill any commitments or obligations. All his money went for drugs. After losing his apartment, he spent about a year on the street, panhandling, selling used books and clothing, and associating with a group of similar homeless men who took drugs together. He finally checked himself into a Veterans Administration drug rehabilitation program after discussions with a street outreach worker. He is living at a shelter, working, and saving money for an apartment. He is drug free.

A MODEL OF HOMELESSNESS

Various societal factors that may have a bearing on homelessness have changed over the past decade. In addition to more general studies, research motivated by an interest in homelessness has documented these changes (e.g., Wright and Lam (1987) for housing; Rossi (1989) for housing and extreme poverty; and Lamb (1984) for deinstitutionalization). These efforts have concentrated on the national level, and have not made specific analytic connections to changes in the rate of homelessness.

Many other research efforts have examined the personal characteristics and circumstances of the homeless. Examples include Farr et al. (1986) for downtown Los Angeles; Rossi et al. (1986) and Sosin et al. (1988) for Chicago; Roth et al. (1985) for Ohio; and Vernez et al. (1988) for California. Burt and Cohen (1989a, 1989b) report personal characteristics from a nationwide random sample of urban homeless soup kitchen and shelter users, and Wright and Weber (1987) report data from a very large self-selected sample of users of special health clinics. These studies show that a disproportionate share of homeless people suffer from mental illness, alcohol or drug abuse, or a criminal record.

To attribute the problems of homelessness entirely to personal character- istics of individuals would be an oversimplification, as would a view that considered only societal explanations. In part rooted in personal vulnerabilities that increase the risk for particular individuals, homelessness is also a problem of housing availability and affordability. The causes of homelessness include structural factors, personal factors, and public policy. Most important, home- lessness is associated with poverty and the accompanying inability to afford housing; for millions of people, including many with disabilities, the combined effects of labor market opportunities and government programs are not enough to alleviate poverty.

Homelessness is a housing problem in two respects. First, some cities have clear-cut housing shortages, regardless of cost (Milgram and Bury, 1987). Second, even in cities with "enough" housing at what would seem a reasonable rent (say, no more than $300 a month), these units are beyond the means of very poor households. Many of the people who fall off the bottom of the economic ladder do so because their disabilities and deficits (physical, mental, addictive, educational, social) make them more vulnerable, and poorer. Their presence among the homeless represents a failure of social and mental health support programs, and the absence of any coordinated efforts that include government housing resources.

Figure 1-1 shows a schematic model of homelessness that incorporates the complex interactions of these many factors. The relationship between household income and housing cost is central. It is worth emphasizing that rising housing prices do not necessarily mean that housing has become less affordable— provided household resources increase proportionately. Similarly, a decline in housing costs will not improve affordability if household resources fall even faster. In general, as resources decrease while housing costs remain stable or increase, households must pay a larger proportion of their income for housing and must forego other essential purchases. This has happened in the 1980s (Leonard, Dolbeare, and Lazere, 1989). As the cost of housing in a given area begins to exceed a reasonable proportion of household income, one would expect to see homelessness increase.

Many factors influence both the level of household income and the availabil-

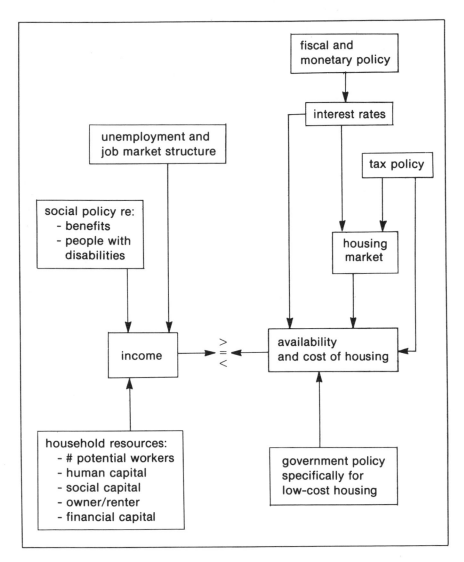

Figure 1-1 Factors Influencing Homelessness

ity and cost of housing, as Figure 1-1 shows. Household income is influenced by social policy as it pertains to public benefit programs and to the treatment of people with disabilities; by the structure of the job market in a local area, wages, and local unemployment; and by household resources. The resources of a particular household in turn depend on:

- The number of actual and potential workers in the household.
- The household's human capital (education, physical and mental health, work experience).
- The household's social capital (family resources, friendship resources, participation in supportive neighborhood networks).
- The household's physical capital (whether it owns or rents its dwelling).
- The household's financial capital (savings, pension rights, eligibility for and participation in public benefit programs).

As poverty increases, presumably single individuals find it harder to pay for housing on their own, and the relatives or friends with whom they might share housing are also stretched to the limit and less able to help out. Increasing poverty and less effective safety-net programs are likely to strain all low-income households, reduce the personal and financial resources available to avoid homelessness, and increase the probability of homelessness among the most vulnerable and poorest of the poor. When housing becomes less affordable, many households try to cope by sending another worker into the labor force or doubling up in housing so that more earners share the same rent (Levy, 1987; Mutchler and Krivo, 1989). Very poor people who live with others are significantly less likely to become homeless than are equally poor people who live alone (Sosin, Colson, and Grossman, 1988, p. 59). Virtually all people who eventually become homeless have tried one or more of these strategies along the way.

The housing side of the equation is as complex as the income side. Government policy specifically focused on low-cost housing influences the availability and cost of housing. But an equal if not greater influence is exerted by the factors in the upper right quadrant of Figure 1-1. Fiscal and monetary policy affect interest rates; interest rates and tax policy in turn influence the housing market (construction, rehabilitation, maintenance, abandonment); ultimately, interest rates, tax policy, and the housing market all affect housing cost and availability. If this view is correct, then policymakers concerned about homelessness should avoid focusing too narrowly on low-income housing subsidies; fiscal, monetary, and tax policies may have a far more pervasive influence on the housing market.

For the very poor, life is usually precarious. Any one of a variety of events can precipitate an episode of homelessness. Since local conditions may influence the likelihood of these events, the principal causes of homelessness may vary from one part of the country to another. A few cities, such as New York, Boston, or Los Angeles (where much of the early research on homelessness was done), may have an actual shortage of units. From their perspective, it may appear that the best remedy is the construction or rehabilitation of low-cost rental units. In many other cities, however, housing is available at reasonable cost, but because of unemployment or low wage rates, many households do not have enough income to afford even quite cheap housing. In these cities a more promising response would be to apply a range of remedies including housing subsidies, job development, retraining unemployed workers, and supported housing for the disabled. Still other cities have experienced tremendous increases in drug addiction, and their homeless population may include a large proportion of crack cocaine users. These communities may need to expand their drug treatment capacity, but they also need to develop programs that offer viable alternatives to drug activities for the most vulnerable subpopulations.

THE PLAN OF THE BOOK

This book is my attempt to advance public debate about the causes of homelessness in the 1980s. In Part One, Changing Conditions, I trace changes at the national level in a variety of factors that seem likely to affect homelessness. In effect, these chapters constitute a case study that relies on an implied association between changes in such factors as income or housing cost and changes in homelessness. Part Two, based on a newly assembled data set, then presents a multivariate analysis of the relationship of proposed causal factors to homelessness in the urban United States between 1981 and 1989.

Chapter 2 summarizes what is known about the characteristics of homeless people, who are predominantly single males (representing about 70 percent of homeless adults), followed by women alone and women with children. The discussion focuses on attributes that may make an individual particularly vulnerable to becoming homeless. In subsequent chapters the search for causes will focus on the factors that would most strongly affect those groups at highest risk for homelessness.

The remainder of Part One uses data available at the national level to develop an understanding of potential causal factors and their relationship to homelessness. Chapters 3 through 6 examine changes during the 1980s in four major factors hypothesized to affect homelessness: housing, housing policy, and housing subsidies (Chapter 3); household incomes, poverty, inequality, unemployment, and labor market structure (Chapter 4); public benefit programs (Chapter 5); and programs and policies for the chronically mentally ill and chemically dependent (Chapter 6).

Part Two, Impact on Homelessness, presents the results of analysis of a new data set designed to make possible, for the first time, analyses of factors affecting homelessness both cross-sectionally and longitudinally. Public data sources were tapped for measures of the hypothesized causal factors (independent variables); rates of homelessness were measured for a large sample of cities early and late in the decade, using a consistent methodology. Statistics pertinent to the four major causal factors discussed in Chapters 3 through 6 were assembled for two periods—1979 through 1981 and 1987 through 1989 (when available)—for each of the 182 U.S. cities with populations of 100,000 or more in 1986. In addition, I obtained counts of the number of shelter beds available to the homeless in these cities in 1981 and in 1989, along with the opening dates of shelters that were established after 1981. (It was then possible to estimate the number of shelter beds available in 1983 and 1986). Using local population figures, I converted these shelter bed counts into rates of homelessness. Regression techniques were then used to test the strength of the hypothetical causal relationships.

Chapter 7 explains the method by which I counted shelter beds and converted them into homelessness rates. It also traces the development of shelter resources throughout the urban United States during the 1980s. Chapter 8 discusses the variables representing the causal factors, and their sources. Chapter 9 describes the results of my regression analyses, demonstrating the independent and interactive effects of the hypothesized causal factors on 1989 homelessness rates and on the increase in rates that cities experienced between 1981 and 1989. Chapter 10 examines which variables allow the best predictions of homelessness rates, without concern for the causal connections between the predictor variables and homelessness. Chapter 11 summarizes the most important findings and discusses them in the context of appropriate policy responses.

CHAPTER TWO

Who Are the Homeless?

■   What kinds of people become homeless? With some understanding of the characteristics of the current homeless population, we will be better able to investigate the causes of the problem. That is, if most homeless people were poor renters before they became homeless, it will make sense to focus on rental rather than ownership housing as we examine changes in housing. If most homeless families are headed by women, our examination of income and benefits will focus on changes that affect this type of household most. If most homeless people are single low-skilled young men, we will look for housing, labor force, and public policy changes that hit this group especially hard.

It is very important to distinguish between the *attributes* of the homeless and the *causes* of homelessness. Some analysts maintain that homelessness is not a housing or income problem at all, but rather stems from the personal problems of individuals, such as mental illness or chemical dependency (Butler, 1989; Kondratas, 1989). Others (e.g., Rossi, 1989) attribute the overall level of homelessness in the country to larger societal factors, such as income levels in relation to housing prices; personal characteristics and problems then influence which individuals among the many extremely poor people actually become homeless.

I believe that personal characteristics can make a person more vulnerable to homelessness, but that we must look elsewhere for causes. Some members of society have always had less earning power than others; there have always been people with personal problems and disabilities (e.g., addiction, mental illness, physical disability). Until the 1980s, however, these people were less likely to become homeless. Do they now constitute a larger proportion of the population, so that individual attributes have made the population more vulnerable? This is not the explanation, as subsequent chapters will show. Yet vulnerable individuals are now less able to keep a roof over their heads. As we will see, the circumstances they face have changed: a person at risk of homelessness was more likely to be able to maintain housing in the 1970s than in the 1980s.

Most of this book explores these changing circumstances. To guide the search for relevant changes, this chapter describes some basic characteristics of homeless people.

THE URBAN INSTITUTE STUDY

Most of the information presented in this chapter comes from the first national study of the urban homeless, conducted in 1987 by the Urban Institute and directed by the author. (The study methodology and results have been described in Burt and Cohen, 1988, 1989a, 1989b, 1989c, 1990; and Cohen and Burt, 1990.) Since it seemed likely that the vast majority of the homeless would be found in cities (where shelter and other services are located), we drew a sample of homeless people who used soup kitchens or shelters in twenty cities that were statistically representative of all cities with more than 100,000 people in 1984.[1] After obtaining permission from facility operators to speak with clients, we interviewed a random sample of 1,704 homeless persons drawn from users of soup kitchens and shelters. Since homeless persons who did not use either soup kitchens or shelters were not included in our study, the results are biased toward service users.

Although many excellent single-city studies of homelessness are available, it has been difficult to generalize to the national level because of differences in sampling, methodology, and substantive focus. The Urban Institute study avoids this problem, because it was national in scope and used the same sampling and analysis methodology in all cities.

Within the literature on homelessness, there has been little agreement on the size and make-up of the homeless population, even on such basic characteristics as household composition. Particular controversy has surrounded the question of how many of the homeless are "families," and how many are the "new homeless." (The concept of the "new" homeless usually refers to families—especially two-parent families—and people with stable work histories and no personal problems whose homelessness can be attributed directly to economic circumstances such as layoffs, plant closings, and unemployment.) The Urban Institute data are well suited to resolve some of these questions,

---

[1]We first stratified the 178 cities with 100,000 or more 1984 population by region and city size. All cities over 1 million were automatically included (New York, Los Angeles, Philadelphia, Chicago, Detroit, Houston). The additional 14 cities in the sample were selected randomly from the remaining strata. Within each city we enumerated every soup kitchen and shelter that served the homeless, stratified them by type (soup kitchens, shelters with meals, shelters without meals) and size, and selected a target sample of 400 (the actual provider sample was 381).

since they are statistically representative of the entire urban service-using homeless population, including those who use soup kitchens but do not use shelters. When reasonable assumptions are made about the homeless in metropolitan areas outside of central cities and in nonmetropolitan areas, and about the presence of children in homeless households, extrapolation from our sample suggests that the total U.S. homeless population was between 500,000 and 600,000 on any given night in March 1987. Less than half of these people (229,000) were service users in cities over 100,000 (Burt and Cohen, 1989a, Chapter 2).[2]

Our unit of analysis is the homeless household, rather than the individual. The most effective policy approaches are likely to involve working with all the people in the household as a unit. Solving the problems of homeless children, for example, will usually involve assistance to their parent(s) rather than treating each homeless family member as an autonomous person. Thus all tables in this chapter present data for households.

Our respondents (homeless adults) were asked who accompanied them to the shelter or soup kitchen. A single person (man or woman) unaccompanied by either children or other adults was counted as a one-person household. An adult accompanied by either a child or a spouse, or both, counted as a family household. We also enumerated two other types of household: people accompanied by nonrelatives, but neither spouse nor children; and people accompanied by one or more relatives other than a spouse or child.

Table 2-1 indicates that single men made up 73 percent of the adult urban homeless service-using population in 1987. Single women represented 9 percent, and women who had children with them made up another 9 percent. Of these women accompanied by children, 88 percent were the single-parent heads of their families; the remainder were accompanied by a spouse as well as children. One percent of the homeless adults were men with children; 24 percent of them were also accompanied by a wife. Thus two-parent families—the

---

[2]Our sampling and weighting procedures make it very likely that our sample captures a large proportion of the total urban homeless population—perhaps as much as 75 to 85 percent. The usual count of the homeless covers a one-night period and classifies people as either in shelter or not. The biggest problem comes in estimating the size of the nonsheltered ("street") population. Our sample includes a large proportion (29 percent) of individuals who do not use shelters but do use soup kitchens. We count these people as service users, although in other studies they would be counted as part of the street population. We also made an adjustment for frequency of use that increases the weight of people who use services less than seven days a week, many of whom would be counted as "street" people in any one-day estimate. This adjustment produces a seven-day estimate that is about 75 percent larger than our one-day estimate. All analyses are based on data weighted for the seven-day estimate. We believe these methods capture a very large proportion of all urban homeless adults, and virtually all homeless families with children. The homeless in the suburbs and in rural areas are not represented, however.

Table 2-1 Demographic Characteristics (weighted percentages)

	Men			Women		
	Single Men (*N* = 1042)	Men with Children (*N* = 28)	Other Men (*N* = 93)	Single Women (*N* = 240)	Women with Children (*N* = 264)	Other Women (*N* = 33)
Percentage of Sample	73%	1%	7%	9%	9%	2%
Race						
Black	40	42	24	47	56	29
Hispanic	9	0	15	7	22	0
White, not Hispanic	48	57	56	40	17	66
Other	2	1	5	6	5	6
	100	100	100	100	100	100
Age						
Under 25	12	24	16	21	28	31
25–34	31	16	47	29	47	37
35–44	26	43	22	24	22	31
45–64	29	17	15	25	3	0
65+	3	0	0	1	0	0
	100	100	100	100	100	100
Mean Age	39	36	34	37	30	31

Marital Status						
Currently married	7	56	18	9	18	64
Divorced/separated	31	10	14	37	27	3
Widowed	5	10	6	5	5	0
Never married	57	23	62	49	50	33
	100	100	100	100	100	100
Homeless Household Composition[a]						
Two-parent family	0	24	0	0	12	0
One-parent family	0	76	0	0	88	0
Married, no children	0	0	16	0	0	64
With other relatives	0	0	30	0	0	10
With nonrelatives	0	0	54	0	0	26
Alone	100	0	0	100	0	0
	100	100	100	100	100	100
Education Completed						
Grades 0-7	10	1	14	4	9	0
8-11	40	7	35	33	48	22
High school graduate	31	65	26	42	32	64
Some post-high school	14	27	14	16	8	6
College graduate	5	1	12	4	1	5
Some post-college	1	0	0	0	2	3
	100	100	100	100	100	100

Note: *N* refers to unweighted sample size. All percentages are based on weighted data. Percentages may not sum to 100 because of rounding.

[a] Respondents were coded as "with other relatives" only if no spouse or child was present; "with nonrelatives" was coded only if no relatives were present.

epitome of the "new homeless," who are often used to make the case that the homeless in the 1980s are "just like you and me"—constituted only 1 percent of homeless households. The remainder of the homeless were men (7 percent) or women (1 percent) accompanied by another adult, but without children. Among these women, about two-thirds were with a husband; 10 percent were with other relatives; and a quarter were with nonrelatives. Among the remaining men, 54 percent were with nonrelatives, 16 percent were with a wife, and 30 percent were with other relatives.

Fully 82 percent of the homeless households we enumerated consisted of a single person; 10 percent included children, 2 percent were married couples without children, and another 6 percent contained two or more adults, but no spouses or children. The adults accompanied by children had an average of 2.2 children with them. If one considers the population of homeless individuals, 15 percent were children, 8 percent were their parents, and 2 percent were married couples without children. Thus 25 percent of homeless individuals were members of households that would commonly be considered "families" (either households with children or married couples without children); these family households made up only 12 percent of all homeless households.

Recent writing about the homeless has stressed that families represent a large and growing share of the homeless population. Certainly more families were homeless at the end of the decade than at the beginning, when there were virtually no shelter facilities for homeless families, and no apparent demand for them, other than battered women's shelters. Nevertheless, claims that families now represent one-third or one-half of the homeless are exaggerated. Because policies to alleviate family homelessness are likely to differ from those directed at reducing homelessness among singles, this exaggeration might lead to inappropriate resource distribution if it is not corrected.

Methodological differences probably explain a large part of the discrepancy between the Urban Institute's statistics on families and those of other studies (Burt and Cohen, 1989a). First, homeless families tend overwhelmingly to be in shelters; very few sleep on the streets. Thus studies that take their samples exclusively from shelters will overestimate the proportion of families in the total homeless population. Second, many reports obscure the difference between households and individuals; when 30 percent of the individuals in a sample are homeless parents and their children, reports tend to say that "30 percent of the homeless are families." (Even by this measure, our data suggest only 25 percent of homeless individuals belong to homeless family units.) Finally, homeless families are steadier users of shelters, and their continuous stays are longer. When they use shelters, they tend to stay for seven nights out of seven, whereas single individuals' use of shelters is more erratic. Any one-night count will overestimate the proportion of the population that are steadier users and users with longer stays.

Conceivably the Urban Institute estimates of families are low because they come only from urban settings. Suburban and rural localities might have more homeless families. Yet a study of the homeless in Fairfax County, a well-to-do Virginia suburb of Washington, D.C., also found that family groups comprised 11 percent of homeless households (Goplerud, 1987). Vernez et al. (1988) found that homeless families accounted for fewer than 10 percent of homeless households in urban/suburban Alameda County and in rural Yolo County, both in California.[3] But in Orange County, California, with characteristics similar to Fairfax County, families constituted as much as 40 percent of homeless households (Vernez et al., 1988). Finally, even if families do represent a larger proportion of homeless households in suburban and rural areas, the resulting bias in the Urban Institute estimates is likely to be offset in the national picture by the fact that members of the urban street population who use neither shelters nor soup kitchens, and who were also excluded from our sampling frame, are overwhelmingly single.

Tables 2-1 through 2-4 present basic descriptive data about the homeless adults in the Urban Institute study, distinguishing single men and women, men and women with children, and men and women with other adults (some of whom are with spouses, but without children). Clearly the subgroups among the homeless differ dramatically. The discussion focuses on the three largest groups—single men, single women, and women with children.

The typical homeless person is a single male, these findings suggest. On average, he has been homeless and jobless longer than people in any other subgroup. He has a lower likelihood of current earned income than anyone except women with children, and a very high probability of institutionalization for criminal offenses and for chemical dependency treatment. Yet half the members of this group have at least completed high school; one in six has been homeless for no more than three months, and one in five has never been in jail, prison, a mental hospital, or an inpatient chemical dependency treatment program.

Women with children are more likely than other homeless people to be members of minority groups, but minorities represent a larger proportion of the overall homeless population than of the general population, as many studies have shown. Single men are the group most likely to be forty-five or older, followed by single women. In each of the four largest subgroups (together comprising 97 percent of the homeless population), including women accompanied by children,

---

[3]In Ohio, Roth et al. (1985) reported that rural homeless were almost three times as likely as urban homeless to be married (18.5 percent vs. 6.7 percent). However, they gave no data on the proportion of households with children, including never-married households, which are probably more prominent in urban areas. It is therefore impossible to tell from the published data what proportion of Ohio's urban and rural homeless households were family households by the definition used in this chapter.

Table 2-2 Length of Homelessness and Joblessness (weighted percentages)

	Men				Women		
	Single Men (N = 1042)	Men with Children (N = 28)	Other Men (N = 93)	Single Women (N = 240)	Women with Children (N = 264)	Other Women (N = 33)
Length of Current Spell of Homelessness						
3 months or less	16%	17%	24%	35%	41%	43%
12 months or less	49	96	48	64	70	86
2 years or more	34	1	35	26	15	7
4 years or more	21	1	25	17	7	0
Mean number of months:	41	7	40	33	16	8
Percentage Currently Working at Steady Job[a]	5	39	4	4	10	9

Percentage Never Worked at Steady Job[a]	13	0	9	14	25	15
Length of Current Spell of Joblessness[b]						
3 months or less	9	6	7	12	11	12
12 months or less	39	58	30	46	35	50
2 years or more	47	40	47	43	51	21
4 years or more	33	2	38	31	37	21
Mean number of months	50	20	45	41	46	23

Note: *N* refers to unweighted sample size. All percentages are based on weighted data. Percentages may not sum to 100 due to rounding.
[a] A "steady job" was defined as three months or more with same employer.
[b] Includes only respondents who are not currently working but who have worked at a steady job at some time in the past. The variable measures the number of months since they last held a steady job.

Table 2-3 Income and Income Sources During 30 Days Before Interview (weighted percentages)

	Men			Women		
	Single Men (N = 1042)	Men with Children (N = 28)	Other Men (N = 93)	Single Women (N = 240)	Women with Children (N = 264)	Other Women (N = 33)
Percentage Getting Any Income From:[a]						
Working	22%	77%	49%	27%	15%	26%
AFDC	1	33	0	2	33	0
General Assistance	10	10	5	16	36	20
SSI	3	2	3	14	3	1
Family	7	8	15	13	4	9
Friends	7	8	8	11	5	5
Handouts	16	8	44	21	4	22
Mean Income Per Person	$144	$96	$64	$184	$121	$45
Percentage Getting Food Stamps Last Month	13	10	12	22	53	21
Average Food Stamp Benefit Per Person	$60	$59	$41	$62	$34	$60

Note: *N* refers to unweighted sample size. All percentages are based on weighted data. Percentages may not sum to 100 due to rounding.
[a] Percentages do not sum to 100; respondents named multiple sources, and table does not show several minor sources.

49 percent or more have never been married. The comparable figure for American adults is 22 percent. Women with children are less likely to have graduated from high school, followed by single men and other men. Overall, only 51 percent of the adult homeless population have completed high school, a proportion well below the American average of 81 percent, but similar to that of adults below the federal poverty line (57 percent). Thus homeless adults resemble other poor people more than they resemble the American average (see also Sosin et al., 1988).

It is often claimed that "the homeless are just like you and me." If this phrase is taken to mean a short period of homelessness, a stable and relatively recent work history including current work effort, a high school diploma, and an intact marriage, it fits only the two smallest groups among the homeless: men with children and other women. These groups together constitute only 3 percent of homeless households and can hardly be considered representative.

The homeless subgroups are all similar in some important respects. They all receive very little total cash each month, and relatively few receive benefits from public safety-net programs. They are thus very poor. Indeed, other studies find few differences between homeless people and other very poor people (Rossi, 1989; Sosin et al., 1988). These findings support the notion that homeless people are very poor before they become homeless, and that additional burdens or problems precipitate the homeless episode. Women with children are the most likely to receive public welfare benefits, both Aid to Families with Dependent Children and General Assistance. They are less likely ever to have held a steady job; 25 percent have never worked at the same job for three months or more, compared with a sample average of 14 percent. However, 10 percent of women with children are currently working, a larger proportion than for any other subgroup except men with children. Clearly the category of women with children encompasses very diverse behavior patterns.

The probability of past suicide attempts is much higher in all subgroups of homeless people than the national average of about 3 percent. Moreover, a larger proportion of homeless people are sufficiently demoralized or depressed, as measured by the CES-D depression scale developed by the Center for Epidemiological Studies at the National Institute for Mental Health, to warrant immediate clinical attention. In the National Health and Nutrition Examination Studies, the average CES-D score for adults is 9.4, and 16 percent of respondents score above the level signaling potential need for treatment. In our data CES-D scores for all groups are close to double the national average, and three to five times as many people are seriously depressed or demoralized. The CES-D measures a person's current emotional state and does not necessarily reflect mental illness. The high scores of most homeless people are undoubtedly due in part to the stresses and discouragements associated with living as a

Table 2-4 Personal Problems (weighted percentages)

	Men			Women		
	Single Men (N = 1042)	Men with Children (N = 28)	Other Men (N = 93)	Single Women (N = 240)	Women with Children (N = 264)	Other Women (N = 33)
Percentage of Total Sample	73%	1%	7%	9%	9%	2%
History of:						
Mental hospitalization	19	38	19	27	8	8
Inpatient chemical dependency treatment	37	48	39	19	7	18
Neither	52	44	59	61	89	75
Either	40	26	23	31	8	24
Both	9	30	17	8	3	1
History of Time Served in						
Jail for 5+ days	60	43	64	23	15	20
State or federal prison	29	4	31	2	2	1
Neither	35	57	32	77	85	80
Either	40	39	42	21	13	20
Both	25	4	26	2	2	1

Percentage with No Institutional History	26	40	26	52	80	71
Percentage with History in Three or All Four Types of Institutions[a]	20	31	23	5	3	1
Other Mental Illness Indicators						
Percentage ever attempted suicide	20	22	27	27	14	13
Percentage above CES-D clinical cutoff[b]	48	56	44	46	59	40
Mean CES-D score[b]	16.9	18.3	15.6	15.8	17.4	14.0

Note: *N* refers to unweighted sample size. All percentages are based on weighted data. Percentages may not sum to 100 because of rounding.

[a] Mental hospitalization, chemical dependency inpatient treatment, jail, prison.

[b] Scale developed by NIMH Center for Epidemiological Studies to measure depression. Short (six-item) version used in this study.

homeless person. They contradict to some degree the idea that many people voluntarily choose a "homeless lifestyle."

There are also similarities among the subgroups of women that distinguish them from all the male groups. Women are more likely to have been homeless for a very short time (less than three months), and they were much less likely to have had chemical dependency inpatient treatment or to have been in jail or in prison. With respect to mental illness, there are significant differences among groups of homeless women. Single women are more likely than men overall to have histories of mental hospitalization, women with children and other women less likely.

This brief description of the homeless suggests that any search for causality should begin with factors that affect single men, including those that may promote their "singleness" or isolation from larger households. Thereafter, attention should focus on factors affecting female-headed families and single women.

CAUSAL FACTORS

Among the personal factors that may push an individual into homelessness, two of the most important are mental illness and chemical dependency (here considered together) and social isolation.

Institutionalization

Slightly more than half of the homeless adults in the Urban Institute sample had been institutionalized in a mental hospital, a chemical dependency inpatient program, or a state or federal prison. When jails as well as prisons are included, the proportion ever institutionalized rises to two-thirds.[4] Three-quarters of single men have had at least one of these four experiences. Women are far less prone to multiple institutionalizations. Only one in twenty single women has experienced three or all four types, and the proportions are even lower in the other female subgroups.

---

[4]Jails are run by local authorities, prisons by states and the federal government. People go to jail for misdemeanors, to prison for felonies. Many homeless people spend time in jail for minor infractions. Given the overcrowded state of the American penal system, usually it takes more than one felony conviction before a person serves a prison term. In general, people with prison records can be assumed to have committed more serious crimes than people who have only served time in jail. With respect to mental illness and chemical dependency prevalence and treatment, Chapter 6 supplements the Urban Institute findings with results from local studies that provide far more extensive information.

Table 2-5 presents background information on the experiences of homeless persons with a history of both mental hospitalization and chemical dependency inpatient treatment (9 percent of the sample); mental hospitalization only (10 percent); chemical dependency inpatient treatment only (24 percent); and no treatment history (57 percent).

Homeless people with neither type of institutionalization are more likely than other groups to be nonwhite (63 percent), female (26 percent), young (mean age of thirty-five), and never married (62 percent). Those with chemical dependency treatment only are the most likely to be white (59 percent), male (93 percent), older (mean age of forty-four), and ever married (61 percent). Those with chemical dependency treatment only are also most likely to be currently married (19 percent, versus 6 to 8 percent for all other groups). Respondents in our sample who reported chemical dependency treatment only are closest to the stereotypical profile of the traditional homeless person or skid row bum.

Educational attainment in our sample is strongly related to institutionalization history. Among those with neither mental hospitalization nor chemical dependency treatment, 31 percent had some post-high school education (compared with 18 percent or less for the other groups), and another 35 percent had high school diplomas (compared with high school diploma rates of 27 to 33 percent for the other groups). From the data available one cannot tell whether mental illness or chemical dependency affected schooling completed or whether people with poor educational credentials were more likely to suffer from mental illness or substance abuse. Whatever the causal order, policymakers should recognize that educational deficits and personal problems often occur together. This combination is particularly discouraging for hopes of long-run self-sufficiency. A large subgroup of the homeless population is very likely to require supported work, supported housing, or both if they are to avoid homelessness.

Data on work experience reinforce this impression. Relatively few people in any group were currently working, while those with a history of mental hospitalization were least likely to have ever worked. In this subgroup, about one in four had never held a steady job. Homeless persons who had been institutionalized had been out of work for four to five years, on average, compared with a mean of thirty-eight months for those with neither type of treatment history. People whose only institutionalization experience was chemical dependency treatment were the most likely ever to have worked at a steady job (defined as three months or more with the same employer). However, among those who had once worked but were not currently working, those with a history of chemical dependency treatment also had the largest average number of months of current joblessness. Among homeless respondents with neither type of institutionalization, 43 percent were currently

Table 2-5 Characteristics of Homeless Adults, by Institutionalization Experiences (weighted percentages)

	Neither (N = 1048)	Mental Hospitalization Only (N = 160)	Chemical Dependency Only (N = 347)	Both (N = 127)	Total Sample (N = 1682)
Percentage of Total Sample	57%	10%	24%	9%	100%
Percentage Male	74	79	93	88	81
Percentage White	37	55	59	53	46
Age					
≤34	59	44	26	38	48
≥45	20	19	47	31	30
Mean age	35	37	44	40	38
Percentage Never Married	62	53	39	52	55
Education					
High school diploma	35	33	27	27	32
Post-high school education	31	14	18	12	19

Percentage Currently Working at Steady Job[a]	6	3	5	7	6
Percentage Never Worked at Steady Job[a]	14	26	5	23	14
Mean Number of Months					
Homeless	33	35	46	48	37
Jobless[b]	38	50	64	51	48
Health Status					
Fair or poor	31	58	27	52	35
Poor	9	29	9	32	13
Number of Health Problems					
Three or more	9	19	20	39	15
Four or more	2	16	12	22	8

[a] A "steady job" was defined as three months or more with same employer.
[b] Includes respondents who are not currently working but who have worked at a steady job at some time in the past. The variable measures the number of months since they last held a steady job.

working or had held a steady job within the twelve months preceding our interview; the comparison figures were 21 percent for those with mental hospitalizations and 30 to 33 percent for those with only chemical dependency treatment or both. The record suggests that many people with severe mental illness or chemical dependency problems do not seem likely to be able to support themselves through work.

Chemical dependency treatment is also strongly associated with criminal behavior, as reflected in state or federal prison terms. More than half (52 percent) of those with both mental hospitalization and alcohol or drug treatment and 41 percent of those with chemical dependency treatment only had served prison time, presumably for felonies. Only 15 percent of those with no history of institutionalization reported prison terms.

Finally, poor health plagued a very high proportion of homeless people, especially those with other problems as well. Thirty-five percent of the whole sample and 31 percent of those who had never been institutionalized perceived their health as fair or poor, compared with 20 percent of poor Americans and only 10 percent of the total U.S. population. The homeless with a history of mental hospitalization, whether or not coupled with chemical dependency treatment, were extremely likely to rate their health only fair or poor.

Other studies (e.g., Wright and Weber, 1987) report that physical health problems are among the top ten precipitating causes of homelessness. The homeless people in our study appear to be no exception. Further, those with mental health or substance abuse problems also report more current health problems, including upper respiratory tract infections, arthritis and rheumatism, high blood pressure, problems with walking (including missing limbs), and heart disease or stroke.

To recapitulate, roughly four in ten homeless adults had histories of institutionalization for mental illness, chemical dependency, or both; many of them also have little education and spotty work histories. It should be emphasized, moreover, that because the Urban Institute study registers only histories of institutionalization, it undoubtedly fails to identify many homeless people who suffer significant mental health and chemical dependency problems, but who have not been institutionalized.

These findings suggest that many homeless people have severe impairments that limit their likelihood of becoming or remaining self-sufficient. Any societal factors that might increase mental illness or chemical dependency, or that might reduce levels of public or private support for people with these problems, will also probably increase their numbers among the homeless. They are so vulnerable that very small changes might be enough to precipitate a homeless episode, and their capacities are often too limited to allow them to assemble the resources needed to find housing.

To understand the causes of homelessness for these people, it will be especially important to examine the linkages between personal problems, available resources, and housing options. For instance, if many mentally ill people used to live in single-room-occupancy hotels (SROs) or in boarding or lodging houses, and if these facilities have either disappeared or become prohibitively expensive, then homelessness among the mentally ill will increase even if the number of the mentally ill outside mental institutions stays the same. Or if families become poorer and their space becomes tighter, they may not be able to continue providing a home for a mentally ill or a chemically dependent member. As we will see, people with histories of institutionalization are more likely to have lived alone before becoming homeless. All other things equal, this isolation increases their risk of homelessness in the face of crisis.

Social Isolation

Literal homelessness is usually the final step in a process that involves gradual or sudden loss of resources coupled with gradual or sudden loss of connection to family or friends who might help in a crisis. In research on users of Chicago soup kitchens and other emergency food programs, Sosin et al. (1988) found three factors that differentiated people who had and had not ever been homeless: living alone, alcohol consumption, and having been in out-of-home placement as a child. The last category is a special case of "loss of connection"; individuals who start their adult life without any family ties may be particularly vulnerable to becoming homeless after a financial crisis. In the only other study that considers out-of-home placement, Piliavin et al. (1987) report that 38 percent of their Minneapolis homeless sample had been in foster care as children.

I cannot prove that living alone causes homelessness. I can, however, explore the living situation of people in the Urban Institute sample immediately before their present homeless episode. Overall, about one-third of this sample lived alone, compared with about 14 percent of all U.S. adults. Those who were homeless alone or "traveling" with nonrelatives were most likely to have lived alone before becoming homeless. Thirty-five percent of single men and 39 percent of single women lived alone, compared with only 1 percent for people whose homeless household included children, a spouse, or another relative.

Further, people who had been institutionalized for mental illness, chemical dependency, or criminal behavior were more likely than others to live alone. Among people with no history of institutionalization, about one in four had lived by themselves before becoming homeless. The comparable figures are 35 percent for people with either mental hospitalization or chemical dependency inpatient treatment, and 43 percent for people with both types of institutional-ization. People with both who also had served time in prison (4 percent of the whole sample) were the most likely to have lived alone before homelessness (56 percent).

One cannot tell from a sample of the homeless whether nonhomeless people with similar personal histories are more likely to live alone than the general population or whether these problems in themselves make a person living alone more vulnerable to homelessness. It is, however, very plausible that having a severe mental illness, an addiction to alcohol or drugs, or a criminal record will strain relations with family and friends. The result might be social isolation and living by oneself. It is also very plausible that these problems make it more difficult to cope with the periodic crises that face the very poor. As we have seen, slightly more than half of the homeless adults in our sample had at least one of these institutionalization experiences (mental hospitalization, chemical dependency treatment, or prison). When social isolation is combined with conditions that may impair coping, vulnerability to homelessness appears to be high. In later chapters we will examine changes in the numbers of one-person households, and changes in the supports available to people living alone who have potentially debilitating conditions.

IMPLICATIONS

This profile of the urban homeless reveals several population characteristics that should guide our analysis of the factors that may have caused an increase in homelessness in the 1980s. First, we will want to look at factors affecting poverty, since virtually all of the homeless come from the ranks of the very poor. We will want to focus as much as possible on what has happened to single men with little education, and to people living alone. Among families, factors affecting poor female-headed families will be the focus. And we will need to ask what changes may have increased the probability that people with mental illness or chemical dependency will become homeless.

It will also be important to look at changes in the availability of housing for people like those in our sample. If many people with these characteristics used to live in SROs or boarding houses but this type of accommodation is disappearing, homelessness may result from a confluence of factors: dwindling housing opportunities, stable or increasing numbers of people with particular problems, and shrinking financial resources.

CHAPTER THREE

Housing Availability

■ Both analysts and advocates have frequently attributed the growth of homelessness in the United States during the 1980s to problems with the housing market (Hartman, 1986; Hombs and Snyder, 1982; Hopper and Hamberg, 1986; Rossi, 1989; Wright and Lam, 1987). Reference is often made to the lack of affordable housing, and the federal government is blamed for reducing housing expenditures. An association between housing cost or availability and homelessness has been shown in a few studies based on the sample of cities and midrange estimates of homelessness developed by the Department of Housing and Urban Development in its 1984 study (Department of Housing and Urban Development, 1984). The housing variables used include median rent and vacancy rate (Quigley, 1990), and the percentage of rental units with rents of $150 or less (Elliott and Krivo, 1991).

Clearly I believe that housing affordability and homelessness are related. But "housing affordability" is a slippery term, and it is important to understand its elements. One component is the housing stock itself—whether there are enough units, in the right places, of the appropriate size and condition, to accommodate the families who need housing. The second factor is whether the families that need housing have the resources to afford the units that exist or that might be built. A third consideration is whether the families that need housing will be prevented from occupying available units because of discrimination based on race, presence of children, welfare receipt, or other criteria.

To examine changes in housing affordability, I look first at changes in the national housing market during the 1980s. This chapter aims to give a general sense of the structure of the housing market and of the national-level factors and changes in the market that may have contributed to homelessness. I will concentrate on the rental housing market since the very poor people most vulnerable to homelessness are typically renters. Changes in ownership housing

31

also will be reviewed briefly, because they may influence the availability and price of rental housing. I will also present some data for the 1970s, since changes in the rental market and the renting population during that decade set the stage for what has happened in the 1980s.

CHANGES IN THE HOUSING STOCK

The U.S. housing inventory has changed substantially in the past two decades. In 1970 there were 68 million housing units: 40 million owner-occupied, 24 million renter-occupied, and the remaining 4 million vacant or other. The number of housing units increased to 87 million by 1980, with 52 million owner-occupied, 29 million renter-occupied, and 6 million vacant or other. Thus in the 1970s owner-occupied stock increased by 30 percent and renter-occupied stock increased by 21 percent (Downs, 1983, Table 1-1; see also Sternlieb and Hughes, 1985). Vacant stock increased by 50 percent, but most of the increase occurred in units that were seasonally vacant, occupied only occasionally, or for other some reasons not available for rental; the number of units vacant and for rent declined. The number of owner-occupied units had risen to 58 million by 1987, an increase of 11.5 percent over 1980. An additional 1 million units were vacant and for sale, and 6 million were vacant for other reasons. By 1987 there were 33 million occupied rental units and slightly less than 3 million vacant rental units—an increase of 15 percent in the renter-occupied stock since 1980 (Apgar, 1989, Table 3).

Federal government programs (public housing, Section 8, and Section 235) contributed 1.5 million new or substantially rehabilitated units to this total from 1970 through 1979 and 0.9 million units from 1980 through 1989 (Dolbeare, 1990, personal communication). The 1.5 million rental units added in the 1970s through federal programs represented 31 percent of the total growth in rental stock in that decade. In comparison, the 877,000 units added from 1980 to 1989 through federal programs represented only 14 percent of the rental units added in that period. The declining share of federally supported new housing is particularly important because all these units were "affordable," in the sense that eligible tenants received subsidies to bring rent payments down to federal guidelines (25 percent of household income through 1980, increasing to 30 percent of income in stages beginning in 1981). Privately developed units are typically not affordable in this sense. In most cases a low-income household would have to pay more than 25 or 30 percent of its income to cover rental costs, and would not receive a subsidy.

During the 1970s, federally funded new construction and substantial rehabilitation programs added an average of 197,000 rental units a year; during the 1980s this figure dropped to 93,000 units a year, a decline of 53 percent. The decline is even more striking if the comparison focuses on the years before and after the policies of the Reagan administration took hold. Additions to the rental stock from federally subsidized programs averaged 160,000 per year during the 1970-1981 period, but only 67,000 in the 1982-1989 period—a drop of 66 percent. As we will see, there is an absolute shortage of appropriate rental units to accommodate poorly housed families (that is, the problem is not simply an inability to afford what exists). In this context the reduced federal contribution to the low-cost housing stock is particularly significant.

Loss of SRO Units

Perhaps the housing stock change most relevant to homeless and very poor persons is the loss of residential hotel rooms (SROs) and accommodations in boarding or lodging houses. In the deteriorating neighborhoods of many big cities, very poor single individuals could formerly occupy these units for very low rents (Hoch and Slayton, 1989). The quality of this housing varied considerably; the worst was little better than today's shelters. But small pensions or earnings from day labor were sufficient to make it affordable. People living in these so-called incomplete units usually shared bathrooms and often lacked access to complete kitchens (although they may have had a gas or electric ring and a small refrigerator), but they were not on the streets or in shelters. Summarizing the research on skid row housing and shelter in the late 1950s and early 1960s, Rossi (1989) concluded that very few of the people living in these neighborhoods were sleeping on the streets or in shelters; that is, there was little homelessness in today's sense.

Since the early 1900s, SROs and similar very inexpensive housing have been considered an undesirable urban phenomenon, an appropriate target for demolition or conversion (Hoch and Slayton, 1989). In the 1960s massive urban renewal projects often eliminated entire deteriorated neighborhoods. More recently, the loss of units through conversion has accelerated. In rejuvenating neighborhoods, many remaining hotels and large houses once used for boarding or lodging facilities have been renovated, altered, and sold or rented to higher-income households.

It is difficult to document the loss of this type of housing for the country as a whole. Lee (1980) analyzed the nationwide disappearance of skid rows, but did not estimate the number of housing units lost. Green (cited in Baxter and Hopper, 1984) estimated the loss at about 1,116,000 units nationally. Some cities have made their own assessments. In Chicago, some 18,000 SRO units (19 percent of the stock) were lost or converted between 1973 and 1984 (Chicago Department of Planning, 1985). More than half the SRO units in downtown Los Angeles were demolished between 1970 and 1985 (Hamilton, Rabinowitz and Alschuler, Inc., 1987). Seattle lost half its downtown rental stock; Boston lost 94 percent of its rooming houses; Nashville lost all but one of its SROs by the early or mid-1980s (Wright and Lam, 1987). In New York, the Housing and Preservation Department estimated that approximately 50,000 SRO units remained in the city in 1986. All but one residential hotel on the Bowery had been removed by 1987 (Jackson, 1987). Because of differences in definitions, estimates of the number of SROs in New York City in 1970 vary greatly. Between 30,000 and 100,000 units were lost during the 1970s and 1980s, however, and even the most conservative calculation indicates that 38 percent of the SRO stock has been lost or converted. Hoch and Slayton (1989, p. 174) summarize information for New York and other cities:

> New York City lost 30,385 units in 160 buildings between 1975 and 1981, for a decrease of 60 percent overall. In San Francisco 5,723 (17.7 percent) of 32,214 units disappeared between 1975 and 1979. Denver, which had forty-five SRO hotels in 1976, had fewer than seventeen left in 1981. In Seattle the number of SRO units dropped by 15,000 between 1960 and 1981. San Diego lost 1,247 units in thirty hotels between 1976 and 1984 and has only about 3,500 units left. Smaller cities lost hotels as well. Portland eliminated 1,700 units in the 1970s. Cincinnati lost 42 percent of its SRO units during the 1970s and has only fifteen hotels remaining with 875 units.

The relevance of these losses becomes clear when one examines who lives, or did live, in SROs and boarding or lodging houses. In the late 1970s about 20 to 25 percent of all people with chronic mental illness other than senility—some 300,000 to 400,000 persons—lived in this type of facility (Burt and Pittman, 1985). One recent study (Hoch and Spicer, 1985) found one-fourth of Chicago SRO residents were disabled and 8 percent were retired. Two-thirds were in the labor force, with 24 percent unemployed and looking for work, 7 percent employed part time, and 34 percent employed full time. Almost one in four received General Assistance, and more than one in four received pension benefits from various sources. Four in five were male, and 94 percent were not currently married, although half of these had been married at some point.

SRO residents are thus quite similar to homeless individuals in many ways; the major difference lies in their incomes. In Chicago SRO residents had an average monthly income of $580, compared with $168 for homeless people in Chicago, and $137 for homeless people in all U.S. cities over 100,000 population (Burt and Cohen, 1989). These incomes derive primarily from pensions and benefits. As Rossi comments (1989, p. 113), SRO residents are not only more likely than homeless people to "have these sources of income, but the amounts derived from each are greater." The loss of, or inability to obtain, these sources of income would obviously increase the homeless population. So would the destruction of SRO housing or an increase in its price beyond the means of its current residents.

CHANGES IN HOUSEHOLD NUMBERS, TYPES, AND TENURE

The total number of U.S. households has grown during the 1970s and 1980s, as a function of housing choices as well as population growth. In addition, both decades saw shifts in home ownership. To the extent that these changes reflect constraints due to decreasing resources or decreasing purchasing power in the housing market, they also may affect increases in homelessness.

In general, more households formed in the 1970s than would be expected merely on the basis of population growth. Both owners and renters shifted to smaller households, with renters moving further in this direction. Downs (1983, pp. 22-23) reports that "in 1970, 23.6 million renter-occupied units contained 64.3 million persons, or 2.73 persons a unit. From 1970 to 1980 the number of renter-occupied units increased by 21.4 percent, but the total number of persons living in them rose only 1.2 percent. Hence in 1980 28.6 million such units held only 65.1 million persons, or an average of 2.28 in each unit." The average unit also became less crowded, since the average number of rooms per unit remained about the same. The number of owner-occupied units rose 29.9 percent during the 1970s, whereas the number of persons occupying these units rose only 19.4 percent. This shift is smaller than that experienced by renters, but in the same direction. Sternlieb and Hughes (1985) report similar analyses and findings.

Several factors contributed to the shift to more and smaller households in the 1970s. During that period, Mutchler and Krivo (1989) demonstrate, households that had once been doubled up were able to afford separate units, reflecting both higher per capita incomes (for whites and Hispanics) and greater housing availability because of higher vacancy rates and more newly built housing (for whites and blacks). Smith et al. (1984) have also documented the effects of housing availability and affordability on household size and structure. Demographic trends in divorce rates, later age at marriage, and maintenance of independent households by the elderly all contributed to the shift to smaller households. Builders responded to the demand for housing created by the demographic trends and rising incomes by constructing units suited to the newer household types. By 1980, fewer people than in 1970 lived in households with their adult children, their elderly parents, or other "nonspouse adults."

During the 1970s rates of home ownership were stable or increased in all age groups. In contrast, the 1980s have seen a reversal in home ownership, especially in households with younger heads, and an increase in poverty among renter households that is likely to constrain housing choices. Tables 3-1, 3-2, and 3-3 show these shifts.

In the late 1970s inflation and tax policies (both bracket creep and deductions for mortgage interest and real estate taxes) made home ownership a good investment and an important hedge against inflation (Downs, 1983, p. 33; Sternlieb and Hughes, 1985, pp. 16-20). For households with heads of age thirty

Table 3-1 Home Ownership Rates, by Age of Household Head, 1973-1988 (percentages)

	1973	1976	1980	1983	1988
Age of Head					
Under 25	23.4	21.0	21.3	19.3	15.5
25–29	43.6	43.2	43.3	38.2	36.2
30–34	60.2	62.4	61.1	55.7	52.6
35–39	68.5	69.0	70.8	65.8	63.2
40–44	72.9	73.9	74.2	74.2	71.4
45–54	76.1	77.4	77.7	77.1	76.0
55–64	75.7	77.2	79.3	80.5	79.6
65–74	71.3	72.7	75.2	76.9	78.2
75+	67.1	67.2	67.8	71.6	70.4
All households	64.4	64.8	65.6	64.9	63.9

Source: William C. Apgar, Jr., et al., "The State of the Nation's Housing, 1989." Joint Center for Housing Studies of Harvard University, Exhibit 13.

and older (Table 3-1), the proportion of ownership rose between 1973 and 1980. An analysis of household types (Table 3-2) shows ownership increasing for all categories except single parents under thirty-five with children. That picture changed considerably in the 1980s. In 1988, for household heads forty-four and younger, home ownership rates were at their lowest since 1973. Ownership among the very youngest group declined by 27 percent between 1980 and 1988, while households with heads in their late twenties and in their thirties experienced drops in ownership of 11 to 16 percent.

Besides the young, households with children were most likely to remain in or shift to rental housing in the 1980s. This was true for both married-couple and female-headed families. Indeed, by the end of the decade, a larger proportion of households with children were classified as poor renters. As Table 3-3 shows, the total number of poor renter households increased by 56 percent between 1974 and 1988. Single parents with children and "other" household types contributed disproportionally to this growth. Over this period, poor renters came to represent a larger proportion of all households, and of households with children and "other" elderly households.

These patterns have significant implications for homelessness. A particularly important change is the increase in the proportion of poor renters that are single-parent families. These families generally spend larger proportions of their low incomes for rent. Not only do they suffer excessive rent burdens, but they are more likely than two-parent families to live in crowded or structurally unsound housing, in unsafe or undesirable neighborhoods, even when paying more than a third of their income for rent (Ahrentzen, 1985; Birch, 1985). These circumstances place particular strains on female-headed families and must contribute to their highly disproportionate presence among homeless families. (Burt and Cohen (1989a, 1989b) report that 80 percent of homeless families have female heads.)

A second important observation is that as the 1980s progressed, young families were more likely to remain in the rental market. In the past, young

Table 3-2 Proportion of Households That Are Renters, by Household Type and Age, 1973, 1980, 1988 (percentages)

		1973	1980	1988
Household Type				
Single	<25	92.3	88.5	89.6
	25–34	82.0	75.2	75.7
	35–44	72.0	63.2	61.0
	45–64	49.3	48.4	45.4
	65+	42.2	40.8	39.3
Married, with	<25	61.1	61.2	70.6
Children	25–34	33.2	28.9	37:2
	35–44	19.0	14.6	18.8
	45–64	14.3	12.3	14.0
	65+	a	a	a
Married, No	<25	73.9	66.4	77.4
Children	25–34	54.6	41.7	46.5
	35–44	33.2	24.8	23.7
	45–64	16.3	11.6	11.5
	65+	18.5[a]	15.0[a]	10.9[a]
Single Parent	<25	86.3	89.9	96.8
with Children	25–34	68.3	68.2	76.2
	35–44	51.9	49.9	53.0
	45–64	38.6	35.5	41.5
Other Households	<25	92.4	90.1	88.2
	25–34	82.0	70.6	70.3
	35–44	48.5	46.1	52.4
	45–64	33.2	32.0	32.7
	65+	30.7	27.7	25.0

Source: William C. Apgar, Jr., et al., "The State of the Nation's Housing, 1989." Joint Center for Housing Studies of Harvard University. Percentages calculated from Appendix Table 13.
[a]For household heads 65 and over, the categories "with children" and "without children" are combined.

Table 3-3 Composition of Poor Renter Households, 1974 and 1978

	Numbers (in 1000s)			Poor Renters as a Percentage of Household Type		Household Type as a Percentage of All Poor Renter Households	
	1974	1988	Percentage Growth	1974	1988	1974	1988
Head Aged Under 65							
Single	1,014	1,507	48.7%	12.7	11.4	20.4	19.5
Married, with children	820	1,085	32.3	3.3	4.5	16.5	14.0
Married, no children	287	292	1.7	2.0	1.6	5.8	3.8
Single parent with children	1,384	2,715	96.2	29.6	36.0	27.9	35.1
Other	414	838	102.5	10.3	10.3	8.3	10.8
Subtotal	3,919	6,437	64.3	6.9	9.0	78.9	83.2
Head Aged 65+							
Single	859	1,025	19.3	14.6	11.8	17.3	13.2
Married	113	140	23.6	1.8	1.8	2.3	1.8
Other	74	140	89.6	4.4	6.4	2.3	1.8
Subtotal	1,046	1,304	24.7	7.6	6.7	21.1	16.8
Total	4,965	7,742	55.9%	7.0	8.5	100%	100%

Source: William C. Apgar, Jr., et al., "The State of the Nation's Housing, 1989." Joint Center for Housing Studies of Harvard University. Numbers of households and percentages based on figures in Appendix Table 9.

families typically bought their first home in their late twenties or early thirties. Yet Apgar et al. (1989) suggest that by 1989 only 11.5 percent of renter households with heads aged twenty-five to thirty-four could qualify financially to purchase a typical starter home. Since the early 1970s, both the down payment requirement and the monthly mortgage payment had increased significantly as a percentage of first-time buyer income (by 50 percent and 25 percent, respectively). Higher-income renters' inability to buy placed upward pressure on rents. Changes in rent burden in relation to household income, as will be seen below, were one result.

CHANGES IN COST AND AVAILABILITY

Is there a housing crisis in the United States? If so, does it contribute to homelessness? Strong opinions have been sounded on both sides of this question, and accompanied by statistical support. It can easily be shown, for example, that there are "enough" vacant rental units in the country to house all renter households; the average vacancy rate nationwide was 7.7 percent in 1988, for example. For such reasons, Weicher, Villani, and Roistacher (1981) have argued that there is no crisis. Further, conservatives argue "that the homeless problem, as such, is not really directly attributable to a crisis in affordable housing" (Beirne, 1989, p. 27). From the premises of economic theory, some have argued that a completely free market in housing would respond to the need for lower-priced rental housing by building it, that owners of vacant higher-priced units would lower their prices rather than keep the units off the market, or that units created for the higher-priced rental housing market would ultimately "filter down" to the poor (see Gilderbloom (1985, 1986) and Gilderbloom and Appelbaum (1988) for a description and critique of these traditional assumptions).

However, figures that apply to the entire U.S. housing stock cannot answer the question of whether housing shortages contribute to homelessness. Rather, we must ask whether access to housing has worsened for the very poorest households in this country, who are most vulnerable to homelessness. Therefore, we must examine the data more closely from the perspective of the very poor; this usually means renters, and households below the poverty level. The geographical distribution of units must be considered, since realistically households must be able to find available units of the appropriate size and condition in their own cities and neighborhoods. Further, we must focus on housing that is very cheap, and available to households with children, to members of minority groups, and to individuals with significant physical or mental disabilities. Only then will we be able to identify groups for whom the rental housing crisis may be real and potentially overwhelming.

I begin by looking at the total number of rental units available in the United States, and at occupied units. As Table 3-4 shows, there appears to have been a healthy growth in the number of units available for rental between 1970 and 1987. In fact, vacancy rates actually increased, to a reasonably "available" level of 7.7 percent in 1987. Data from the Census Bureau's Current Population Survey for 1988 also show a rental vacancy rate of 7.7 percent.

However, Table 3-4 also shows substantial regional variation in vacancy rates; moreover, regional rates do not always shift in parallel with the national average. From 1975 to 1988, the Northeast had a consistently tighter housing market than other regions of the country. The South had relatively high vacancy rates throughout the period; after 1984 its rates were more than twice those of the Northeast. Everywhere but in the Northeast, the rental housing market loosened up after 1985.

To begin to analyze whether there is a housing crisis for the poor, Table 3-5 examines changes in the number of units and vacancy rates by rent level. Now the picture becomes more ominous. Between 1981 and 1987, there was an absolute loss of almost 1.2 million units renting for $300 or less (in 1987 dollars); the percentage change was greatest in the very lowest-cost units, those renting for less than $150. These losses continued a trend established in the 1970s, when 6 percent of units renting for $300 or less (in 1988 dollars) were lost (Apgar et al., 1989, Appendix Table 6). In comparison, the number of units renting for more than $300 grew by 4.4 million—an increase almost four times as large as the loss in the low-cost stock.

Vacancy rates in the lowest-cost units were substantially lower than in the more expensive units for both 1981 and 1987, and median rents for vacant units in 1987 were significantly higher than median rents for all units in that year—a pattern not seen in 1981. This pattern suggests that low-income renters seeking an apartment in 1987 faced a much tighter market, in which housing would absorb a larger proportion of their income than in 1981.

Any effort to understand whether available housing is adequate for the population needing shelter must attempt to distinguish the housing issues from the income issues. An interesting approach was taken by Milgram and Bury (1987), using data from the American Housing Surveys conducted in 1982 and 1983 in twenty-five metropolitan areas. Using simulation techniques, these researchers attempted to "move" every family living in physically inadequate or overcrowded conditions into standard-quality vacant units where they would not be crowded, without regard to whether the family could afford to pay for the unit. They found that no housing market area had enough rental units to house renter families living in unsatisfactory conditions. Even if ability to pay were not an issue, the simulations indicated, from 5 to 94 percent of these families could not be appropriately rehoused (depending on the city and on simulation assumptions). Even in suburban areas, the range was 0 to 36 percent. Differences in

Table 3-4 Rental Housing, 1970-1987

	Total Units (in thousands)		Vacancies	
	Available	Occupied	Number	Rate
Year				
1970	24,105	22,806	1,299	5.3%
1980	28,990	27,415	1,575	5.4
1987	35,354	32,602	2,752	7.7
Percentage Change				
1970–1980	20.3%	20.2%	23.7	—
1980–1987	21.9	18.9	68.4	—
1970–1987	46.7	43.0	108.4	—

Rental Vacancy Rates, by Region

	1975	1980	1981	1982	1983	1984	1985	1986	1987	1988
Northeast	4.1%	4.2%	3.7%	3.7%	4.0%	3.7%	3.5%	3.9%	4.1%	4.8%
Midwest	5.7	6.0	5.9	6.3	6.1	5.9	5.9	6.9	6.8	6.9
South	7.7	6.0	5.4	5.8	6.9	7.9	9.1	10.1	10.9	10.1
West	6.2	5.2	5.1	5.5	5.2	5.2	6.2	7.1	7.3	7.7
Total	6.0	5.4	5.0	5.3	5.7	5.9	6.5	7.3	7.7	7.7

Source: Bureau of the Census, "Current Population Surveys/Housing Vacancy Survey," Series H-111 (excludes renter-occupied or vacant for rent mobile homes).

41

Table 3-5 Rental Units and Vacancies, by Price, 1981 and 1987 (rent-specified units only, in 1,000s) (contract rent in 1987 dollars)

	1981			1987			1981-87 % Change in Units
	Total	Vacant	Rate	Total	Vacant	Rate	
Contract Rent							
$0-150	5,045	193	3.8	4,362	165	3.6	-8.2%
150-300	11,463	537	4.7	10,690	859	8.0	-6.8
300-400	6,158	307	5.0	7,483	651	8.7	+21.5
400-500	3,146	152	4.8	4,276	351	8.2	+35.9
500+	2,299	173	7.5	4,276	436	10.2	+86.0
Total	28,111	1,363	4.8	31,357	2,462	7.9	+11.5
Median Contract Rent in 1987 $	281	286	—	304	330	—	—

Source: William C. Apgar, Jr., "Recent Trends in Rental Vacancies." Working Paper 89-3, Joint Center for Housing Studies of Harvard University, 1989, Table 3.

vacancy rates were only part of the story, explaining less than half of the variance in undersupply. The mismatch between supply and demand was greatest for larger families, but even one- and two-person households faced constraints in most areas. (No efficiency units remained vacant after the simulated moves in any central city, or in five suburban areas.) The researchers concluded that shortfalls do exist in the rental housing stock, independent of price, in most of the metropolitan areas examined.

These simulation results parallel the experience of households who attempt to obtain housing under federal Section 8 certificate and voucher programs. Over half of these vouchers are returned unused because the recipients could not find acceptable housing within the allowed time period (usually two months). Large households were least successful, minority group members were less successful than nonminority households, and younger families were less successful than the elderly.

Milgram and Bury (1987) address the affordability issue by estimating what subsidy would enable a family to pay no more than 30 percent of its income for the rental unit to which it was moved by the simulation. The average subsidy required ranged from $88 to $332; in 1982 and 1983, depending on the area, between 29 and 100 percent of these hypothetically rehoused families would have needed a subsidy to afford their new unit.

The affordability problem documented by Milgram and Bury reflects an increase in real rents between 1970 and 1988 (Table 3-6). Inflation-adjusted median gross and contract rents rose substantially during the 1980s in the country as a whole, with the Northeast and West showing increases approximately three times as great as those in the Midwest and South.[1] These increases also substantially exceeded real rent increases during the 1970s. In fact, during the 1970s the inflation-adjusted median contract rent actually fell in all regions of the country, while the inflation-adjusted median gross rent fell in the Midwest and South. The 1980s reversed these trends.

Rent Burden

An increase in rents does not necessarily mean that housing has become less affordable, since incomes could have increased even more. It is therefore important to look at the relationship between rents and available household incomes.

---

[1]Gross rent is the total cost of housing, including utilities; contract rent is the amount on the lease, which often does not include utilities. Gross rent burden is the proportion of household income absorbed by gross rent; contract rent burden is the proportion of household income absorbed by contract rent.

Table 3-6 Rent Levels and Rent Burdens 1970, 1980, and 1988
(all rents in 1988 dollars)

				Change (percent)		
	1970	1980	1988	1970 –1980	1980 –1988	1970 –1988
Median Gross Rent ($)						
Northeast	341	350	420	+2.6%	+20.0%	+23.2%
Midwest	345	322	345	−6.7	+7.1	0
South	317	311	334	−1.9	+7.4	+5.4
West	380	389	470	+2.4	+20.8	+23.7
All	346	343	393	−1.0	+14.3	+13.3
Gross Rent Burden						
(% of income)						
Northeast	20.7	27.2	29.0	+31.4	+6.6	+40.1
Midwest	21.6	26.5	28.9	+22.7	+9.1	+33.8
South	24.6	25.2	26.2	+2.4	+4.0	+6.5
West	24.5	28.1	31.5	+14.7	+12.1	+28.6
All	23.0	27.2	29.6	+18.3	+8.8	+28.7
Median Contract Rent ($)						
Northeast	303	297	370	−2.0	+24.6	+22.1
Midwest	305	270	290	−11.5	+7.4	−4.9
South	268	251	270	−6.3	+7.6	+0.7
West	350	348	427	−0.6	+22.7	+22.0
All	308	291	338	−5.5	+16.2	+9.7
Contract Rent Burden						
(% of income)						
Northeast	18.4	23.1	25.5	+25.5	+10.4	+38.6
Midwest	19.1	22.3	24.3	+16.8	+9.0	+27.2
South	20.8	20.3	21.2	−2.4	+4.4	+1.9
West	22.6	25.2	28.6	+11.5	+13.5	+26.5
All	20.5	23.1	25.5	+12.7	+10.4	+24.4

Source: William C. Apgar, Jr. et al., "The State of the Nation's Housing, 1989." Joint Center for Housing Studies of Harvard University. Data derived from Tables A1 through A5.

The rent burden on households, calculated as median rent divided by the median gross income of renter households, has increased in every part of the country during the last two decades (Table 3-6). (The change has been smallest in the South.) Nationally, between 1970 and 1988 renter households experienced increases on the order of 24 to 29 percent in the burden of real rents they had to carry. Although the 1980s saw the greatest proportional increases in inflation-adjusted rents, the increase in rent burden was larger in the previous decade, because of declines in renters' median household income. Some of this change was due to the shift of higher-income renters into home ownership, leaving the renter population with higher proportions of low-income households (Downs, 1983; Sternlieb and Hughes, 1985).

Thus, even at the beginning of the 1980s renters faced increasing financial pressures from housing costs, which reduced the proportion of their income available to purchase other essentials. Across the entire 1970-1988 period, gross rent burdens on renter households increased by more than one-fourth in real terms in every section of the country except the South (40 percent in the Northeast, 34 percent in the Midwest, and 29 percent in the West). The Midwest shift is especially instructive because it shows that rent burden can increase substantially even when real rents fall. (Median household incomes of renters in the Midwest declined even faster than rents.) Other analyses also document these increasing rent burdens (General Accounting Office, 1985; Sternlieb and Hughes, 1985).

The severity of the housing crunch for low-income renters can be assessed by comparing the number of affordable units (renting for 30 percent of household income or less) with the number of renter households. This test shows a widening gap between available affordable units and the needs of poor households. Table 3-7, based on Dolbeare (1988), shows the shortfall in rental housing affordable to the bottom income quartile of renter households.

The vast majority of bottom-quartile renter households have incomes that fall below the official poverty line. At least since 1980, the number of these households has exceeded the number of units available for a rent no greater than 30 percent of the income level marking the top of the quartile. This gap increased steadily during the 1980s, a trend that is projected to continue. In 1980 the shortfall in affordable units amounted to 27 percent of bottom-quartile households; that figure had risen to 35 percent in 1985 and is projected to be 42 percent in 1990. To make matters worse, many units that poor renters could afford are occupied by households with higher incomes. The result is that most households in the bottom quartile of renters occupy units that cost more than 30 percent of their incomes.[2]

---

[2]These calculations used 30 percent of the income marking the division between the bottom quartile and the next higher quartile in calculating an affordable rent. But the incomes of most people in the bottom quartile are lower than this maximum. Therefore the percentages in Table 3-7 are only lower-bound estimates of the shortfall in affordable housing. Using data from the 1987 American Housing Survey, Dolbeare calculates that fewer than one in six households in the bottom income quartile occupied units costing less than 30 percent of their income (personal communication).

Table 3-7 Undersupply of Low-Cost Rental Units, 1970-1985, Projected to 1990

	1970	1980	1985	1990
Top Income for Bottom Quartile of Renters	$3,066	$5,742	$7,580	$9,418
Number of Households in Bottom Quartile (1000s)	5,890	7,148	8,070	8,992
Affordable Rent Limit for Bottom Quartile (30% of income)	$77	$144	$189	$235
Rental Units with Rents Below 30% Threshold (1000s)	6,622	5,209	5,224	5,239
Gap/Surplus of Affordable Units (1000s)	+732	−1,939	−2,846	−3,753
Number of Units Below 30% Threshold Occupied by Households in Bottom Quartile of Renters (1000s)	2,899	2,704	3,384	4,064
Occupancy Gap (1000s)	−2,991	−4,444	−4,686	−4,928
Constant 1985 Dollars Bottom quartile limit	$8,493	$7,496	$7,580	$7,664
30% of bottom quartile	$212	$187	$189	$192

Source: Cushing Dolbeare, "Why a Housing Entitlement Program?" Paper presented at Urban Institute Housing Seminar, December 1988.

The Concept of "Shelter Poverty"

Data presented earlier documented increasing rent burdens for all renters in the years between 1970 and 1988. Nevertheless, because these figures include renters at all income levels, rent burdens remain below 30 percent of income in 1988 in all but one instance (gross rents in the West). Since the Department of Housing and Urban Development now considers a rent equivalent to 30 percent of income affordable, perhaps the situation is not as bad as it has been painted. Before reaching this conclusion, however, we must look specifically at the situation for poor households. In addition, it would be good to consider conflicting demands on household income and ask what poor households really can afford to pay in rent.

Among poor renter households, 72 percent paid more than 35 percent of their income for rent in 1978. This proportion had risen to 79 percent by 1985. Still more disturbing, 44 percent of these poor renters paid more than 60 percent of their income for rent in 1978, and 55 percent did so in 1985 (Leonard, Dolbeare, and Lazere, 1989, Table 1). Clearly, the proportion of poor renters whose housing is "unaffordable" is large and growing.

Poor owners also bear high housing cost burdens. In 1978, 55 percent of this group paid more than 35 percent of their income for housing and 65 percent did so in 1985. Among poor owners, 31 percent paid 60 percent or more of income for housing in 1978, and 38 percent in 1985 (Leonard et al., 1989, Table 1).

But even these figures do not tell the whole story. Defining affordability in terms of a percentage of household income ignores the fact that households of different sizes have different needs. In absolute terms, moreover, households with high incomes will have much more money left over after paying 30 percent for housing than will low-income households. High-income households will therefore be better able to afford everything else than will low-income households.

The concept of "shelter poverty," first discussed by Stone (1983), attempts to develop a more meaningful measure of affordability. Using the Bureau of Labor Statistics' (BLS') "urban family budget" for a "lower" standard of living, Stone (1983) and Leonard et al. (1989) calculated how much households of a given size must spend for all necessities. Subtracting the housing cost component then yielded an estimate of the cost of everything else a low-income family must buy. Comparing this figure with actual income indicates how much a household can afford to pay for housing.

Using this approach, Leonard et al. (1989) calculated that 39.6 percent of renter households had affordability problems in 1985, a proportion only slightly higher than would result from applying the 30 percent of income standard (38.3 percent). This overall result masks differences among households of different sizes. The proportion with affordability problems actually dropped for one- and two-person households, and increased for all households of three or more (Leonard et al., 1989, Table A-II). The larger the household, the higher the proportion with problems. Dolbeare (1988) also estimated the proportion of all households (both owner and renter) whose incomes are so low that nonshelter requirements (based on the BLS "lower" budget) consume their entire income. By this standard, she found, 11 percent of all households, and 19 percent of female-headed households, could not afford to pay anything for housing.

These data on housing burden and shelter poverty show that housing costs for poor people have been high and increasing, especially for female-headed households. The effect on homelessness is twofold. First, the poorer the household and the more of its income it must expend on housing, the less able it will be to absorb relatives or friends who may lose their housing. As households become poorer, they cannot protect others against homelessness. Second, when housing takes the lion's share of a household's available resources, any crisis or other need for money increases the probability that the family will fall behind in rent, and perhaps be evicted. Thus the household itself runs an increased risk of becoming homeless. It is not surprising that the profile of homeless families (Burt and Cohen, 1989b; Sullivan and Damrosch, 1987) is quite similar to that of the families hardest hit by housing costs.

Discrimination in Housing Markets

Discrimination in housing markets against minorities and against households with children may further strain the resources of some poor households. Residential segregation based on race and ethnicity has been well documented (Denton and Massey, 1989; Galster, 1987; Massey and Denton, 1987, 1988, 1989; Massey and Eggers, 1990; Wienk et al., 1979). This segregation is not simply the residue of past discrimination; it continues unabated for minority households seeking both rental and ownership housing today (Turner, Struyk, and Yinger, 1990). In addition, some observers have suggested that the concentration of poverty in central cities has created an underclass that is a cultural and behavioral phenomenon as well as an economic one (Bane and Jargowsky, 1988; Jargowsky and Bane, 1990; Ricketts and Sawhill, 1988; Wilson, 1987). Massey and Eggers (1990) combine these two themes to demonstrate that residential segregation arising from racial discrimination tends to increase poverty. Discrimination may therefore contribute to homelessness through its effects on poverty.

Discrimination may encourage homelessness in another way as well. Low-cost housing in or near ghetto neighborhoods is a prime target for disinvestment, abandonment, or conversion (Brady, 1983; Smith, Duncan, and Reid, 1989; Smith and Williams, 1986). Disinvestment leads to deterioration in the housing stock as well as inadequate provision of utilities; renters get lower-quality housing for their money. Ghetto housing also runs the risk of complete abandonment, or of gentrification. Arson for profit is also commonplace, for it facilitates either complete disinvestment or conversion (Brady, 1983). The consequence is a reduction of either the total number of rental units in the stock or the number of low-cost units.

Households with children also face discrimination in rental housing. Working with a national sample of renters and their rental agents, Marans and Colten (1985) found that one-fourth of rental units prohibited children altogether. An additional 50 percent of units had restrictions on the number or ages of children, sharing of bedrooms, or location within a building or rental complex. They also found that the extent of restrictions depended on the racial composition of neighborhoods. Families with children faced greater discrimination in predominantly white neighborhoods than in predominantly black neighborhoods.

The facts of housing discrimination and their association with poverty are drawn together in Elliott and Krivo's (1991) analysis of factors associated with homelessness. They found that the proportions of black people and female-headed families with children in a city's population were significantly related to homelessness as well as to poverty and income inequality.

This review of available data has identified three aspects of the housing problem that may have a bearing on homelessness. First, many metropolitan areas simply do not have enough units available to house all families in physically adequate dwellings without overcrowding. The undersupply of larger units is particularly acute. Vacancy rates as ordinarily computed do not capture the adequacy of supply once household size and unit size are taken into consideration. Second, the 1980s saw a severe increase in affordability problems. Because household incomes have not kept pace with housing costs, rent burdens have increased for many households, but especially for the poor. Third, rental housing does not operate as a free market for many of the households with the most acute housing needs and financial constraints—most notably, large families, households with children, and members of minority groups. Discrimination thus compounds the problems created by shortfalls in standard quality units and by escalating rent burdens.

FEDERAL POLICIES AFFECTING HOUSING

Advocates for the homeless often claim that cuts in the budget of the Department of Housing and Urban Development played a major role in creating the problems of the 1980s. Between 1981 and 1989, they point out, the federal budget authority for subsidized housing dropped more than 80 percent, from $32 billion to $6 billion. These startling figures may have important implications for the availability of low-cost housing in the 1990s. However, their import for the 1980s is not as straightforward as it might seem.

In fact, federal subsidies reached more households and a larger proportion of the poverty population in 1989 than in 1981. (Chapter 5 provides greater detail on these changes.) Although federal spending was much reduced, it reached more households, for two reasons. First, these funds were used to subsidize residence in existing housing rather than to build new housing; second, they financed five-year subsidy commitments to renters rather than fifteen-year commitments (which in itself meant that a given dollar amount could serve three times as many households).

The fifteen- to five-year change should have decreased the financial pressure on low-income renters somewhat, since more households were covered by a subsidy. Any negative impact would be felt only in the future, if Congress or the administration failed to renew existing subsidy commitments. To date, however, commitments have been renewed as they expired, and provisions of the National Affordable Housing Act of 1990 assure renewals of all commitments in the future.

But renters in the 1980s may have been hurt by an accompanying shift from unit-based to tenant-based subsidies. The former fifteen-year subsidy commitments had been unit based; if one tenant moved, the landlord was still assured of rental income from the next tenant through federal subsidy. The shorter commitments are mostly tenant based; if tenants move, the subsidy goes with them. Conceivably the shorter time commitment and tenant control of the subsidy might discourage some landlords from renting to subsidized tenants, whereas the longer fifteen-year unit-based commitments provided enough incentives and guarantees to attract landlords.

The change from new construction to vouchers for existing stock could have a negative impact under certain circumstances. In the past, government assistance has produced rental housing both through direct construction (public housing) and through construction subsidies and assurance of an adequate rental stream to private developers (Sections 8, 202, and 235). In principle, certificates or vouchers to subsidize rents in existing units could raise the purchasing power of poor households enough that private landlords and developers would hold existing units or build new ones for that market. However, the experience of the 1980s suggests that unless the federal government guarantees developers a profit for holding or building low-income housing, they will cater to the middle and upper end of the rental market rather than the poor. The current value of certificates and vouchers (i.e., the level of rent they would support) does not appear to be high enough to tempt landlords or developers to serve subsidized households.

The shortfall in affordable rental housing described earlier is probably due in part to federal withdrawal from new construction and substantial rehabilitation of rental units. Approximately the same number of new rental units have been added to the housing stock, on average, in each of the last twenty years. But the proportion of the incremental rental stock that was developed to meet the needs of low-income households was significantly higher in the 1970s than in the 1980s. New federal incentives available since 1987 have partially reversed this shift.

To understand how the federal government may have influenced homelessness, one must look more carefully at the range of policies that affect the creation and maintenance of housing, and make it affordable. Government can build housing itself or use a variety of policies to induce private developers to build. Federal policies begun in the 1930s stimulated housing production for the middle class for five decades through new approaches to financing home ownership. These included providing new payment schedules and insurance backing for mortgages through the Federal Housing Administration (and later the Veterans and Farmers Home Administrations), creating a secondary market for mortgages through the Federal National Mortgage Administration, and subsidizing home ownership through tax deductions for mortgage interest and property taxes (Struyk, Turner, and Ueno, 1988). These practices made home ownership affordable for many households, increasing owner occupancy from about 45 percent in the 1920s to over 60 percent by 1960.

Federal policies aimed at increasing housing options for the poor have included building housing directly (public housing, mostly in the 1950s), stimulating production by the private sector (after 1960), and offering income assistance to enable tenants to afford existing units (from the mid-1970s). Mechanisms to stimulate building new units included production subsidies through below-market interest rates and favorable tax treatment, plus rent supplements to assure a steady income stream despite the very low tenant incomes (Struyk, Turner, and Ueno, 1988).

Since the 1930s, housing production for both the poor and the middle class has been subsidized through federal policies. Hoch and Slayton (1989, Chapter 4) discuss the private sector's inability, since the 1920s, to build profitably for the poor without government subsidy or assistance. But it is also true that since the 1930s the private sector has not been able to build profitably without subsidy or assistance for the vast majority of moderate- and middle-income households. For either group, housing becomes more affordable under conditions of favorable government policies.

Changes in direct federal housing subsidy programs during the 1980s are likely to have been less significant contributors to homelessness than other elements of federal policy that influenced the profitability of rental housing for low-income people. These include tax treatment of investments in low-rent housing, and factors affecting interest rates (huge budget deficits and efforts to control inflation through monetary policy).

Ownership of rental housing is presumably motivated by a desire for profits. Production of, maintenance of, and investment in rental housing should therefore respond to factors that affect its profitability. Rents are one such factor, but they are not what kept rental housing profitable in the 1970s. By Downs's (1983, p. 3) estimates, rents in 1980 would have had to be 30 percent higher than they were to support the rental market values of 1970, and 77 percent higher to support those of 1960. In fact, "the real value of rental housing properties in the United States *sustainable from rents alone* appears to have fallen substantially since 1960—perhaps by 50 percent or more" (Downs, 1983, p. 3, emphasis in original).

One reason rents stayed as low as they did is that the incomes of renting households could not sustain significant increases. Downs (1983) and Sternlieb and Hughes (1985) describe the flight of higher-income renters to home ownership during the later 1970s, as real costs of home ownership were reduced by very high inflation and the availability of relatively low fixed-rate mortgages, coupled with tax policies that allowed deductions for mortgage interest and real estate taxes. In other words, home ownership became very cheap in relation to renting for higher-income tenants. Each of these factors is very much influenced by federal policy.

The departure of higher-income families changed the composition of the rental sector, Sternlieb and Hughes (1985) explain: "While renters have increasingly been drawn from the pool of the less affluent, nominal rents have grown relatively modestly—and this in the face of rather impressive increases in some of the principal operating-cost components. The degeneration in effective market demand for rental units was surely the root cause, but it was made possible in many cases by a much less broadly acknowledged fact: the existence of relatively inexpensive fixed-rate mortgages" (pp. 19-20).

Although rents stayed relatively low, investment in rental property remained profitable at least until 1980. According to Downs several factors were responsible:

1. Tax shelter helped offset low net operating income because deductible losses benefit high-bracket investors.

2. Leverage, the advantage gained by borrowing most of the cost of each investment, magnified the positive effects of depreciation deductions and increases in property values during the inflationary 1970s.

3. Low real rates of interest occurred in the late 1960s and throughout the 1970s because lenders failed to foresee rising inflation [or were constrained by regulation from raising interest rates].

4. Anticipated appreciation resulted in many cases from the possibility of converting rental units to condominiums. It was also stimulated by a rising belief among most investors that real estate was a good hedge against inflation.

All four factors helped raise yields on equity investments in rental units far above their current earnings from rents (Downs, 1983, pp. 3-4).

In short, tax code provisions, housing price inflation, and low interest rates interacted to increase landlords' profits. During the 1980s, however, higher real interest rates and new types of financing, such as variable-rate mortgages, changed the incentives to invest in rental housing. The pressures on the money supply created by large federal deficits, coupled with monetary policy focused on controlling inflation, kept interest rates high for much of the early 1980s.

By allowing accelerated depreciation and tax shelter for investment in all rental housing, with some special provisions for low-income housing limited partnerships, the Economic Recovery and Tax Act of 1981 encouraged some private investment in housing for low-income renters. Exemption from federal taxes also encouraged private investment in industrial development bonds, issued by state and local housing agencies and used extensively to finance construction of low-income housing. By some estimates, these bonds financed 20 to 30 percent of all new construction of rental housing units in the early 1980s

(Apgar et al., 1985). By federal law, at least 20 percent of these units had to be reserved for low- and moderate-income renters (those with incomes below 80 percent of their area's median renter income). Before 1986, however, this income limit was not adjusted for family size, so many units went to one- or two-person households that were not poor. The Tax Reform Act of 1986 corrected this problem by lowering the income cutoff to 60 percent of the area median and adding an adjustment for family size.

Other aspects of the 1986 act effectively reduced the remaining incentives to invest in low-cost housing. First, the reduction of the maximum tax rate diminished the value of real estate interest deductions. Second, the act lengthened the term of real estate depreciation from fifteen years for low-income rentals to twenty-eight years, and reduced accelerated depreciation. Third, it eliminated the unearned tax benefits for high-income passive investors in housing tax shelters. Fourth, it eliminated special tax treatment of capital gains, thereby reducing profit at the time of sale. Fifth, it limited the tax-exempt status of industrial development bonds. DiPasquale and Wheaton (1989) estimated a 5 percent rise in real rents over the next ten years as a consequence of the act. To put this increase in perspective, they observe that "over the last 3 decades, real rents have varied by less than 20%" (p. 3).

In many respects the Tax Reform Act of 1986 reduced the incentives for investing in any housing. Within these overall constraints, it made one change intended to encourage the production of housing for low-income renters. The 1986 act established a three-year program for low-income housing tax credits, which was extended in fiscal 1990 and again in fiscal 1991. In 1988, $304 million was available for these tax credits and $202 million was used, making possible the construction or rehabilitation of 57,000 units of housing for low- and very-low-income renters. An additional 11,000 units were acquired for this use without rehabilitation (which did not add units to the stock, but did convert them from market rate to low-income use). The 57,000 new and rehabilitated units are equivalent to about 7 percent of the average of 773,000 rental units added per year from 1981 to 1987. In fact, almost three times as many new or rehabilitated units were generated through these tax credits as through Section 8 and Public Housing (20,700). Figures for production using low-income housing tax credits in subsequent years are expected to be even higher, since all available credits have been allocated. On net, the Tax Reform Act of 1986 has probably increased the tax benefits of low-income housing production, while lowering the overall incentives to invest in any housing.

Clearly, many federal policies affect the production and availability of low-cost housing. At least during the 1980s, tax, deficit spending, and inflation-control policies probably had a larger impact on the rental stock, and thereby presumably on homelessness, than policies directly related to subsidized housing for the poor. The increased number of subsidies established in the 1980s could conceivably have a net positive effect on the stock by reducing abandonment and deterioration. Countering any such trend, however, would be the pressures brought by growth and downtown revitalization efforts toward converting low-rent urban housing to more profitable uses. Any assessment of the overall effect of government housing policies on homelessness must focus on the net gain or loss of units suitable to the population in need, however created or rendered affordable.

SUMMARY AND CONCLUSIONS

In the early 1980s the existing rental stock in many metropolitan areas could not have accommodated all renter households in standard-quality housing, even if cost were no consideration. As the decade progressed, moreover, low-income renters were forced to devote an increasing proportion of their income to housing costs. Two things happened simultaneously: rents increased, and renter households had less money to spend. The income reduction was due in part to shifts in the types of households that made up the renter population, as we saw earlier. Later chapters will explore the factors affecting the remaining renters' available resources: reductions in the real wages of low-skilled workers, and reductions in the real value of public benefits.

Whatever its source, the reduction in real renter income during the 1980s puts a good deal of pressure on poor renter households. Yet the vast majority of poor renters continue to be housed, although their rent burden may leave them with little money for other essentials. Even the poorest of poor renters, however, have more money at their disposal than does the average homeless household (Rossi, 1989).

Poor renters in the 1980s are more likely than those of the 1970s to be single-person or one-adult households (usually female headed). Both household types are more vulnerable to a crisis affecting the only earner or adult than are husband-wife households. Single-person and one-adult households are less able to support disabled or unemployed family members. Should they lose housing following some crisis (e. g., loss of a job or of government benefits), they are less likely to have the cash to get back into the housing market. Thus their circumstances, combined with increasing housing costs, put them and their wider network of family and friends at higher risk of homelessness.

A reduction in the absolute number of low-cost units will increase the risk of homelessness if rent burdens increase. If all other things were equal, one would expect federal withdrawal from the production of new or substantially rehabilitated low-cost units to exacerbate homelessness, inasmuch as lower supply would result in higher prices, and higher burdens. But it is not clear that the number of low-cost units (or of units effectively rendered low-cost through subsidies that reduce renter payments to 30 percent of income) has indeed gone down in the 1980s, relative to demand.

Additions to the rental stock in any given year represent a relatively small proportion of the entire stock. Thus changes in the number of additions for a single year are unlikely to affect the availability or price of rental units immediately. Although the number of units added through federal new construction and substantial rehabilitation programs began to decline in the late 1970s, this change would take some years to affect the availability of low-cost rental units. Even with this slowdown, one would need to assess other factors before concluding that the total affordable rental stock had changed.

It appears that the purely private market cannot afford to produce low-price housing and thus has no independent effect on availability. Four other factors are important:

1. The rate at which poor households receive subsidies that make relatively more costly rental units affordable for them, and the amount of the subsidy (essentially, reducing the cost from the nominal rent level to a lower level).
2. The rate at which low-priced or low-rent units are being removed from the existing housing stock available to low-income renters, through gentrification, conversion to other uses, demolition, or abandonment.
3. The rate at which low-rent units are being created through other mechanisms subject to federal policy, such as tax-sheltered real estate development partnerships, industrial development bonds, or, more recently, low-income housing tax credits.
4. The rate at which the private market builds housing that attracts the higher-income renters who currently compete with low-income households for the inadequate supply of low-rent units.

We saw earlier that subsidies (certificates or vouchers) covered a higher proportion of poor households during the late 1980s than was true for earlier years, even though the number of poor households increased significantly. We also saw that the number of units available in the housing stock, independent of price, was inadequate to meet the need for standard-quality rental housing in the early 1980s. Between 1981 and 1987 1.2 million units were lost from the low-cost stock (although some of these may have been "lost" only in the sense that their rents increased beyond $300, leaving them still potentially affordable with subsidies). Concurrently, several mechanisms created by federal policy have led to significant additions to the affordable stock. However, it is not easy to determine the total number of additional units and their rents, and until the 1990 census data can be analyzed, their joint impact will not be known. Until we can examine the simultaneous effects of all these factors on the availability of affordable housing, it may be premature to blame the crisis of homelessness on the federal shift from creating new units to subsidizing existing ones.

Real rent burdens, and hence the risk of homelessness, have increased in the 1980s. The federal policies with greatest influence on these changes are likely to have been those related to taxation, deficit spending, and the control of inflation, rather than the reduction in the budget authority of the Department of Housing and Urban Development, even though that reduction was substantial. (Of course, if budget authority had remained at 1980 levels and been used for five-year subsidy commitments for existing units, four to five times as many households could have been supported.) Further, as we have seen, the "housing problem" is not merely a lack of appropriate rental units, but an inability on the part of poor households to afford what does exist. Thus housing policy per se may be no more influential than federal policies that reduced eligibility for and benefits from income support programs in a period of increasing unemployment and poverty. The next two chapters examine the relevant changes in household income and poverty, and in government income support programs.

CHAPTER FOUR

Changes in Poverty and Household Income

■ Homeless persons are extremely poor. In the Urban Institute's 1987 national interview study of homeless users of soup kitchens and shelters, homeless single men reported a mean income of $143 for the preceding thirty days; single women reported $183; and homeless women with children reported $300 to cover a typical household with a mother and two children. These figures translate to an annual income of about $2,000 for a one-person household (about one-third of the federal poverty level), or $3,600 for a family of three (40 percent of the poverty level) (Burt and Cohen, 1989a, 1989b). Single-city studies of the homeless have found comparably low income levels. Median incomes were even lower; single homeless people reported a median monthly income of $64, or only $768 a year (Burt and Cohen, 1989a).

Even very poor people with homes have substantially higher incomes. Whereas Rossi (1989) reports a mean income for Chicago's homeless of $168 a month in 1985–1986, Hoch and Spicer (1985, cited in Rossi, 1989, p. 107) found that Chicago's single-room-occupancy hotel residents had an average monthly income of $580 in 1985.

Further evidence from Chicago documents that homeless people come from the ranks of the very poor, and resemble other very poor people on many important dimensions. Sosin, Colson, and Grossman (1988) interviewed people using soup kitchens, drop-in centers, and other free meal programs in Chicago. Their sample included some people who were currently homeless, some people who were very poor but had never been homeless, and some people who were currently housed but who had been homeless at some point in their adult lives. People in the study who had been or were currently homeless did not differ from the never-homeless with respect to their work histories, past and current marital status, parenting histories, lifetime earnings, prison or jail experiences, or involvement with drugs. But they were twice as likely to have lived in out-of-home institutions as children. This finding signals a probable breakdown or incapacity in their family of origin while they were still children. If, as a character in one of Robert Frost's poems maintains, "home is . . . where they have to take you in," one predictor of homelessness is the absence of such a refuge when it becomes impossible to take care of oneself. Those who had been homeless at some time were also somewhat more likely than the never-homeless to have problems with alcohol.

These results suggest that the very poor are vulnerable to homelessness, and many of them have experienced at least one episode of homelessness in their adult lives. Moreover, lack of a family network increases an already rather high risk of homelessness, as does behavior that strains one's relationship with family, such as alcohol abuse. The association of homelessness with extreme poverty makes it very important that we understand the increase in poverty during the 1980s, and its differential impact on various groups, if we are to understand the recent growth of homelessness.

This chapter examines national shifts in poverty. Circumstances may differ from one area to another, however, and these local effects will be explored in Part II of this volume. Here I begin by examining changes affecting single people. I then look at changes in the numbers of people in poverty, poverty rates, and the poverty gap for all households and for selected household types. After a brief discussion of increases in inequality, as distinct from poverty, I turn to some potential causes of the shifts in poverty and inequality. These include labor market factors—unemployment, employment structure, wage levels, and the minimum wage—and racial discrimination. Together these changes have decreased the resources available to many poor households between 1970 and 1989, making it more difficult for them to afford housing. The households hardest hit are single young people and female-headed families with children. These are the same households most prominent among the "new" homeless.

SINGLE PEOPLE

Because almost three-fourths of homeless households consist of a single man, and another tenth consist of a single woman, the circumstances of one-person households are of particular importance for understanding the growth of homelessness. In the American population overall and in the subpopulation of poor households, however, one-person households constitute a much smaller proportion of the total. As a result, most statistical presentations do not break out separate results for one-person nonelderly households. This section pulls together the limited data available to suggest what has been happening to single people that might explain their disproportionate presence among the homeless.

As we saw in Chapter 2, 82 percent of the homeless in the Urban Institute study were not accompanied by any other person. Among the single men, 53 percent were young (under thirty-five), and 57 percent had never married; corresponding figures for single women were 50 and 49 percent. Compared with the American population as a whole, this is an extraordinarily high rate of aloneness. The most directly comparable category in available poverty data is "unrelated individuals"—people who do not live in households with others to whom they are related by blood or marriage. Current Population Survey data indicate that from 1982 through 1987, about one in five nonelderly adult unrelated individuals was poor. About half of these people were very poor, with incomes that were less than half the poverty threshold level (U.S. House, 1990, p. 1033). Nonparticipation in the labor force is one important reason for their poverty. About 85 percent of single people work. Among those who work, only 10 percent are poor (Klein and Rones, 1989), suggesting a poverty rate of about 77 percent among those who do not work.

Recent simulation analyses conducted at the Urban Institute indicate that already poor young people and unrelated individuals suffered the largest proportional income losses in the mid-1980s (Michel, 1990). Average inflation-adjusted posttax income for household heads under twenty-five and between twenty-five and thirty-four in the lowest income quintile for their age groups dropped 20 percent and 4 percent, respectively, between 1983 and 1987. The only other age groups to experience a drop in household income were those fifty-five and older in the lowest income quintile for their age. Further, when the population was subdivided by household type, unrelated individuals in the lowest income quintile were seen to have experienced a drop of 6 percent in average inflation-adjusted posttax income between 1983 and 1987. Only the lowest income quintile for families with female heads registered a larger decline (8 percent). In comparison, bottom-quintile married couples experienced an increase of 8 percent during the same years. Evidently poor young people and poor single people got poorer as the 1980s progressed, while other household types held their own or increased their incomes.

During the 1980s, as in previous decades, the proportion of young people who have ever married continued to decline, while the proportion who do not currently live in married-couple households (although they may have married at some time) increased. These trends suggest that more young people may be at risk of homelessness because they live either by themselves or, if they are women with children, in households with only one potential earner. As we will see below, such households are more likely to be poor.

A look at the proportion of men who live with their wives indicates the extent of the change. Among twenty- to twenty-three-year-olds in 1970, 35 percent of white men and 28 percent of black men lived with a spouse. Among twenty-four- to twenty-nine-year-olds in the same year, the figures were 72 and 58 percent, respectively. By 1980, the proportions had shrunk to 24 and 13 percent for the younger age group, and to 56 and 39 percent for the older group.

The proportion of young men in this type of household declined even further by the middle of the 1980s, to 19 percent for white men and 10 percent for black men in the younger group, and to 52 percent for white men and 35 percent for black men in the older group (Mare and Winship, 1991). The decline has been more precipitous for young black men, who are consistently less likely to be married and living with a spouse than are young white men. A parallel development has been a declining rate of participation in the labor force for young black men (but not for young white men or young women of either race), which Mare and Winship (1991) analyze as being responsible for some of the decline in marriage rates.

Taken in combination, these reductions in earnings, labor force participation, and likelihood of marriage have probably contributed to the growth of homelessness among the young and single. With very little money and few or no relatives or other social supports to turn to, many poor single people may be at high risk of homelessness. Where they are available, additional data relevant to single individuals will be discussed in subsequent sections of this chapter. I turn now to a review of the much more extensive analyses available for the entire poverty population.

HOW MANY PEOPLE ARE POOR?

Researchers and policymakers have developed several alternative definitions of poverty. One approach is to count the number of people or households whose incomes fall below the poverty line, a numerical standard developed by the Census Bureau and adjusted annually for inflation. Using this definition, Table 4-1 shows the numbers in poverty and poverty rates for all individuals, elderly individuals, and individuals living in female-headed households, from 1970 through 1988.[1] In this tally, a person is considered poor if the sum of all cash income plus income from social insurance (e.g., unemployment compensation), Social Security, and means-tested benefits (e.g., AFDC, Supplemental Security Income (SSI), General Assistance) is below the official poverty line. The poverty rate is the number of poor people in a category divided by the total number of people, poor and nonpoor, in that category.

As Table 4-1 reveals, there were 3.9 million more poor people in 1980 than in 1970, an increase of 15 percent. Much of this increase was due to simple population growth, but the poverty rate also increased from 12.6 percent to

---

[1]The category "individuals in female-headed households" includes both families with children and multiperson households without children headed by a woman (e.g., two sisters living together). It excludes one-woman households, however; the many poor elderly women who live alone are included in the figures on aged individuals, but are not counted among female-headed households.

Table 4-1 Numbers in Poverty and Poverty Rates, 1970-1988

	Numbers Below Poverty (in 1000s)					Poverty Rates (Percentage of Total)				
	All	Aged	Individuals in Female-headed Families	Black	Hispanic	All	Aged	Individuals in Female-headed Families	Black	Hispanic
1970	25,420	4,793	10,440	7,548	NA	12.6%	24.6%	38.1%	33.5%	NA
1971	25,559	4,273	10,551	7,396	NA	12.5	21.6	38.7	32.5	NA
1972	24,460	3,738	10,284	7,710	2,414	11.9	18.6	38.2	33.3	22.8%
1973	22,973	3,354	8,178	7,388	2,366	11.1	16.3	37.5	31.4	21.9
1974	23,370	3,085	8,462	7,182	2,575	11.2	14.6	36.5	30.3	23.0
1975	25,877	3,317	8,846	7,545	2,991	12.3	15.3	37.5	31.3	26.9
1976	24,975	3,313	9,029	7,595	2,783	11.8	15.0	37.3	31.1	24.7
1977	24,720	3,177	9,205	7,726	2,700	11.6	14.1	36.2	31.3	22.4
1978	24,497	3,233	9,269	7,625	2,607	11.4	14.0	35.6	30.6	21.6
1979	26,072	3,682	9,400	8,050	2,921	11.7	15.2	34.9	31.0	21.8
1980	29,272	3,871	10,120	8,579	3,491	13.0	15.7	36.7	32.5	30.8
1981	31,822	3,853	11,051	9,173	3,713	14.0	15.3	38.7	34.2	26.5
1982	34,398	3,751	11,701	9,697	4,301	15.0	14.6	40.6	35.6	29.9
1983	35,303	3,625	12,072	9,882	4,633	15.2	13.8	40.2	35.7	28.0
1984	33,700	3,330	11,831	9,490	4,806	14.4	12.4	38.4	33.8	28.4
1985	33,064	3,456	11,600	8,926	5,236	14.0	12.6	37.6	31.3	29.0
1986	32,370	3,477	11,944	8,983	5,117	13.6	12.4	38.3	31.1	27.3
1987	32,546	3,491	12,278	9,683	5,470	13.5	12.2	38.3	33.1	28.2
1988	31,878	3,482	12,103	9,426	5,279	13.1	12.0	37.4	31.6	26.8

Source: U.S. House of Representatives, Committee on Ways and Means, *Overview of Entitlement Programs: The 1990 Green Book*, Washington, D.C., Government Printing Office, 1990, pp. 1023-1025.

13.0. The most precipitous increase in poverty occurred between 1980 and 1983, when 6.0 million more people became poor. This was a 20 percent increase in poor persons, and a 17 percent increase in the poverty rate. Even in 1988, when the numbers in poverty had declined somewhat, there were still 2.6 million more poor people than in 1980.

The numbers of poor elderly declined during the period covered by Table 4-1, and their poverty rate dropped substantially in the early 1970s because of indexing and other changes in Social Security. It continued a slow decline in later years. The pattern for individuals in female-headed families is less encouraging. Many more individuals in families headed by women were poor in the 1980s than was true in the 1970s. Yet since the mid-1970s the rate of poverty in this group has fluctuated within a fairly narrow range rather than showing a steady increase or decrease.

Because of changes in Social Security, the aged have become a substantially smaller proportion of the poverty population. They represented 18.9 percent of the poor in 1970, 13.2 percent in 1980, and only 10.9 percent by 1987. On the other hand, people in female-headed households grew as a proportion of the poor, from 43.9 percent in 1970 to 50 percent in 1980 and 52 percent in 1987, with a decline in 1988. The biggest jump for this group thus came in the 1970s.

Single-parent female-headed families with children are poorer than the larger category of female-headed households. Single-parent female-headed families have increased not only in absolute numbers but also as a proportion of all families with children, from 11.5 percent in 1970 to 19.4 percent in 1980, and 25.2 percent in 1988 (U.S. House, 1990, p. 876). As the 1980s progressed, moreover, a larger proportion of female-headed families with children were in poverty; 40 percent were poor in 1979, compared with 47 percent in 1988 (U.S. House, 1990, p. 1030).

Female-headed households with children are precisely the families most likely to become homeless. Among homeless households with children, 80 percent are female-headed single-parent families. Households headed by women are more likely to be poor for two reasons. Not only are their hourly earnings significantly lower than men's, but their conflicting role obligations and childcare responsibilities make it harder for them to work full-time (Ellwood, 1988; Klein and Rones, 1989). Thirty-five percent of the mothers in homeless families had held a steady job (three or more months with the same employer) within the twelve months before being interviewed, but 37 percent had not worked steadily for four years or more (Burt and Cohen, 1989a, 1989b). Because of their lower earning capacity, greater poverty, and greater reliance on noninflation-adjusted public welfare benefits, female-headed households with children are especially vulnerable to homelessness.

As we saw in Chapter 2, there are more than three times as many blacks among the homeless as their share of the total U.S. population would suggest.

Hispanics are also slightly overrepresented among the homeless. If poverty is one root cause of homelessness, we would expect to see rates of poverty for blacks and Hispanics that parallel the data on homelessness. White poverty rates ranged between 8.4 and 9.9 percent during the 1970s, and between 10.2 and 12.1 percent between 1980 and 1988. As Table 4-1 shows, poverty rates for blacks in the 1970 to 1988 period were about three times those of whites. Hispanic poverty rates were also high, more than twice those of whites. Thus poverty rates for blacks in comparison with whites roughly parallel their overrepresentation among the homeless. However, the high poverty rates of Hispanics do not translate directly into the homeless statistics. Apparently other factors are at work that buffer the effects of poverty for Hispanics somewhat more than they do for blacks.

THE ANTIPOVERTY IMPACT OF GOVERNMENT PROGRAMS

Changes in public benefits during the 1980s (detailed in Chapter 5) increased the risk of homelessness for poor families. During the 1970s, noncash food and housing benefit programs served more people, noncash benefits were worth more, and tax policy was less punitive to low-income people than was true a decade later. If noncash benefits and tax effects are considered in assessing poverty, only 21.6 million people would have been considered poor in 1979. The increase from 1979 to 1987 would then be 41 percent, rather than the 20.6 percent calculated under the definition used in Table 4-1. Further, the poverty rate increased 37.4 percent under the expanded definition, compared with 15.4 percent in Table 4-1. By reducing the resources available to poor households, these federal program changes probably made them more vulnerable to financial crisis and ultimately to homelessness.

The Committee on Ways and Means of the U.S. House of Representatives analyzed the ability of various social programs to lift households above the poverty line (U.S. House, 1990). Table 4-2 starts with the numbers in poverty and the poverty rate, and examines the sources of income that remove individuals from poverty. It also shows the changing effectiveness of these mechanisms from 1979 through 1988. The first row of the table shows the number of individuals who would be considered poor if only cash income before transfers was counted. This cash income includes cash from earnings, pensions, savings, investments, self-employment income, and similar sources. The second and third panels show the numbers and percentages of people removed from poverty by various social programs. The final panel shows the poverty rate that would result from different definitions of poverty. As the "cash income before transfers" row of this fourth panel shows, between 19 and 23 percent of all Americans were poor during the 1979 to 1988 period if one counts only cash income before transfers. This poverty rate is considerably higher for every year

Table 4-2 Antipoverty Effectiveness of Cash and Noncash Transfers, 1979-1988

	1979	1980	1981	1982
Number of Poor Individuals[a] *(thousands)*	41,695	46,273	49,184	51,942
Number (thousands) Removed from Poverty by:				
Social insurance (other than Social Security)	1,860	2,257	2,210	2,953
Social insurance (including Social Security)	13,849	14,635	15,275	15,738
Means-tested cash, food, and housing benefits	6,915	6,756	6,206	5,711
Federal taxes	−675	−1,148	−2,280	−2,056
Percentage Removed from Poverty by:				
Social insurance (including Social Security)	33.2%	31.6%	31.1%	30.3%
Means-tested cash transfers	6.3	5.5	4.8	3.9
Means-tested cash, food, and housing benefits	16.6	14.6	12.6	11.0
Means-tested cash, food, and housing benefits and federal taxes	15.0	12.1	8.0	7.0
Povery Rate (percent)				
Cash income before transfers	19.1%	20.6%	21.7%	22.6%
Plus social insurance (other than Social Security)	18.3	19.6	20.7	21.4
Plus Social Security	12.8	14.1	14.9	15.8
Plus means-test cash transfers (official definition)	11.6	12.9	13.9	14.9
Plus food and housing benefits	9.6	11.1	12.2	13.3
Less federal taxes	9.9	11.6	13.2	14.2

[a]Poverty defined by cash income before transfers.
Source: U.S. House of Representatives, Committee on Ways and Means, *Overview of Entitlement Programs: The 1990 Green Book,* Washington, D.C., Government Printing Office, 1990, pp. 1041-1042.

than the official poverty rate after transfers and taxes, given in the last row of the table.

The second panel of Table 4-2 reveals that Social Security is the social program most effective in removing people from poverty. In every year from 1979 through 1988, Social Security lifted more than twice as many people out of poverty as did the means-tested cash, food, and housing benefits that form the core of public welfare spending. The third panel of the table reveals that these means-tested benefits became much less effective in preventing poverty during the 1980s. In 1979, these programs removed from poverty 16.6 percent of those

1983	1984	1985	1986	1987	1988
52,700	50,943	50,462	49,702	49,679	49,145
3,232	2,253	2,254	2,236	1,948	1,848
15,772	15,241	15,291	15,168	15,299	15,295
5,231	5,599	5,682	5,546	5,376	5,493
−2,226	−2,426	−2,351	−2,261	−1,396	−857
29.9%	29.9%	30.3%	30.5%	30.8%	31.1%
3.6	3.9	4.1	4.4	3.7	4.5
9.9	11.0	11.3	11.2	10.8	11.2
5.7	6.2	6.6	6.6	8.0	9.4
22.8%	21.8%	21.3%	20.8%	20.6%	20.2%
21.4	20.8	20.4	19.9	19.8	19.4
15.9	15.3	14.9	14.5	14.3	13.9
15.1	14.4	14.0	13.6	13.5	13.0
13.7	12.9	12.5	12.2	12.0	11.6
14.6	13.9	13.5	13.1	12.6	12.0

who would have been poor on the basis of cash income alone. This figure dropped to 14.6 percent in 1980, then fell even more dramatically to a low of only 9.9 percent in 1983. The drop occurred as a consequence of provisions enacted in the Omnibus Budget Reconciliation Act of 1981, restricting eligibility for the major benefit programs. These were also the years in which the issue of homelessness first forced itself into the national consciousness. The reductions in aid coincided with the worst recession and highest unemployment since the Depression, severely straining people's ability to cope.

HOW POOR ARE THE POOR?

A mechanism such as the poverty line that divides people into two groups, those who are poor and those who are not, is too simple in some important respects. It

Table 4-3 Reduction in the Poverty Gap Due to Cash and Noncash Transfers, 1979-1988

	1979	1980	1981	1982	1983
Poverty Gap (millions of 1987 dollars)					
Cash income before transfers	$100,276	$111,613	$118,235	$123,562	$126,720
Plus social insurance (other than Social Security)	93,481	103,424	110,471	114,739	116,617
Plus Social Security	51,881	58,398	63,763	68,480	71,431
Plus means-tested cash transfers	35,981	41,415	46,782	51,287	53,231
Plus food and housing benefits	28,176	32,239	37,441	40,687	42,409
Less federal taxes	28,628	32,945	38,734	42,119	43,988
Percentage Reduction in the Poverty Gap Due to:					
Social insurance (excluding Social Security)	6.8%	7.1%	6.6%	7.1%	8.0%
Social Security	41.5	40.6	39.5	37.5	35.6
Means-tested cash, food and housing benefits	23.7	23.4	22.3	22.5	23.1
Cash only	15.9	15.2	14.4	13.9	14.4
Noncash (food and housing)	7.8	8.2	7.9	8.6	8.7
Percent increase in poverty gap due to federal taxes:	0.4	0.6	1.1	1.2	1.2
Percentage of poverty gap remaining after all programs and federal taxes	28.5	29.5	32.8	34.1	34.7

Source: U.S. House of Representatives, Committee on Ways and Means, *Overview of Entitlement Programs: The 1990 Green Book,* Washington, D.C., Government Printing Office, 1990, pp. 1041-1042.

makes no distinction between the person whose income is only $1.00 below the poverty line and the person with only one-half or one-quarter that amount. To measure degrees of poverty, researchers developed the concept of the "poverty gap," which indicates the amount of money it would take to lift every poor person out of poverty. The poverty gap will be quite small if all poor people have incomes just under the poverty line, and will be very large if all poor people have incomes very far below the poverty line.

In 1979 the United States' poverty gap based on cash income before transfers was $100 billion (in constant 1987 dollars). It grew to $127 billion by 1983 and shrank only to $124 billion by 1988 (see Table 4-3). These changes

1984	1985	1986	1987	1988
$122,517	$122,327	$122,905	$124,246	$121,956
114,939	115,427	116,299	117,820	116,403
69,047	68,280	68,678	69,419	67,000
50,671	50,480	50,987	51,650	50,184
40,021	39,929	40,316	40,434	38,962
41,747	41,601	41,948	41,394	39,772
6.2%	5.6%	5.4%	5.2%	4.6%
37.4	38.6	38.7	38.9	40.5
23.7	23.2	23.1	23.3	23.0
15.0	14.6	14.4	14.3	13.8
8.7	8.6	8.7	9.0	9.2
1.4	1.4	1.3	0.8	0.7
34.1	34.0	34.1	33.3	32.6

were due almost entirely to the increase in the numbers of poor people, rather than to greater impoverishment among those already poor. Social Security reduced the poverty gap by 48 percent in 1979 and 1980, by 46 percent in 1981, and by 44 to 45 percent for 1982 through 1988. It is primarily elderly households that receive Social Security payments, which have helped to reduce poverty among the aged significantly (as shown in Table 4-1). Means-tested cash transfers reduced the poverty gap by 16 percent in 1979, and by 13 to 15 percent from 1980 through 1988. The imputed value of noncash means-tested benefits (food stamps, school feeding programs, and housing) further reduced the poverty gap by 7 to 9 percent from 1979 through 1988.

Throughout the decade, the program with the greatest impact on the poverty gap was Social Security; its effect was approximately three times that of means-tested cash transfers and about twice that of cash and noncash means-tested transfers combined. All programs became less effective as the 1980s progressed, removing a smaller proportion of the poverty gap. At the same time, the added burden due to federal taxes was greater in the 1980s. As a consequence, the proportion of the poverty gap remaining after all income transfers jumped from 29 percent in 1979 to 33 to 35 percent from 1981 through 1988 (U.S. House, 1990, pp. 1041-1042). This represents about a 20 percent increase in impoverishment and a sharp departure from the practice of the 1970s, when antipoverty programs were much more effective in reducing poverty in periods of both economic growth and recession (Danziger, Haveman, and Plotnick, 1986).

After analyzing the factors contributing to the increase in poverty between 1979 and 1988, the Committee on Ways and Means of the U.S. House of Representatives concluded that:

> changes in means-tested programs added 2.9 million people to the poverty population, changes in market income added 0.1 million, and changes in the social insurance programs [including Social Security] added roughly 0.9 million. Population growth and all other changes added an additional 3.0 million. In percentage terms, the largest contributing factor was the reduced effectiveness of means-tested welfare programs (38 percent), followed by population growth (33 percent), changes in demographics (17 percent), and the reduced effectiveness of social insurance programs (11 percent). (U.S. House, 1990, p. 1053)

> Population growth, changes in market incomes and other residual changes accounted for 53 percent of the increase in the aggregate poverty gap, followed by social insurance programs (22 percent), means-tested programs (23 percent), and changes in federal tax policy (2 percent). (p. 1054)

Individuals in single-parent families with children accounted for 53 percent of the total increase in the number of poor persons, although they make up only 12 percent of the population. These families were hit hardest by changes in means-tested programs. All other household types were underrepresented among the poor. Elderly households were most remarkable in this respect; despite considerable growth in the number of elderly households, the number in poverty actually declined.

INEQUALITY

Wealth and earnings have never been evenly distributed across the population. It appears, however, that inequality among U.S. households has increased since the early 1970s, primarily because of demographic shifts and changes in the types of jobs available. Sectoral shifts (e.g., from manufacturing to services) play a relatively small role, since inequality has increased among workers within each sector, as well as for the work force as a whole (Blackburn, Bloom, and Freeman, 1990; Blackburn and Bloom, 1987; Bluestone, 1990; Bluestone and Harrison, 1988; Massey and Eggers, 1990; Maxwell, 1989; Minarik, 1988; Moon and Sawhill, 1984). During the 1970s, most of the growth in inequality came from higher earnings at the top end of the distribution (the rich got richer); in the 1980s increased inequality derived from lower earnings in the lowest income quintile (the poor got poorer) (Burtless, 1990b; Michel, 1990).

In principle, inequality presumably has less effect on the risk of homeless-ness than does the absolute level of poverty. Inequality could increase while poverty declined, and vice versa. However, the fact that both inequality and absolute poverty increased during the 1980s may be important for policy toward the homeless. An awareness of greater inequality could incline the public to support programs to help the homeless or very poor in the interest of fairness. Alternatively, if middle-income households are themselves under financial stress, they may be less sympathetic to the very poor and homeless (Levy, 1987; 1988). Conscious of how hard they must work to maintain their standard of living, with sometimes marginal success, the middle class may be unwilling to assist poor people whom they see as doing little to help themselves. Ehrenreich (1989) describes this pattern at some length. The widespread characterization of the 1980s as "the me generation" suggests a widespread perception that many people were committed to taking care of themselves first, and others not at all. Finally, increasing inequality may widen the gap between policymakers and the people toward whom policy is directed. The realities facing poor people thus may be obscured, and public policies may fail to address some of the most difficult circumstances that maintain poverty.

Efforts to explain the recent increases in poverty and inequality have focused on such factors as unemployment, low earnings, shifts in the labor market, and race discrimination. The remainder of this chapter explores the evidence for some of these propositions.

LIVING STANDARDS AND THE CHANGING REWARDS OF WORKING

Unemployment

In periods of high unemployment, which typically coincide with economic recession, unemployment is a strong contributor to poverty. It cannot provide the entire explanation, however. During the 1980s, unemployment was substan-tially reduced after the end of the 1981–1982 recession, yet poverty persisted.

Table 4-4 shows the annual fluctuations in the civilian unemployment rate from 1977 through 1988. The changes in this official rate reflect the major periods of downturn and upturn in the economy. Rates increased by two-thirds from 1979 through 1983, and then decreased through 1988 by 43 percent.

Earlier, unemployment rates had increased 73 percent between 1970 and 1975 and decreased by almost one-third between 1975 and 1979. These fluctuations are far more dramatic than the changes in the numbers in poverty (Table 4-1), suggesting that other factors contribute to poverty.

The unemployed include persons who have lost or left their jobs as well as new entrants and re-entrants to the labor force. As Table 4-4 shows, job loss explains a particularly large share of unemployment in the years surrounding the recession of the early 1980s. Although re-entrants and new entrants represented smaller proportions of the unemployed during this time, their absolute numbers increased. This pattern suggests that as some people lost jobs, other family members who had left or never entered the labor force tried to compensate by looking for work.

During the period shown in Table 4-4, blacks experienced unemployment rates more than twice those of whites; women who maintained families experienced rates two to three times as high as those of married men; and part-time workers had rates somewhat higher than full-time workers. These discrepancies were reduced during the 1981–1982 recession, as the rates for whites, men, and full-time workers grew closer to those of minorities, women, and part-time workers (U.S. House, 1990, p. 483). Overall, unemployment changes contributed to the increase in poverty during the recession of the early 1980s. However, they made a greater difference for households whose risk of poverty would ordinarily have been relatively low. Individuals who were already at high risk of unemployment and poverty, because of work experience, education, sex, or race, were less affected by trends in unemployment.

When workers who had been unemployed in the early 1980s got new jobs, they often did not return to their previous level of earnings. The Bureau of Labor Statistics reports that for workers displaced during the years 1983 through 1988, 14 percent were still unemployed in 1988, and 10 percent had had to accept part-time work when they wanted full-time work. Among those who found new full-time jobs, 38 percent took pay cuts. Outcomes for workers displaced in the 1979 to 1984 period had been still worse. Losses were greatest for older workers and for those with lower skill levels. These were also the workers most likely to leave the labor force involuntarily (Bluestone and Harrison, 1982; Schervish, 1985; U.S. House, 1989, pp. 490-494).

While levels of unemployment hit a postwar high in the early 1980s, the value and coverage of unemployment insurance were reduced beginning about 1984, as discussed in some detail in Chapter 5. The consequence of lower unemployment coverage can be seen in Tables 4-2 and 4-3, in the rows describing the antipoverty effects of social insurance programs. Since 1984 only about one-third of the unemployed received insurance coverage through unemployment compensation, compared with an average of almost half in earlier years (U.S. House, 1990, p. 479). Obviously both the depth of the 1981–1982

Table 4-4 Unemployment Rates, Total, and by Reason, 1977-1989

	Yearly Average Unemployment Rate	Unemployed (1000s)	Reasons for Unemployment (percentage of total)			
			Job Losers	Job Leavers	Re-entrants	New Entrants
1977	7.1%	6,991	45%	13%	28%	14%
1978	6.1	6,202	42	14	30	14
1979	5.8	6,137	43	14	29	13
1980	7.1	7,637	52	12	25	11
1981	7.6	8,273	52	11	25	12
1982	9.7	10,678	59	8	22	11
1983	9.6	10,717	58	8	23	11
1984	7.5	8,539	52	10	26	13
1985	7.2	8,312	50	11	27	13
1986	7.0	8,237	48	13	26	13
1987	6.2	7,425	48	13	27	12
1988	5.5	6,701	46	15	27	12
1989	5.3	6,528	46	16	28	10

Source: U.S. House of Representatives, Committee on Ways and Means, *Overview of Entitlement Programs: The 1990 Green Book*, Washington, D.C., Government Printing Office, 1990, p. 484.

recession and the reduction in unemployment benefits contributed to the poverty of the 1980s.

Unemployment may be the first step toward homelessness for many men. In a very informative study conducted on Nashville's skid row, Peterson and Weigand (1985) interviewed tramps—homeless men who would probably be classified as unemployed in most labor surveys, but who regularly seek short-term or day labor jobs, support themselves by work (as opposed to panhandling or illegal activities), and perceive themselves as working men. Their stories revealed a process of descent that began for many with the loss of a job, often through plant closings, other displacement, or temporary disability or illness. Most of the respondents had grown up "in relatively stable working-class or lower middle-class families and descended to the tramp life through a series of progressively less stable jobs" (p. 219):

> In case after case, we see men who have *lost* skills, men for whom past job experience is now unavailable and irrelevant for their current job seeking and ways of life. The exigencies of their lives have caused them to become deskilled and cut off from the supports of home and family. Rather than *gaining* human capital through job experience, they are cumulatively disadvantaged so that the jobs for which they can successfully compete are successively less desirable, lower paying, more physically dangerous, and less secure. (p. 222, emphasis in original)

The job restructuring that has taken place over the last twenty years, coupled with the severe unemployment of the early 1980s, may have created the conditions to start many less advantaged men on the path to eventual homelessness.

Poverty increased during the 1980s, and many of the jobs created in the latter part of the decade did not pay enough to lift a family above the poverty line. Living standards declined, and a two-tier job structure developed in the United States. The differences in earning power between more-skilled and less-skilled people increased, augmenting income inequality. The people most affected by these changes were also the ones most vulnerable to homelessness.

Many writers have described the stagnation or decline in U.S. living standards during the 1980s, or the need for two earners to maintain a family's living standards, even in the middle class (e.g., Friedman, 1988; Levy, 1987; Litan, Lawrence and Schultze, 1988; Newman, 1988). Some attributed the decline largely to the loss of manufacturing and other high-paying jobs and their replacement with low-paying jobs (e.g., Harrison and Bluestone, 1988; Burtless, 1990a).

Low Earnings

During the 1980s it became much harder for Americans to rise above poverty even when they expended significant work effort. In 1987 about one-third of all poor persons over sixteen worked or looked for work for at least half the year. About two-thirds of the working poor who usually worked full-time had earnings of less than $167 a week—not enough to rise above poverty. Households with only one potential wage earner naturally had a greater chance of being poor. When that one wage earner was a woman, or a black person of either sex, the odds of poverty were still greater, because of the lower earnings of women and minorities. These circumstances affected female-headed families and single workers most. In 1987 women who worked and maintained families comprised 17 percent of the working poor and had a poverty rate of 17.7 percent. Unrelated individuals who worked were 30.3 percent of poor workers. However, because many single people make good salaries, only 9.8 percent of unrelated individuals, taken as a group, were poor (Klein and Rones, 1989; McLanahan, Sorensen, and Watson, 1989; Smith and Vavrichek, 1987).

More than half of all poor families in metropolitan areas and more than two-thirds of other poor families included at least one worker during the 1980s. Their situation worsened over the decade. The number of married-couple families with children who remained poor despite the presence of at least three-fourths of a full-time worker increased by 19 percent between 1979 and 1987, from 0.96 to 1.14 million families; 4.8 percent of these households were poor in 1987, compared with 4.1 percent in 1979. The changes were even more dramatic among working female-headed families with children; poverty in this category rose 60 percent, while the poverty rate increased from 11.1 to 14.8 percent (U.S. House, 1990, p. 1031).

A number of federal policies are intended to reduce the poverty of working people. Among these, the federally mandated minimum wage has drawn considerable analytical attention as a possible explanation of poverty increases during the 1980s. From 1968 through 1973, the minimum wage was $1.60. Between 1974 and 1981 it rose in gradual increments to $3.35, almost keeping pace with inflation until 1979. It stayed at $3.35 between 1981 and 1989 (although legislation enacted in late 1989 raised the minimum to $4.25 by 1991, in two increments). Between 1980 and 1988, the minimum wage lost about 23 percent of purchasing power, compared with just 3 percent from 1970 to 1980.

At the end of the Reagan administration, the real purchasing power of the minimum wage was lower than at any time since the 1950s. It had also fallen as a share of average wages. The minimum averaged about 50 percent of average hourly earnings in the 1950s and 1960s and over 45 percent in the 1970s, but had dropped to 39 percent of average wages by 1985. Finally, a full-time year-round worker earning the minimum wage during most of the 1960s and 1970s could have earned enough to raise a family of three just above the poverty threshold. By the mid-1980s this was no longer true (Smith and Vavrichek, 1987).

In 1989 the poverty line for a family of four was an income of $12,675 a year. To earn that much by working a forty-hour week, year round, an individual would have to make at least $6.09 an hour. If, as is more likely, full-time work means a thirty-five-hour week for fifty weeks a year, the hourly rate needed rises to $7.24. These figures are 60 and 90 percent more than the minimum wage (of $3.80 in April 1990). In other words, two full-time earners working at the minimum wage could just barely raise a family of four out of poverty.

The federal government's failure to raise the minimum wage probably accounts for some increased poverty in the 1980s. In principle, if all people working for the minimum wage were second or third earners in households that included a better-paid primary earner, then the level of the minimum wage might not affect the poverty rate. In that case one would expect the household poverty rate among workers earning the minimum wage in 1987 ($3.35) to be the same as for workers earning a wage equivalent to the buying power of the minimum wage in the years before the 1980s (when the minimum was routinely adjusted to be about half of average wage rates). Klein and Rones (1989) have made this comparison for 1987. They found a household poverty rate of 34.5 percent among people working full-time at $3.35, but only 24.5 percent among those working full-time at $4.18.[2] This finding suggests that if the minimum wage level had kept pace with inflation during the 1980s, fewer people would be poor.

Analyses by Mincy (1990) suggest that this difference is relatively small, but not insignificant. The impact of changes in the minimum wage is limited by the fact that many workers at this pay level are not the sole support of a household. Teenagers held 19 percent of minimum wage jobs in 1986, and adult women held 59 percent. Most of the teenagers and perhaps as many as half the women lived in households with two or more workers. Nevertheless, if the minimum wage in 1987 had kept pace with inflation, Mincy estimates that the number of poor families would have been reduced by 8.7 percent in that year. In addition, an inflation-adjusted minimum wage would have eliminated 11.1 percent of the poverty gap that these families experienced in 1987. Even workers who remained poor, that is, would have been less poor if the minimum wage had been adjusted for inflation.

Other studies have shown that minimum wage changes have small but real effects on the well-being of poor people (Gramlich, 1976; Minimum Wage Study Commission, 1981). Gramlich's analyses showed that low-wage adult

---

[2]The $4.18 figure results from adjusting $3.35 (the minimum wage in 1987) for inflation using the Consumer Price Index, version U-XI. Workers' poverty status was determined by their household's poverty status, not by their own earnings. A minimum-wage earner would not be counted as poor if he or she lived with other persons who earned enough to raise the household above poverty.

workers gain more than they lose from minimum wage increases; this effect was clearest for adult females, whose median wage has consistently been a smaller multiple of the minimum wage. The Minimum Wage Study Commission concluded that increases in the minimum produce a net gain for the poorest one-fifth of households. However, its analyses also showed that "higher taxes and reduced benefits offset roughly half of the earnings gains . . . the effects of the tax-transfer system have limited the impact of minimum wage increases on the net income of the poorest households" (p. 103). Also, Gramlich finds considerable "leakage" of effects into higher-income households, since 25 percent of the increased earnings associated with a higher minimum wage go to households with incomes above the median (and considerably above the poverty threshold).

Both Gramlich and the Commission conclude that the minimum wage is considerably less efficient than other mechanisms for increasing the incomes of the poor. The minimum wage probably cannot be raised enough to have a major impact on the well-being of poor households, because doing so would create more significant disemployment and inflation effects, as well as greater leakage or spillover to higher-income families. These findings imply, and the Minimum Wage Study Commission explicitly states, that shifts in "direct government transfer payments or some variant of a negative income tax would be more effective tools for fighting poverty" (p. 85).

Unfortunately for poor people, the federal government's tax and transfer policies worked in the opposite direction in the 1980s. As Tables 4-2 and 4-3 show, tax policies did not increase either the poverty rate or the poverty gap by more than 0.6 percent in 1979 and 1980. These effects doubled in 1981 and abated only in 1987 as the provisions of the Tax Reform Act of 1986 began to take effect. Far from using tax policy to aid the poor, the Reagan administration added to their tax burdens while diminishing the ability of other federal programs to reduce poverty.

Among men, younger persons with fewer skills and less education are most likely to be employed in low-wage jobs. Earning power for this segment of the male work force declined significantly during the 1980s (down 10 percent between 1979 and 1987 for men with less than a high school education), reducing their ability to support families, or perhaps even themselves. Between 1973 and 1987 they lost ground in terms of both absolute earnings (down 13 percent) and earnings relative to other segments of the working population. They also experienced higher rates of unemployment (Blackburn, Bloom, and Freeman, 1990).

The decreasing ability of low-skill males to earn a living helps explain their predominance among the homeless, and also may contribute to the size of the family homeless population. Previously unpublished data from the Urban Institute's 1987 national survey show that 8 percent of the homeless are single

Table 4-5 Changing Employment and Pay Levels, by Industry, 1980-1988

	1980	1984	1988	Percentage change, 1980-1988	Share of Total Private Employment 1980	1988
Employment Levels (millions)						
Total	90.4	94.5	105.6	+16.8%	—	—
Total Private	74.2	78.5	88.2	+18.9	100%	100%
Goods-producing	25.7	24.7	25.2	−1.6	34.6	28.6
Mining	1.0	1.0	0.7	−29.8	1.4	0.8
Construction	4.3	4.4	5.1	+17.9	5.9	5.8
Manufacturing	20.3	19.4	19.4	−4.3	27.4	22.0
Service-producing	48.5	53.8	62.9	+29.7	65.4	71.3
Transportation/communications/utilities	5.1	5.2	5.5	+7.8	6.9	6.2
Wholesale trade	5.3	5.6	6.0	+14.3	7.1	6.8
Retail trade	15.0	16.5	19.1	+27.1	20.3	21.7
Finance/insurance/real estate	5.2	5.7	6.7	+29.4	7.0	7.6
Services	17.9	20.8	25.6	+43.1	24.1	29.0
Government	16.2	16.0	17.4	+7.0	—	—

Average Weekly Earnings (current dollars)[a]			Inflation-Adjusted Change[b] (percent)
Total Private	$235	$293	$322	-3.9%
Goods-producing	305	396	437	+0.7
Mining	397	504	539	-4.8
Construction	368	459	493	-6.2
Manufacturing	289	374	418	+1.6
Service-producing	205	256	287	-1.7
Transportation/communications/utilities	351	438	484	-3.2
Wholesale trade	268	342	379	-0.6
Retail trade	147	174	184	-13.7
Finance/insurance/real estate	210	279	326	+8.3
Services	191	247	290	+6.3

Source: Current Labor Statistics: Employment Data, *Monthly Labor Review*, January 1990, Tables 20 and 21.
[a] Adjusted for hours worked and average hourly wage. Retail Trade and Services are particularly low because both hours worked and average wage are low.
[b] Adjusted using CPI-U-X1, a version of the Consumer Price Index for urban areas (CPI-U) that treats the cost of home ownership consistently across the time period of interest.

males under the age of twenty-five, and another 22 percent are single men aged twenty-five to thirty-four. Families headed by women under twenty-five make up 26 percent of all homeless families in the same data set; 41 percent of those homeless families are headed by women between the ages of twenty-five and thirty-four. These young female family heads (about 12,000 in total) are far outnumbered by the 52,000 young single men. One interpretation of these data is that low-skilled young men who cannot earn an adequate living are less likely to support families. The mothers of their children must then cope with poverty and potential homelessness on their own. This pattern may affect up to two-thirds of homeless families.

It is not only minimum wage or low-skilled workers who have lost earning power. Average annual earnings from employment, adjusted for inflation, have decreased for men in all but one age and education category since 1973. Only young college-educated men maintained their earning power, and even they did not increase it. For all women, and especially for those with college educations, real average annual earnings from employment rose substantially, but are still only about 60 percent of male earnings for people of the same age with equivalent educations. Young men (twenty-five to thirty-four) with high school educations lost the most purchasing power (21 percent) between 1973 and 1986. Men aged thirty-five to forty-four lost about 12 percent of their earning power during the same years, while forty-five- to fifty-five-year-old men lost 8 percent (high school graduates) and 4 percent (college graduates). College-educated women aged thirty-five to forty-four gained the most—38 percent. Gains for other groups of women ranged from 6 to 30 percent, with higher-educated women generally making larger gains (Litan, Lawrence, and Schultze, 1988/1989; see also Levy and Michel, 1991).

Shifts in the Labor Market

A shift in the distribution of American jobs is responsible for some of this drop in earning power. Between 1979 and 1987 low-wage jobs—those in which a full-time year-round worker could not earn at least $11,611, the poverty level for a family of four in 1987—grew "dramatically relative to middle and high wage jobs. Half the 11.8 million payroll jobs created between 1979 and 1987 were low-wage jobs. Moreover, the share of low-wage jobs for many groups of workers and regions of the country has increased while the share of middle-wage jobs has dropped" (U.S. House, 1989, p. 512).

In general, between 1980 and 1988 industries with a history of paying relatively well have come to account for a smaller share of all American jobs, while those that have historically paid least have grown most, both absolutely and as a proportion of all private-sector jobs. Table 4-5 shows these shifts in employment and pay levels by industry. The better-paying jobs tend to be in the goods-producing sector, where the absolute number of jobs shrank over the decade, and average weekly pay barely kept up with inflation. Some of the best-paying components of the service sector (e.g., transportation, communications, utilities) have slipped in real average weekly earnings over the decade while growing more slowly than other segments of the service sector. Simultaneously, the lowest-paying service area (retail trade) expanded by 27 percent and also saw the largest loss in real average weekly wages.

Many analysts have explored the relative roles of demand-side and supply-side factors in reducing earning power in the 1980s. Factors on the demand side include business cycles; shifts in the proportion of jobs found in different industrial sectors (goods producing versus service producing); shifts in the distribution of jobs within industrial sectors (i.e., fewer middle-wage jobs and more low-wage jobs); and technological change, which may create more high-paying and low-paying jobs. Supply-side analysis has concentrated on the changing size of different age cohorts (particularly the baby boom) and on the education and skills of potential workers. Also examined were mechanisms that set or directly influenced wage levels, such as the minimum wage, union activity, and union membership (Blackburn, Bloom, and Freeman, 1990; Bluestone and Harrison, 1982, 1988; Burtless, 1990b; Harrison and Bluestone, 1988; Levy, 1987; Minarik, 1988; Stanback and Noyelle, 1982).

To summarize briefly, the business cycle and the sectoral shift from manufacturing to services each have some effect. At the bottom of the income distribution, however, their influences on earnings appear to be less important than within-sector changes, technological change, the effects of wage-setting mechanisms, cohort size, and returns to education. Interactions among these factors are also significant; for example, the highest levels and the fastest-growing increases of wage inequality occur within the service sector, which also gives most differential rewards for post-high school education.

The Role of Race in Poverty and Inequality

Across the nation, in every study of the homeless, members of minority groups appear in numbers disproportionally larger than their share in the local population. This pattern is to be expected if poverty is the key underlying factor in homelessness. As we saw earlier, blacks and Hispanics have poverty rates significantly higher than those of whites (Table 4-1). A recent analysis of poverty, inequality, and residential concentration by race across sixty metropolitan areas (SMSAs) allows us to see very clearly the position of different urban racial groups on these critical dimensions.

Massey and Eggers (1990) report that changes in median income and national trends in poverty and inequality mask substantial differences by minority status and region. Specifically, "among whites, family incomes

underwent a significant and almost universal upward shift" in the 1970s
(p. 1166). However, for metropolitan blacks in the Northeast and Midwest, the
1970s saw sharp increases in the numbers of both the affluent and the poor.
But the poor grew proportionally more, so median incomes fell. Black family
incomes in the South and West showed moderate growth, in a pattern similar
to that of white families in these regions. Hispanic incomes either dropped
overall in this same period or became more unequally distributed. In either
case the proportion of families in poverty increased, with families in the
Northeast experiencing the most severe shifts toward poverty. Massey and
Eggers conclude: "This interregional and intergroup heterogeneity suggests
that much of the increase in income inequality noted at the national level
reflects a widening gap between affluent whites and poor minority groups,
especially blacks and Hispanics" (p. 1168).

The experience of the 1980s cannot be analyzed in comparable detail until
the 1990 census data are available. Still, the Current Population Surveys
provide some clues to income trends of racial and ethnic groups in the 1980s.[3]
Median incomes for all racial groups declined in the first half of the decade to
levels lower than in the 1970s. For both blacks and whites, the late 1980s saw
some improvement, which Hispanics did not share. In all three groups, the
proportion of households at the lower end of the income spectrum increased.
Among white and black households, on average 26 to 27 percent more
households had incomes under $5,000 (in 1988 dollars) throughout the 1980s
than in the 1970s. The parallel figure for Hispanics is 43 percent. In general,
this shift appears to derive from the increased impoverishment of households
that were already poor or near-poor. That is, proportionally more households
in each group earned less than $10,000 in the 1980s than in the 1970s, and the
lowest income categories grew the most (Bureau of the Census, 1989, Table
2). Cotton (1989) also documents that the trends in poverty for blacks
extended through the 1980s. The evidence suggests that economic difficulties
persisted and worsened for blacks and Hispanics. White households appear to
have shared in this impoverishment during the 1980s more than they did during
the 1970s.

Moreover, Massey and Eggers (1990) find severe concentrations of
poverty (the "underclass" phenomenon) only among poor blacks in the
Midwest and blacks and Hispanics in the Northeast. Poor whites and Asians in
all regions, and blacks and Hispanics in the South and West, are not highly
concentrated geographically. To the extent that geographic concentrations of

---

[3]The Current Population Survey (CPS) is conducted monthly by the Census Bureau. In March
of every year the CPS collects detailed data about income and employment that can be used to track
income trends for the years between decennial censuses.

poverty may contribute to homelessness over and above household poverty, one would expect to see higher rates of homelessness in cities where these patterns prevail.

SUMMARY AND CONCLUSIONS

The 1980s have seen an increase in poverty and inequality, and witnessed very high levels of unemployment. These patterns continue trends that for many households began in the 1970s. The primary causes of the increase in poverty are changes in market income (people do not make as much from working), changes in means-tested benefit programs (fewer people get benefits, and some recipients get lower benefits), population growth, changes in social insurance programs (primarily unemployment insurance coverage), and changes in federal tax policy.

The changes described in this chapter have had their greatest effect on the very groups with the highest risk of becoming homeless: minorities and low-skilled men, unrelated individuals, and families headed by women. Indeed, the characteristics of homeless adults closely parallel the patterns of poverty and related phenomena discussed in this chapter. It is important to recognize these parallels, because the press and advocates for the homeless often ignore poverty as a root cause of homelessness. The claims that "the homeless are just like you and me," and that most people are "just a paycheck or two away from homelessness," are meant to arouse sympathy and support for policies to aid the homeless, on the premise that people will be more willing to help others like themselves. But this strategy may prove to be misguided if sympathy and commitment dwindle when middle-class Americans come face to face with the facts. Efforts to prevent homelessness must do something substantial about the poverty and low earning potential that underlie the problem.

CHAPTER FIVE

Changes in Income Support Programs

■ Many homeless people have struggled to maintain an economic position that allows them to afford housing, until some final crisis precipitates an episode of homelessness. They may borrow money, leave bills unpaid, double up with other family members or with friends, split up a household (e.g., leaving older children with relatives), leave town to look for work, and use free services such as soup kitchens or health clinics to stretch their resources. Research indicates that currently homeless people have tried most or all of these approaches while they still had homes. Even with all of these strategies, however, they may not be able to afford to stay in housing.

Social policies and programs might be able to intervene in the downward economic spiral that sometimes leads to homelessness. A number of federal social safety-net programs were designed to help very poor people avoid complete destitution of this type. Because of limitations on eligibility, payment levels, and funding, however, these programs do not reach all needy people at risk of homelessness. The growth in homelessness in the 1980s, therefore, may be due in part to changes in the safety-net programs that reduced eligibility, the purchasing power of benefits, or coverage of the eligible population.

The most important federal safety-net programs are Aid to Families with Dependent Children (AFDC) and Supplemental Security Income (SSI), which provide monthly cash benefits, and the Food Stamp Program, which provides coupons that can be exchanged for food in grocery stores. We will also consider federal programs to subsidize or supplement the cost of housing (rent and utilities) for the poor, disabled, and elderly, and the state-federal unemployment compensation system.[1]

---

[1] I do not examine changes in Medicaid for two reasons, although federal expenditures for the program have increased greatly. First, the effect of increases have been felt almost entirely in services to the elderly, who have a very low risk of homelessness. Second, Medicaid clearly improves health outcomes for its recipients, but households without Medicaid are far more likely to

Finally, we will look at General Assistance (GA) programs (also called General Relief, Public Assistance, or Home Relief), which are funded and administered by states, counties, or cities. GA is usually the only program for which single persons without disabilities are eligible. Often, however, it is restricted to unemployable individuals (disabled or elderly); relatively few jurisdictions provide GA for healthy people who are able to work.

The eligibility criteria of the federal programs examined in this chapter make it impossible for them to meet the needs of all very poor people. Only needy families with children may receive AFDC, and in most states AFDC income ceilings are below federal poverty income guidelines. SSI is available only to needy elderly, blind, or disabled people. Food stamps are available to low-income people with gross household incomes up to 130 percent of federal poverty guidelines and net monthly incomes at poverty level or below. Federal housing subsidies reach only about one-fourth of all poor households, because of spending limits on the programs. Unlike AFDC, SSI, and food stamps, housing subsidies are not entitlements. By law (until October 1991), single adults who are not elderly or handicapped may not receive more than 15 percent of federal housing subsidies. Under current funding limits this restriction means that most poor singles do not receive federal housing assistance.

Poor single able-bodied individuals—the most prominent category of homeless adults—are not eligible for any federal cash transfer programs, although they can receive food stamps. Their only recourse is to locally administered General Assistance programs, which provide relatively low monthly payments and usually require employables (if they are eligible at all) to work or look for work.

AID TO FAMILIES WITH DEPENDENT CHILDREN

Aid to Families with Dependent Children (AFDC) is an entitlement program that serves primarily single-parent families with children. Any family that meets state eligibility criteria is entitled to benefits; the program has no spending cap. AFDC was created by the Social Security Act of 1935 to provide "cash welfare payments for needy children who have been deprived of parental support or care because their father or mother is absent from home continuously (85.2 percent of the children [in 1986]), is incapacitated (3.2 percent), is deceased (1.9 percent), or is unemployed (7.4 percent)" (U.S. House, 1989, p. 517). In nine

---

forego medical care than to pay for equivalent medical services. Receipt of Medicaid benefits thus does not free up household resources for other uses; Medicaid simply provides a benefit that household members otherwise would not get. The health status of poor children with and without Medicaid clearly bears out this view.

out of ten AFDC families, no adult male is present and the mother is the only adult in the household. Receipt of AFDC categorically entitles a household to Medicaid (96 percent participate) and usually implies receipt of food stamps (82 percent participate) (U.S. House, 1989, p. 1103).

AFDC is a combined state-federal program. Each state defines its need standard (the amount the state estimates is required to provide necessities such as rent and food), sets benefit levels (which are below the state's own need standard in almost two-thirds of the states), establishes income and resource limits within federal guidelines, and administers the program. Benefit levels differ widely. The maximum monthly AFDC grant for a three-person family in January 1990 ranged from $118 in Alabama and $120 in Mississippi to $694 in California and $846 in Alaska. The Alabama benefit provided only 14 percent of the Census Bureau's poverty threshold for a three-person family, while the California benefit provided 84 percent. When states are ranked by size of maximum AFDC benefit, the median grant for a three-person family is $364, which puts the family at 44 percent of the poverty threshold (U.S. House, 1990, pp. 553-555).

AFDC benefits have been losing their purchasing power steadily for two decades (Table 5-1). Adjusted for inflation, AFDC benefits were worth considerably less per family in the 1980s than in the 1970s; average monthly benefits per person also declined, but not nearly as much. Between 1970 and 1980, the average family monthly benefit declined 27 percent, compared with 4 percent for benefits per person. The low point (not shown in Table 5-1) came in 1982, when real benefits were about 4 percent lower than for 1984.

The discrepancy between individual and family figures is largely explained by the fact that average family size dropped from 4.0 persons in 1970 to 3.2 in 1975 and to 3.0 in 1980, and has remained at about 3.0 throughout the 1980s. The average per person benefit showed the greatest drop (7 percent) between 1980 and 1984, and most of this decline had occurred by 1982. These reductions were related to provisions of the Omnibus Budget Reconciliation Act of 1981 (OBRA).

The purchasing power of the average family AFDC benefit may be of more practical relevance to the risk of homelessness than the individual benefit. The average AFDC family had only $385 a month in 1984 with which to purchase housing and all other necessities, compared with $568 a month in 1970. Although the 1970 family had one more child, both households probably occupied approximately equal units, and the 1984 family probably had to spend more on housing than did the 1970 family. The reduction in family size would not appreciably reduce their required monthly expenditures for housing; the 1980s family would thus be left with far less money for all other necessities.

OBRA changes, largely in the treatment of earned income, left almost 500,000 families completely ineligible for AFDC benefits, while another 300,000

Table 5-1 Historical Trends in Average, Maximum, and Mean AFDC Payments, 1970-1989[a]

	1970	1975	1980	1984	1985	1986	1987	1988	1989
Current Dollars									
Average Monthly Benefit									
Per family	$178	$210	$274	$322	$339	$353	$359	$370	$381
Per person	46	63	94	110	116	120	123	127	131
Maximum State Benefit in July for a Family of Four with no Income									
Per family	375	497	563	660	800	823	833	866	899
Per person	94	124	141	165	200	206	208	217	225
Constant 1989 Dollars[b]									
Average Monthly Benefit									
Per family	568	482	412	385	391	401	393	388	381
Per person	147	145	141	131	134	136	135	133	131
Maximum State Benefit in July for a Family of Four with no Income									
Per family	1,196	1,141	847	789	923	935	911	909	899
Per person	299	285	212	197	231	234	228	227	225

Source: U.S. House of Representatives, Committee on Ways and Means, *Background Material and Data on Programs within the Jurisdiction of the Committee on Ways and Means*, Washington, D.C., Government Printing Office, 1990, p. 563.
[a] Among fifty states and the District of Columbia.
[b] Constant dollars were calculated using the CPI-U monthly Consumer Price Index series.

families had their benefits reduced. Together, these households represented about 21 percent of 1981 AFDC families. In March 1979, 12 percent of AFDC families had earned income, averaging $382 per month. By May 1982 the proportion of AFDC families with earned income had dropped to 5 percent, and their earnings to $261 a month (U.S. House, 1990, p. 582). The families that suffered most under OBRA were working people.

When the General Accounting Office assessed the effects of the 1981 OBRA, it found that many AFDC families who lost eligibility (1) suffered a substantial loss of income that they could not make up; (2) had fallen below the poverty level; (3) had not replaced the health coverage formerly provided by Medicaid; and (4) faced more emergency situations, such as refusal of medical care because of lack of funds, or running out of food (U.S. House, 1990, pp. 627-628).

Poor children have also suffered under OBRA changes. From 1970 through 1981, on average 72 percent of all poor children received AFDC.[2] From 1982, when the OBRA changes took effect, through 1987, on average only 54 percent of poor children got AFDC (U.S. House, 1989, p. 560). Thus, during the Reagan years the share of poor children covered by AFDC benefits shrank by one-fourth.

Although data are scarce, in 1980 it was extremely rare to find households with children among the homeless. Virtually no shelters accommodated families with children. During the recession of 1981–82 the presence of families with children among those seeking emergency housing and food assistance was noted as a distinct change and was viewed as a sign of how deeply the recession had hurt poor households. By 1987, however, about 10 percent of homeless households included children. Eight out of ten of these family households were headed by a single woman; all were very poor (Burt and Cohen, 1989a, 1989b). These are the very families that AFDC is designed to help, and indeed about one-third did receive AFDC benefits.[3] However, their income from AFDC and other sources was not enough to pay for housing and other expenses. Changes in AFDC during the 1980s may have increased the likelihood of homelessness for some poor families, by eliminating eligibility or reducing the face value of benefits, particularly for those who worked. In addition, the purchasing power of

---

[2] Poor children are those belonging to families whose cash income, including any government transfer payments, was below the federal poverty threshold.

[3] An additional one-third of homeless families received General Assistance (Burt and Cohen, 1989a, 1989b), which localities probably used as stopgap funding while AFDC applications were being processed. The conditions that made some families homeless may also have made them eligible for AFDC for the first time (e.g., women leaving a battering situation might only be eligible once they left), helping to explain the low level of benefit receipt among households that on the surface appear to be eligible for AFDC and in great need.

benefits eroded in many states, making it harder for some AFDC families to pay housing costs and thus increasing their risk of homelessness.

SUPPLEMENTAL SECURITY INCOME

The Supplemental Security Income program (SSI), begun in late 1974, is an entitlement program that supplements the incomes of poor aged, blind, or disabled people. It provides cash assistance (up to $386 a month for an individual and $579 for a couple in 1990) that, at its maximum, brings an individual or a couple up to about 75 percent or 89 percent of the poverty threshold, respectively (U.S. House, 1990, p. 723). SSI is indexed to the Consumer Price Index in the same way as Social Security payments, so its purchasing power has not eroded in the 1980s. Further, adjustments in July 1983 and January 1984 actually increased the real value of benefits by 4 to 5 percent. Complicated program rules determine the precise level of benefit for a given recipient.

Many states supplement federal SSI payments, which are uniform across the country. For individuals living independently, twenty-six states and the District of Columbia provide supplemental assistance, ranging from $2 to $384 depending on the state (Table 5-2). These supplemental payments are not indexed to inflation. Only six states have adjusted their supplemental payments to meet or exceed inflation; thirteen states paid $35 a month or less in 1989, and five of these paid $15 or less. As the final column of Table 5-2 shows, state supplements lost value in real terms virtually everywhere, with a median loss of 48 percent from 1975 to 1989. Thus state supplements are worth only half as much today as they were at the beginning of SSI; only in eleven states do they amount to $50 or more a month.

Some states attune the level of their supplement to the going rate for a room in a boarding or lodging house. This practice has helped disabled individuals to maintain themselves in the community as long as they are eligible for SSI. All but seven states[4] supplement living expenses for SSI recipients in a protective, supervisory, or group living situation. These payments also help disabled people maintain housing in the community. The level of supplement varies by state.

SSI is relevant to homelessness primarily because it is aimed at people with disabilities that prevent them from working. From 1975, the first full year of SSI operation, through 1988, the proportion of recipients who were disabled grew from 45 percent to 66 percent. Even among SSI recipients younger than sixty-five, more than half were disabled in 1988 (U.S. House, 1989, p. 695). With federal SSI payments and state supplements, many of these disabled

---

[4]Arkansas, Georgia, Kansas, Mississippi, Tennessee, Texas, and West Virginia.

Table 5-2 State SSI Supplements for Aged Individuals Without Countable Income Living Independently

	July 1975	July 1980	Jan. 1985	Jan. 1986	Jan. 1987	Jan. 1988	Jan. 1989	Percentage Change (constant dollars) 1975–89[a]
Alaska[b]	$142	$235	$261	$269	$292	$305	$317	0%
California	101	164	179	197	220	221	234	+4
Colorado	27	55	58	58	58	58	58	0
Connecticut	NA	NA	NA	NA	NA	393	384	—
District of Columbia	0	15	15	15	15	15	15	—
Hawaii	17	15	5	5	5	5	5	−87
Idaho	63	74	78	72	73	73	73	−48
Illinois[c]	NA	NA	NA	NA	NA	NA	NA	—
Maine	10	10	10	10	10	10	10	−55
Massachusetts	111	137	129	129	129	129	129	−48
Michigan	12	24	27	28	29	30	30	+11
Minnesota[d]	31	34	35	35	35	35	35	−49
Nebraska	67	75	61	62	51	43	38	−74
Nevada	55	47	36	36	36	36	36	−71
New Hampshire	12	46	27	27	27	27	27	0
New Jersey	24	23	31	31	31	31	31	−42

New York	61	63	61	72	72	72	86	−37
Oklahoma	27	79	60	64	64	64	64	+6
Oregon	17	12	2	2	2	2	2	−95
Pennsylvania	20	32	32	32	32	32	32	−29
Rhode Island	31	42	54	56	56	59	61	−13
South Dakota	0	15	15	15	15	15	15	—
Utah	0	10	10	10	9	9	9	—
Vermont	29	41	53	56	57	58	60	−8
Washington[e]	36	43	38	28	28	28	28	−65
Wisconsin	70	100	100	102	102	103	103	−34
Wyoming	0	20	20	20	20	20	20	—
Median[f]	31	43	36	36	36	36	36	−48

Source: U.S. House of Representatives, Committee on Ways and Means, *Background Material and Data on Programs within the Jurisdiction of the Committee on Ways and Means*, Washington, D.C., Government Printing Office, 1989, p. 716.

[a] The percentage decrease in constant dollars was computed by inflating July 1975 to January 1989 by the CPI-U price index. A January 1989 figure of 361.6 was used. The July 1975 CPU-I was 162.3.

[b] 1975 and 1980—less if shelter costs are less than $35 monthly.

[c] State decides benefit on a case-by-case basis.

[d] Payment level for Hennepin County. State has ten geographic payment levels.

[e] State has two geographic levels; the higher, paid in King, Pierce, Kitsap, Snohomish, and Thurston Counties, is shown.

[f] Among the states with payment, Connecticut and Illinois are classified as having a payment above the median.

individuals can remain in the community, either in independent situations or in supervised living arrangements.

Although most studies of the homeless estimate that between 25 and 30 percent suffer from severe mental disorders (Rossi, 1989, p. 154), only 4 percent get SSI (Burt and Cohen, 1989a, p. 43). In all likelihood many mentally disabled homeless are eligible for, but not receiving, federal SSI and state supplements to assist with housing. Some may have received SSI in the past but lost eligibility; others may never have had contact with an agency that could help them apply (the application process is quite difficult, especially for someone with a mental disability).

In 1987 the nonaged disabled represented 54 percent of SSI recipients; 26.9 percent of this group were disabled by mental retardation, and another 24.1 percent (12.6 percent of all SSI recipients) by some other mental disorder. Only one other condition (nervous system and sense organs) accounted for more than 10 percent of the disabled. Altogether, about 415,000 individuals suffering from mental illnesses received SSI in 1987, representing about 23 percent of the approximately 1.8 million people in 1987 estimated by the National Institute of Mental Health to be chronically mentally ill (Steering Committee on the Chronically Mentally Ill, 1980).

In March 1981 the Department of Health and Human Services (DHHS) decided administratively to tighten eligibility requirements and accelerate case reviews for SSI and SSDI (Social Security Disability Insurance) recipients. Thus new applicants found it more difficult to qualify for SSI, and many disabled SSI recipients were disqualified and lost their benefits. Among those hardest hit by this process were people disabled by mental illness and those with musculoskeletal disorders. Under pressure, DHHS stopped these reviews after several years until a more reasonable set of criteria could be developed that did not prejudice the outcome for many individuals with clear incapacities (Burt and Pittman, 1985, pp. 82-89). Many professionals who worked with the mentally disabled believed that the risk of homelessness went up during the period of these reviews, however. In addition, the burden of proof to establish eligibility for the mentally disabled increased (Burt and Pittman, 1985, pp. 112-113).

Countering the "antimental" mood of the executive branch in the early 1980s, Congressional action from 1983 onward has called for active efforts to enroll eligible homeless persons in the SSI program. Specific measures include prerelease arrangements for people leaving psychiatric facilities; emergency "while you wait" payments for clearly eligible new enrollees; disregarding the cash value of food and shelter assistance received from nonprofits in calculating benefit levels; provisions for continued receipt of benefits during short hospital and shelter stays (up to three and six months, respectively); and demonstration projects to do outreach and on-the-spot enrollment in localities frequented by the homeless (U.S. House, 1989, pp. 686-688).

FOOD STAMPS

The Food Stamp Program (FSP) is designed to enable poor households to purchase food that provides a nutritionally adequate low-cost diet. It is an entitlement program; all those who qualify may receive benefits. Further, it is the only federal program available to all poor people without restrictions based on household type (e.g., single-parent families), age, or disability. As such the FSP offers a resource to virtually all poor households and is especially valuable to those households whose demands on cash income are so great that little remains to buy food.

To qualify for food stamps, poor households must have gross incomes of no more than 130 percent of the poverty threshold (slightly more liberal rules apply to elderly and disabled households), and net incomes, after allowable deductions, of no more than 100 percent of poverty. The rules establishing benefit levels are very complex. Eligible households receive monthly allotments of coupons that can be exchanged for food at grocery stores. The FSP distributed $12.5 billion worth of coupons in 1989 to 18.8 million individuals in about 7 million households.

The Food Stamp Program has changed dramatically over the years, reaching its present form only in 1979, the year that the purchase requirement was eliminated.[5] Food stamps have been indexed for inflation since 1973, and available in all states since 1975.

Between 1979 and 1983, the year of maximum enrollment, FSP participation rose from 15.9 million to 21.6 million individuals, an increase of 36 percent. However, because the number of people in poverty also peaked in 1983, the FSP increase did not represent an increase in the percentage of poor people served by the program. In both 1979 and 1983, 61 percent of poor people participated in the FSP (this proportion fluctuated in the intervening years). Since 1983, participation has dropped by 13 percent to 18.8 million in 1989. The percentage of poor people served also dropped slightly, to 59 percent (again with intervening fluctuations) (U.S. House, 1990, p. 1269).

Average monthly food stamp benefits per person increased 13 percent between 1979 and 1983, from $47 to $50 (in constant 1989 dollars). Since 1983 average benefits have fluctuated between $51 and $53 a month (in 1989 dollars) (U.S. House, 1990, p. 1275).

As a result of legislative changes in 1981 and 1982, about 1 million persons (about 5 percent) lost FSP eligibility, and the remaining recipients suffered some

---

[5]Before 1979 a household needed to exchange a certain amount of cash for a greater dollar value of food stamps (i.e., one had to "purchase" the food stamps). Although the value of the food stamps allowed the household to obtain more food than it could have gotten with the cash, many households did not have the cash to exchange. When this purchase requirement was eliminated, many more households enrolled in the Food Stamp Program.

loss of benefits. The Food Security Act of 1985, the Stewart B. McKinney Homeless Assistance Act of 1987, and the Hunger Prevention Act of 1988 liberalized benefit and eligibility rules, but the net effects on program participation have been relatively small. The Hunger Prevention Act of 1988 also took the historic step of authorizing across-the-board increases in the maximum benefit above any inflation adjustments. These increases will benefit every food stamp household.

Receipt of food stamps clearly improves the adequacy of poor households' diets (Butler and Raymond, 1987; Devaney and Moffitt, 1990; USDHHS and USDA, 1986). Yet recent evidence suggests that food stamp households still do not obtain a nutritionally adequate diet (Neuhauser, 1988), and that the benefits available through food stamps and other food benefit programs combined are inadequate to meet actual food costs (Weicha and Palombo, 1989). Unfortunately, the assumptions underlying the Food Stamp Program often do not reflect economic reality for many poor families. Inflation of housing costs may have exacerbated this problem during the 1980s.

Food stamp benefit levels are determined as follows. Every year the Department of Agriculture establishes the cost of a Thrifty Food Plan for households of different sizes. Food stamp recipient households are assumed to be able to spend 30 percent of their "counted" income on food. Each household then receives food stamp coupons worth the difference between this 30 percent of counted income and the cost of the Thrifty Food Plan for a household of its size.

Until 1983, the Thrifty Food Plan was set at a dollar level 23 percent lower than the average food expenditures of the poorest one-quarter of all households. In 1983 this level was revised to be 24 percent lower than the food expenditures of the average low-income family (for more detailed discussion, see Cohen and Burt, 1989, pp. 37-42). The Hunger Prevention Act provisions added 2 percent to the inflation-adjusted value of the Thrifty Food Plan in 1989 and 1990, and will add 3 percent each year beginning in 1991. The possibility of a further 2 percent add-on has been discussed in Congress. The add-on provides an across-the-board increase in food stamp benefits to every recipient household, adjusted only for the size of household. It is not large, however. The 3 percent add-on translates into an extra $6 or $7 a month in food stamps for the average household; the 5 percent add-on would provide an additional $12 to $13 a month.

Because the dollar value of the Thrifty Food Plan is defined to be low in relation to real food costs, food affordability has been a problem for food stamp households in the 1980s. Even with the add-on, a belated response to the drastic expansion in the need for emergency food services in the 1980s, many households will still be left short (Cohen and Burt, 1989).

Further, the FSP benefits calculations make assumptions about housing expenses that are unrealistic for many poor households. As we saw in Chapter 3, poor households have been forced to spend increasing proportions of their income on housing, leaving little to meet the costs of other essentials. In 1985, 46 percent of poor renters paid 70 percent or more of their income for housing. The comparable figure was 30 percent in 1983, and less than 15 percent in 1975 (GAO, 1987, p. 10). Of course, an even higher proportion of renters (63 percent in 1985) paid 50 percent or more of their income for housing (Leonard, Dolbeare, and Lazere, 1989).

The Food Stamp Program permits an "excess shelter deduction." Households spending more than half of their adjusted income (about 35 to 40 percent of gross income) on shelter costs (after all deductions have been taken) may claim as an additional deduction the amount they pay for shelter that exceeds the "half of adjusted income" threshold, up to a ceiling, indexed for inflation, that stood at $177 a month in 1990. Three-fourths of food stamp households claim an excess shelter deduction, averaging over $130 a month. One-third of this group would deduct even more if their claims were not limited by the ceiling. The average excess shelter deduction increases food stamp benefits by about $40 a month solely because of shelter costs (USDA, 1990). The difference between the additional food stamp benefit and the excess shelter cost, or about $90, must still be borne by the household. Thus it is likely that these very poor households pay half or more of their gross income for shelter. Given the pressure of housing costs on low-income households, the FSP is increasingly less able to meet recipients' nutritional needs, even though benefits are indexed to inflation in food prices and a deduction is permitted for excess shelter costs.

HOUSING SUBSIDIES AND SUPPLEMENTS

If homelessness fundamentally springs from a household's inability to afford housing, then the most direct approach to preventing or eliminating it would be to subsidize the housing expenses of the poor. A variety of federal programs offer such assistance, and many states and some local governments also sponsor housing assistance programs. Chapter 3 described the major programs at the federal and state levels. Here we concentrate on comparing available housing assistance with need, as measured by the number of poor households potentially eligible for assistance. We then look at who gets assistance and what proportion of households with demonstrable need do not receive housing subsidies. To the extent possible, we also identify changes in these programs during the 1980s that may have made it more difficult for poor households to pay for housing. We also examine the types of assistance available from state and local governments.

Federal Housing Subsidy Programs

In 1979 2.9 million housing units were available (eligible for payment) under federal rental housing assistance programs.[6] This number increased to 3.5 million in 1982, 3.9 million in 1985, 4.1 million in 1987, and 4.3 million in 1989. The number of federally assisted households has thus increased substantially during the 1980s. However, the rate of increase—the number of new units added each year—slowed in the later years of the decade (Milgram, 1990, Table D).

Federal housing subsidy programs are not entitlement programs. They have a fixed dollar amount to spend, which has not been sufficient to cover all households that meet income and other eligibility criteria. Households with incomes at or below 80 percent of the median renter income for a local geographical area are eligible for programs of the Department of Housing and Urban Development (HUD), and households below 50 percent of area median (very low income) have priority.

Some housing subsidies are restricted to certain types of households, particularly the elderly; as a result, program coverage varies significantly. The Congressional Budget Office has calculated HUD coverage of very-low-income households for 1988 (see Table 5-3), when only about one-third of all very-low-income households were served by federal housing assistance programs.[7] About the same proportion holds for households with children. More than half of the households consisting of elderly persons without children received a subsidy, however, while those with no elderly persons or children had a less than 20 percent chance of receiving a federal housing subsidy. Federal legislation specifies that no more than 15 percent of total housing subsidies may be awarded to households without categorical eligibility due to age, handicap, or dependent children. This restriction would be less important if funding limits were higher. At current funding levels, however, it has posed a severe limit on assistance to the kinds of people found most often among the homeless.

Did changes between the late 1970s and the 1980s in the proportion of poor households helped by housing subsidies affect homelessness? To answer this question, the number of units subsidized by federal housing programs can be compared with the number of households with incomes below federal

---

[6] These figures cover public housing (including Indian housing), all Section 8 programs, Section 235, Section 236, Rent Supplement, and Section 202 completions. They do not include Farmers' Home Administration programs. Figures are unduplicated for units covered by Section 202 or 236 plus Section 8 or Rent Supplement.

[7] The figures in the last column of Table 5-3 provide the most realistic idea of program coverage for very-low-income households, because some proportion of available units are occupied by households above this income threshold.

Table 5-3 Estimated Distribution of the Eligible Population and the Rental Assistance Available for Various Groups of Households, 1988

Type of Household	Very-Low-Income Renters (thousands)[a]	Assisted Units Available to Group (thousands)[b]	Percentage Served By	
			All Commitments Available to Group	90 Percent of Commitments Available to Group[c]
Elderly, No Children	3,500	1,900	57	51
Nonelderly, No Children	3,500	660	19	17
Households with 1 or 2 Children	3,600	1,380	38	35
Households with 3 or More Children	1,600	620	38	34
Total	12,200	4,650	38	34

Source: Congressional Budget Office, *Current Housing Problems and Possible Federal Responses*, Washington, D.C., U.S. Government Printing Office, 1988, Table 11, p. 55.

[a]Very-low-income renters have incomes at or below 50 percent of area median, adjusted for household size. Estimates of the total number of very-low-income renters are based on the 1985 American Housing Survey, adjusted for growth in the number of households between 1985 and 1988, assuming the number of very-low- and low-income renters grew at the same rate as the number of households in general. Excludes renters that pay no cash rent.

[b]Includes units still being processed at the end of fiscal year 1988.

[c]Since 1981, housing assistance has been targeted almost exclusively toward very-low-income households. A small but unknown proportion of assisted units, however, are still occupied by low-income renters. These figures assume that 90 percent of commitments are received by very-low-income renters, with 10 percent going to low-income renters.

poverty guidelines, to assess the degree to which federal housing programs meet the need for housing subsidies.[8] These calculations suggest that in 1979 the number of subsidized units would have served 29.1 percent of poor households if all subsidies went to these households. The problem was most severe in 1982, when only 26.8 percent of poor households were potentially covered. Thereafter the proportion increased, to 31.3 percent of poor households in 1985 and to 34.7 percent in 1988 (the last year for which poverty statistics are available). Thus the coverage of federal housing assistance programs was at its lowest during the early 1980s, when the country was in recession. At the end of the decade federal housing subsidies covered a higher proportion of poor households than they did in the late 1970s.

This pattern may seem to cast doubt on the hypothesis that federal housing assistance policies—specifically, large reductions in budget authority—played an important role in producing homelessness in the 1980s. Several other aspects of "coverage" need to be explored, however, before drawing a conclusion. These include targeting to particular types of households, the shift in the proportion of income households must pay, and the change from fifteen- to five-year commitments for Section 8 certificates and vouchers.

If housing subsidies make a difference in the risk of homelessness, then we would expect household types to be represented in homeless populations in inverse proportion to their likelihood of getting housing subsidies. This is in fact the pattern revealed by most homeless surveys. Homeless persons are disproportionately less likely to be elderly and more likely to be single or without children. But housing programs disproportionally serve the elderly and households with children. Together these program biases may shape the distribution of household types among the homeless: they will come dispropor- tionally from those who are poor yet are not eligible for or receiving aid through safety-net programs. For this reason the National Affordable Housing Act of 1990 changed the definition of "family" used by Public Housing and Section 8 programs to include single persons, effective October 1, 1991.

Recipients of federal housing assistance have usually had to pay a certain proportion of their income toward housing costs, with the government supplying the difference between the household contribution and the actual cost of a dwelling. The required contribution of the household jumped from 25 percent to 30 percent of income in 1981. Thus each subsidized household

---

[8]To make comparisons over time, which the Congressional Budget Office study did not do, I used the number of U.S. households below the federal poverty threshold as a rough indicator for calculating the proportion of poor households aided by HUD housing assistance programs. Since the number of poor households was estimated on the basis of the number of poor individuals this calculation is not directly comparable to the very-low-income criterion used by the Congressional Budget Office.

experienced a 20 percent increase in its out-of-pocket housing costs, phased in over five years beginning in 1981. The major justifications for this change were budgetary (a desire to control program expenditures) and equity (subsidized households should pay 30 percent, since their unsubsidized poor counterparts were often paying more than 50 percent of income for housing). No evidence was ever offered documenting that poor households had discretionary income available to cover this increase without cutting other essentials from their budget. For very poor households, this change may have increased their risk of homelessness. The 1983 increase in the income tax standard deduction was enacted in part to provide relief to the very poorest households caught in this income squeeze.

The Reagan administration also made less visible changes in regulations that increased the out-of-pocket expenditures of assisted households. These regulations affected adjustments to income—the items and amounts that households can deduct from their gross incomes to arrive at a net income against which the 30 percent co-payment is calculated. Changes during the 1980s reduced the amounts that could be deducted; as a result, the 30 percent co-payment was not merely 5 percentage points more than households paid before 1981, but applied to a higher adjusted income figure. Administration plans called for further tightening of allowable deductions after 1983, but the Housing and Urban-Rural Recovery Act of 1983 forestalled such action.

Finally, most of the commitments made during the 1980s for new assistance units involved five-year commitments to help renters pay for units in the existing housing stock. Earlier, in contrast, most of the new assistance units involved either new public housing units or fifteen-year commitments that provided an assured stream of rents for rentals in the private stock (Milgram, 1990). After 1981, in short, federal housing assistance no longer tended to add new units to the overall stock of low-cost housing. Some have hypothesized that this change added upward pressures on rent levels, thereby reducing affordability.

State Housing Subsidy Programs

Some state and local governments provide housing supplements, usually to households that receive some type of income assistance such as AFDC, SSI, or General Assistance. These programs spend at least $10 billion a year on housing assistance, almost as much as the federal Department of Housing and Urban Development. In some states the housing component of AFDC or GA benefits is made explicit; in others it is implicit. SSI state supplements are also explicitly intended to help recipients with housing costs. In addition to the state supplements described earlier in this chapter, which are for individuals living independently, many states provide special subsidies for SSI recipients who must live in group homes or other supervised residential programs for people with special needs.

Only one study has investigated the housing component of these state and local programs; it reports data for households only for 1983 and subsidy program characteristics only for 1984 (Newman and Schnare, 1988). Therefore conditions at the beginning and end of the 1980s cannot be compared. However, the data from 1983 and 1984 reveal characteristics of these programs that are important to any understanding of how well available subsidies are meeting the need for housing assistance.

The most important program characteristics are the difference between what federal programs pay and what state and local programs pay, and the variations among states and regions. Nonfederal housing subsidies paid through the AFDC system, either as a component of the regular cash grant or as an explicit separate housing allowance, average only about 50 percent of the Fair Market Rent (FMR) defined by HUD to indicate the cost of standard housing.[9] SSI recipients who live in states that provide supplements receive approximately 64 percent of FMR, whereas GA recipients get 68 percent of FMR.

Variations by region are also dramatic. AFDC shelter allowances "average only about 27 percent of the FMR in the South, compared with a high of 64 percent in the West. Under GA, shelter allowances range from 35 percent in the South to 77 percent in the Northeast. Even under SSI, with the least regional variation, shelter allowances average about 62 percent of the cost of standard housing in the South, compared with about 71 percent in the Northeastern states" (Newman and Schnare, 1988, p. 3). Moreover, ten of the sixteen states without any type of General Assistance, and six of the seven states that do not provide SSI supplements for special needs housing, are in the South; no southern state supplements SSI for individuals living independently. Thus there are dramatic regional variations in the probability that poor households will receive adequate shelter assistance.

UNEMPLOYMENT INSURANCE

The Social Security Act of 1935 created the federal-state unemployment compensation (UC) system, to provide financial relief to workers who had lost their jobs recently and involuntarily, and to stabilize the economy during recessions. States establish their own eligibility requirements, with criteria

---

[9]HUD sets Fair Market Rents for each metropolitan area and adjusts them annually for inflation. The value of housing supplements attached to AFDC, SSI, and GA was compared with the FMR for a particular metropolitan area.

related to types of employers, length of employment, circumstances of leaving employment, and availability for work, among other variables. The system is financed by taxing employers on a certain proportion of their payroll expenses. Regular benefits under the UC system cover two quarters (twenty-six weeks); after regular benefits are exhausted, some programs provide extended benefits for an additional one or two quarters. The availability of extended or supplemental benefits has often been tied to periods of economic downturn.

The UC system covers about 85 percent of all employment situations, yet the proportion of unemployed people receiving UC benefits has never reached 85 percent, and it has fallen dramatically in the later 1980s. The closest the system has come to total coverage was in April 1977, when 81 percent of the unemployed received benefits; the low point—27 percent—occurred in October 1987. In general, unemployed people received significantly less financial protection from the UC system during the 1980s than they had in the 1970s (Table 5-4). Indeed, coverage today is lower than ever before.

Table 5-4 Unemployment Rate and Percentage Insured, 1971-1989

	Yearly Average Unemployment Rate	Insured Unemployed (percentage of total)	Exhaustions of Regular State Benefits (in 1000s)
1971	5.9%	52%	1,942
1972	5.6	45	1,811
1973	4.9	41	1,495
1974	5.6	50	1,926
1975	8.5	76	4,195
1976	7.7	67	3,262
1977	7.1	56	2,776
1978	6.1	43	2,030
1979	5.8	42	2,037
1980	7.1	50	3,072
1981	7.6	41	2,987
1982	9.7	45	4,175
1983	9.6	44	4,180
1984	7.5	34	2,607
1985	7.2	34	2,579
1986	7.0	33	2,746
1987	6.2	32	2,408
1988	5.5	32	1,979
1989	5.3	33	1,933

Source: U.S. House of Representatives, Committee on Ways and Means, *Overview of Entitlement Programs: The 1990 Green Book,* Washington, D.C., Government Printing Office, 1990, pp. 460, 479, and 508.

Analyses conducted for the Ways and Means Committee of the House of Representatives indicate that multiple factors contributed to this drop, including:

1. The decline in the proportion of unemployed from manufacturing industries. These industries had higher rates of "coverage" under UC than the industries that replaced them, so eligibility for UC was reduced. This change accounted for 4 to 18 percent of the drop in the insured rate.

2. Geographic shifts in composition of the unemployed among regions of the country. Since states differ in their eligibility criteria, movement of workers will shift the overall insured rate. This change accounted for 16 percent of the drop.

3. Changes in state program characteristics, including: a) increase in the base period earnings requirements; b) increase in income denials; and c) other nonmonetary eligibility requirements. These changes accounted for 22 to 39 percent of the drop in the insured rate.

4. Changes in federal policy; partial taxation of UC benefits (16 percent).

5. Changes in unemployment as measured by the Current Population Survey (1 to 12 percent) (U.S. House, 1990, p. 462).

The number of workers who exhaust their regular unemployment benefits (i.e., remain out of work after twenty-six weeks) is an indicator of the difficulties encountered in finding another job. Predictably, exhaustions vary with the unemployment rate; they were very high during the early 1980s, as was unemployment. If the high level of unemployment in the early 1980s was an important contributor to homelessness, as has been proposed, then the decline in the insured rate may have helped keep homelessness at a high level even when unemployment began to fall in the second half of the decade.

As we saw in Chapter 4, Social Security lifted more than twice as many people out of poverty between 1979 and 1988 as did the means-tested cash, food, and housing benefits examined in this chapter. Social Security had an even greater differential effect on the poverty gap (the amount of money it would take to lift a family out of poverty). Social insurance programs other than Social Security (unemployment insurance, workers' compensation) along with means-tested benefits became much less effective in preventing poverty during the 1980s; the loss was greater in noncash benefit programs than in cash assistance. In essence, changes made in the early 1980s left federal safety-net programs less capable of alleviating poverty than they had been in 1979. Compensatory changes beginning in 1985 have recouped some, but not all, of the loss.

GENERAL ASSISTANCE

General Assistance—also known in different jurisdictions as Public Assistance, General Relief, Home Relief, Poor Relief, and by other names—is the support of last resort for many needy people. Unlike the other safety-net programs just described, it is not governed by any federal statutes. States are under no federal obligation or incentive to offer General Assistance, and vary in their approaches. Some states provide no mandate or standard; others allow counties to decide whether or not to offer a program; still others require all counties to provide a program that meets state standards; and some states administer their own programs.

States and counties also vary in their rules for GA eligibility. Some allow able-bodied individuals to receive benefits (although they usually also require work or search for work); others restrict GA to the disabled and/or elderly not otherwise eligible for SSI; still others use GA only as a stopgap measure to help people cope until their AFDC or SSI applications are approved. Even when widely available, GA benefits rarely provide the level of support available through AFDC or SSI.

Table 5-5 shows the availability of General Assistance by state in 1982, 1984, and 1987. Seventeen states offered no GA, or emergency assistance only, in 1987. In nine states, counties have the option of providing GA, but only a few of the biggest counties do so. In four states, most counties administer state-mandated programs. Statewide programs are limited to unemployables in thirteen states and the District of Columbia, and include employables in addition to the disabled and/or elderly in seven states. Because the data for these three years come from three different studies, they are not always parallel. For instance, for states with county option or county administration, the study of 1987 GA programs (Shapiro and Greenstein, 1988) did not identify benefit levels in the largest county. Hence there are no 1987 dollar figures to parallel those for 1982 and 1984.

The data in Table 5-5 show that GA programs have only a limited ability to stave off homelessness. One-third of all states (seventeen) do not have a General Assistance program of any kind. Poor people in these states—whether they are disabled, elderly, or able to work—will receive no sustaining state or local financial support (although a few of these states may offer some one-time assistance for an emergency). Thus the one-fourth to one-third of single homeless people who are disabled physically or who are mentally ill will receive no financial help in these states unless they qualify for SSI.

In the nine states in which only the largest counties offer a GA program, a needy person will have an incentive to move to the area where benefits are available. In many states with only one or two large cities, homelessness is often regarded as a city problem. It may be that the absence of safety-net resources in nonurban counties impels the needy and disabled into the cities, where they can find services and the possibility of financial support. Thus program availability may create a self-fulfilling prophecy—the cities will indeed become the residence of all people who cannot sustain themselves without help in smaller communities.

Table 5-5 Availability of General Assistance, 1982-1987

	1982		1984		1987		Change in Real Value, 1982–1987[c]
	Type[a]	Benefit[b]	Type[a]	Benefit[b]	Type[a]	Benefit[b]	
States with no GA in 1987 (17)							
Alabama	N	—	N	—	N	—	na
Alaska	A	80	N	—	N	—	na
Arkansas	N	—	N	—	N	—	na
Colorado	N	—	N	—	N	—	na
Florida	N	—	N	—	N	—	na
Indiana	N	—	N	—	N	—	na
Kentucky	N	—	N	—	N	—	na
Louisiana	D	91	D	91	N	—	na
Mississippi	N	—	N	—	N	—	na
N. Carolina	N	—	N	—	N	—	na
N. Dakota	C_L	275	N	—	N	—	na
Oklahoma	N	—	N	—	N	—	na
S. Carolina	N	—	N	—	N	—	na
Tennessee	N	—	N	—	N	—	na
Texas	N	—	N	—	N	—	na
Vermont	A	164	N	—	N	—	na
West Virginia	N	—	N	—	N	—	na
States with County Option, Where Only Urban Counties Have Substantial Programs (9) ($ figures are for largest county)							
Georgia	C_L	225	C_L	225	C_L	—	na
Idaho	C_L	—	N	—	C_L	—	na
Illinois	C_L	144	C_L	154	C_L	—	na

Iowa	C_L	284	N	—	C_L	—	na
Montana	C_L	153	C_L	212	C_L	—	na
Nebraska	C_L	210	C_L	240	C_L	—	na
Nevada	C_L	—	C_L	228	C_L	—	na
New Hampshire	C_L	282	N	—	C_L	—	na
S. Dakota	C_L	185	N	—	C_L	—	na

States with County Administration and Fairly Widespread Availability (4)
($ figures are for largest county)

California	C	228	C	228	C	—	na
Maine	D	216	C	406	C	—	na
Virginia	C	214	C	157	C	—	na
Wisconsin	C	175	C	175	C	—	na

States with Statewide GA, Unemployables Only (14)

Arizona	D	130	D	130	D	173	+15
Delaware	D	107	A	116	D	119	−4
District of Columbia	D	190	D	210	D	239	+8
Hawaii	D	297	A	297	D	297	−14
Kansas	A	194	A	216	D	189	−16
Maryland	A	164	A	126	D	171	−10
Missouri	D	70	D	80	D	80	−1
New Mexico	D	139	A	145	D	156	−3
Oregon	D	195	D	212	D	239	+6
Pennsylvania	A	172[d]	D	177	D	186	−7
Rhode Island	D	63	A	276	D	260	+356
Utah	D	215	A	217	D	217	−13
Washington	D	288	D	303	D	314	−6
Wyoming	A	195	A	145	D	145	−36

Table 5-5 Continued

	1982		1984		1987		Change in Real Value, 1982–1987[c]
	Type[a]	Benefit[b]	Type[a]	Benefit[b]	Type[a]	Benefit[b]	
States with Statewide GA, Employables Eligible (7)							
Connecticut	A	144	A	268	A	315	+89
Massachusetts	D	181	A	244	A	328	+56
Michigan	A	218	A	218	A	223	−12
Minnesota	D	186	A	236	A	203	−6
New Jersey	A	119/178[e]	A	200	A	140	−19
New York	A	246[f]	A	287	A	277	−3
Ohio	A	106	A	128	A	136	+10

Sources: For 1982: Urban Systems Research and Engineering Inc., *1982 Characteristics of General Assistance Programs*, Washington, D.C., 1983. For 1984: Sandra J. Newman and Ann B. Schnare, *Subsidizing Shelter*, Washington, D.C.: The Urban Institute Press, 1988, Tables 7.1 and 7.4. For 1987: Isaac Shapiro and Robert Greenstein, *Holes in the Safety Nets*, Washington, D.C.: Center on Budget and Policy Priorities, 1988, Tables 3 and A8.

[a] N = None, or emergency only; C$_L$ = County admin., limited to one or a few big counties; C = County admin., fairly widespread, no state average available; D = Unemployable, disabled and/or elderly only; A = Any needy person (if a state covers unemployables as long as necessary, but limits employables to brief periods of coverage during any one year, it was coded D, not A).

[b] In nominal dollars.

[c] In constant 1987 dollars.

[d] For Philadelphia; state range was $147–$181.

[e] $119 for employables, $178 for disabled.

[f] For New York City; state range was $177 for low-cost areas; $299 maximum in highest cost areas.

Relatively few states maintain GA programs that accommodate employable individuals; instead, many restrict eligibility to the disabled, elderly, or families awaiting AFDC. Four states (Kansas, Maryland, Pennsylvania, and Wyoming) that served employables in 1982 had changed their programs to exclude these people by 1987. (In Pennsylvania, employables are limited to three months of support in any year.) Further, some states and counties restrict eligibility even among the disabled and elderly to those who have applied for SSI and are waiting for their applications to be accepted. Thus in many locations GA is available and helpful to some homeless and potentially homeless individuals, but not to many others.

Finally, GA benefit levels have been relatively low and shrinking. In 1982, a monthly income of $418 was needed to raise a single nonelderly adult above the poverty threshold. The figure for 1987 was $492 a month. In the latter year, the highest GA benefit ($328, in Massachusetts) supplied only 67 percent of the resources needed to escape poverty. The lowest GA benefit ($80, in Missouri) covered only 16 percent of the poverty line.

Three states that had a GA program in 1982 had dropped it completely by 1987. Further, in most states for which data are available for both 1982 and 1987, GA benefits lost ground to inflation during the decade, declining from 1 to 36 percent in real terms. (In seven states benefits gained against inflation, often substantially.) Thus even in states with relatively generous benefits, recipients will be hard-pressed to maintain themselves in housing on what they receive.

Most of the homeless are single individuals; they are not eligible for AFDC and of all groups are the least well served by federal housing assistance (although after October 1991 they will be eligible to receive more help with housing). Because few of the homeless are elderly, Social Security, SSI-aged, and federal housing assistance restricted to the elderly are irrelevant. (Of course, the success of these programs in alleviating poverty among the elderly has helped keep their numbers small among the homeless.) Some of the homeless are physically or mentally disabled and thus might qualify for SSI-disabled, but very few receive it. Thus for many people, the major federal safety-net programs offer little protection from homelessness. State or county General Assistance programs are often the only recourse for single individuals in need of assistance. As we have just seen, however, General Assistance is not available in a number of states and is restricted in many others to a few counties, and/or to certain categories of persons. Even this program of last resort fails to help major segments of the homeless and at-risk populations. Further, the purchasing power of GA benefits has eroded during the 1980s; even those who receive General Assistance may be forced to choose between necessities.

SUMMARY AND CONCLUSIONS

This chapter has reviewed changes in the major safety-net programs during the 1980s that might have contributed to the increase in homelessness. We have seen that benefits available through several of the programs (AFDC, SSI state supplemental payments, General Assistance) have lost their purchasing power through failures to adjust for inflation. Further, eligibility, co-payments, and other program requirements changed in several programs (AFDC, food stamps, SSI, federal rental assistance) in ways that excluded substantial proportions of those eligible in 1980 and/or increased the burden on the household of those using the benefit. In addition, program coverage has always largely excluded single adults—the most sizable household type among the homeless.

It is therefore plausible that changes in these safety-net programs contributed to the increase in homelessness during the 1980s, especially since the number of households in need of assistance has increased, as we saw in Chapter 4. The fundamental premise of this book has been that homelessness may be increased through changes in any combination of factors that affect housing affordability—the cost of housing on one side of the equation, and a variety of resources to purchase housing on the other side. Safety-net programs provide very poor households with resources they would not otherwise have, which make housing more affordable. Withdrawal of these resources, or a reduction in their value, makes housing less affordable, other things being equal. The national-level data examined in this chapter suggest that there has been a reduction in resources available through safety-net programs, which could have contributed to homelessness. Part Two will examine the effects of changes in these programs as they play out in individual cities.

CHAPTER SIX

Mental Illness and Chemical Dependency

■ Since 1980, as we have seen, there have been significant changes in housing, poverty, and public benefits that may well have contributed to the growth of homelessness. With respect to mental illness and chemical dependency among the homeless, however, little has changed. Studies of skid rows, transients, and vagrants going back to the late nineteenth century show roughly comparable proportions of people with alcohol problems. Studies reporting on mental illness date from the 1950s, and show many mentally ill among the homeless (summarized by Rossi, 1989). Although their proportions are somewhat higher today, the mentally ill have always been part of our skid row populations.

One thing has changed, however: the definition of homelessness. Before 1980, homelessness was usually interpreted to mean detachment from a family-type living arrangement. People living by themselves in skid row hotel rooms were considered homeless, even though they spent every night in shelter paid for with their own resources. Even the U.S. Census Bureau used this terminology as late as the 1960 Census. Studies that report actual sleeping arrangements (summarized in Rossi 1989) reveal that very few skid row residents spent nights on the streets, however.[1] Thus the "homeless" of previous decades often had reasonably stable shelter arrangements, despite severe disability in many cases. Today's homeless, in contrast, are literally without shelter at the time they are identified as homeless. The major issue for this chapter, then, is to understand the reasons for this shift from housing (however inadequate) to literal homelessness among the mentally ill and chemically dependent poor.

---

[1]In Chicago, of 12,000 persons on skid row, only 110 were found on the streets. In Philadelphia, only 64 of 2,000 skid row residents slept on the streets.

MENTAL ILLNESS AND CHEMICAL DEPENDENCY
AMONG THE HOMELESS

Could increases in mental illness, alcohol abuse or alcoholism, and drug abuse help explain the growth of homelessness in the 1980s? To establish the facts about the prevalence of these problems, this section compares the findings of studies of the homeless conducted during this decade and in previous years, and of national studies using samples of housed American adults. After considering each condition separately, the available information about homeless people who have both "addictive" and "nonaddictive" diagnoses will then be summarized. Remedies for these "dual-diagnosis" people are particularly difficult to devise, because the various existing treatment systems are typically so specialized that they reject anyone who has more than one diagnosable condition (e.g., who is mentally ill as well as alcoholic) (Ridgely, Goldman, and Willenbring, 1990). Indeed, this refusal to treat people with multiple conditions may contribute to their risk of homelessness, since each of their conditions may get worse without treatment and render them less capable of self-sufficiency or less tolerable to potentially care-giving family or friends.

Mental Illness

The chronically mentally ill appear to be at great risk for homelessness in the 1980s. Available evidence suggests that they made up a significant part of the homeless population in past decades as well.

The designation "severe mental illness" usually includes the diagnoses of schizophrenia, the major affective disorders (recurrent major depression and bipolar disorder), paranoid and other psychoses, and personality disorders. Two other criteria, disability and duration, are usually considered along with diagnosis in identifying people who would be considered "severely disabled" or "chronic." To meet the disability criterion, the mental illness must interfere with the person's ability to work, handle personal affairs, or perform normal activities of daily living such that self-sufficiency is impossible. To meet the duration criterion, the mental illness and concomitant disability must have lasted, or be expected to last, at least a year.

Population rates of chronic or severe mental illness are very stable across time and place, including non-Western and less developed countries and cultures. In the United States, officials estimate that about 1 percent of the adult (sixteen and over) population—about 1.9 million people in 1989—suffer from a chronic mental illness other than senility without psychosis (Goldman, 1984; U.S. Department of Health and Human Services, 1980). In contrast, most careful studies find that 20 to 50 percent of homeless people have either a current severe mental illness, a history of hospitalization for a severe mental illness, or both (Burt and Cohen, 1989a, 1989b; Rossi et al., 1986; Tessler and

Dennis, 1989; Vernez et al., 1988). Studies of the homeless in seven cities and one state (Ohio), funded by the National Institute of Mental Health (NIMH) in the mid-1980s, included fairly elaborate psychiatric assessments to determine the presence of current mental illness. Their results, summarized by Tessler and Dennis (1989), revealed 20 to 48 percent of the homeless showed symptoms of severe mental illness. Proportions of people with past hospitalizations for mental illness were about the same, 22 to 45 percent. Most experts now work with a conservative assumption that about one-third of the homeless suffer from a severe mental illness. Many more homeless people report current psychological states of high demoralization and depression when they are asked about sleep and eating disturbances, the hopelessness of the immediate future, and current feelings of discouragement. While their responses might be valid indicators of clinical depression among domiciled people, for the homeless they may be no more than a realistic assessment of their situation (Burt and Cohen, 1989a; Farr et al., 1986; Rossi et al., 1986).

Historical comparisons are limited because earlier studies of skid row populations tended to focus on alcohol rather than mental health problems. However, some earlier studies reveal the presence of the mentally ill among skid row residents (summarized by Rossi, 1989). Working in Chicago before deinstitutionalization had significantly reduced the state mental hospital census, Bogue (1963) judged that about 20 percent of skid row residents were chronically mentally ill. Bahr and Caplow (1973) reached a similar conclusion in New York's Bowery. The presence of the mentally ill among skid row and homeless populations may have increased somewhat during the 1980s, but it is by no means a new phenomenon.

Alcohol Abuse and Alcoholism

The proportion of alcohol abusers and alcoholics in the U.S. population has remained relatively constant at least since the late 1960s. About 5 percent of American adults experience moderate levels of symptoms indicating dependence on alcohol, and another 7 percent experience negative social or personal consequences (such as loss of a job, illness, or arrest) that indicate alcohol abuse. If people who abstain completely from drinking alcoholic beverages are excluded from the base, these percentages increase to 7 and 10 percent of drinkers, respectively. Thus approximately 12 percent of American adults (17 percent of those who drink at all) have moderate or more severe drinking problems. Men are approximately twice as likely as women to have drinking problems (14 to 16 percent versus 6 percent); younger people (under thirty-five) have at least double the rate of drinking problems of those thirty-five and older (National Institute of Alcohol Abuse and Alcoholism, 1987).

Studies of alcohol abuse and alcoholism among homeless populations during the 1980s have been summarized by Fischer (1987) and Stark (1987). The fifteen studies reviewed by Stark show prevalence rates ranging from 10 to 45 percent. Summarizing more than forty studies (including many of those reviewed by Stark), Fischer reports rates for mixed-sex or male populations ranging from 15 to 86 percent. The modal rate is about one-third of the homeless. Studies that report separate rates for women generally find significantly lower rates—3 to 15 percent, with one outlier at 32 percent.

The substantial variation among studies reflects the lack of any uniform definition of alcohol abuse and alcoholism; reported rates are based on many different indicators, including daily use, excessive use, drinking problem, binge drinking, use of detoxification service, and psychiatric diagnosis of lifetime alcohol abuse. Moreover, samples were drawn from very different locations and populations. Most of the studies gathered data in only one city, or at most in one state. (The same limitations are found in studies reporting rates of mental illness among the homeless.)

Some unifying perspective is provided by two studies whose data are national in scope. Wright and Weber (1987) report prevalence rates for alcohol abuse, based on clinician judgment, of 47 percent for men and 16 percent for women among homeless persons using special health clinics for the homeless in sixteen large cities. These estimates are probably on the high end, since alcoholics are significantly more likely than nonalcoholics to have multiple health problems and to visit a doctor, clinic, or emergency room (the same is true for the mentally ill).[2] The prevalence data reported by Wright and Weber therefore contain significant bias toward higher rates due to self-selection.

As reported in Chapter 2, the Urban Institute study of the homeless who use soup kitchens or shelters in large U.S. cities found that 37 percent of the men, 19 percent of the single women, and 7 percent of the women with

---

[2]The data on number of health problems were given in Chapter 2, Table 2-5, based on the results of the Urban Institute study. Differences between those with and without a history of mental hospitalization are highly significant (p < .00001), as are differences between those with a history of chemical dependency treatment and those without. Their health problems make homeless persons with these histories more likely than others to visit doctors, clinics, or emergency rooms. Among alcoholics, 77 percent sought treatment in these settings within the year before being interviewed, compared with 59 percent of homeless persons without a history of treatment for alcoholism. A history of mental hospitalization also predicted heightened use of medical services—74 percent of those with this history but only 63 percent of others sought treatment in the previous year. Both differences are significant at (p < .0001). Conversely, 39 percent of medical service users, but only 21 percent of nonusers, had histories of chemical dependency treatment. The corresponding figures for those with mental hospitalizations were 22 percent versus 15 percent. Piliavin, Westerfelt, and Elliott (1989) also report that the mentally ill in their Minneapolis sample were overrepresented among clinic users.

children had undergone inpatient treatment for chemical dependency. Since 80 percent of homeless adults are male, these data suggest that at least one-third, and probably a larger proportion, of homeless populations in the 1980s had problems with alcohol.

The studies conducted in the 1980s confirm that alcohol abuse and alcoholism are at least as prevalent as severe mental illness among the homeless. Alcohol problems are more than twice as prevalent among the homeless as among males in the general public. Alcohol abuse probably plays some causal role in increasing the risk of homelessness, by reducing earning capacity and leading to downward mobility, cognitive impairments, and disruptive or bizarre behavior that strains the tolerance of family and friends. Abuse of alcohol is probably also exacerbated by the stresses and circumstances of living as a homeless person.

While it is hard to obtain historical data on mental illness among the homeless, many studies document alcohol problems in this population. Stark (1987) summarizes twenty-three studies, conducted in every decade from the 1890s through the 1970s. Their findings are very similar to more recent studies: prevalence rates ranged from 7 to 58 percent, again with a median around 30 to 35 percent. Not too much has changed, it seems, with regard to the prevalence of alcohol problems among homeless populations in the United States.

Drug Abuse

Information on the use and abuse of illicit drugs comes from several sources: household surveys (1980 to 1988), longitudinal surveys of high school seniors and high school graduates through their twenties (1975 to 1988), and medical reporting (Drug Abuse Warning Network, 1976 to 1985 and 1986 to 1989; federally supported drug treatment facilities, 1979 to 1984). Household surveys and the longitudinal surveys of seniors and young adult high school graduates show prevalence rates gradually declining since 1980. Annual use of all illicit drugs peaked in 1979; annual prevalence of marijuana use peaked in 1981. Cocaine is the only exception, with increasing rates of annual use through 1985, and consistent drops since 1986. Crack cocaine was not identified separately before 1986, which was its highest year for high school seniors and young adults (Johnston et al., 1989; National Institute on Drug Abuse, 1989).

These general population data cannot be used to draw inferences about risk of homelessness. As we saw in Chapter 2, about half of homeless adults have not completed high school or obtained an equivalency degree, and all are extremely poor. General population data, in comparison, are weighted heavily toward the better educated and more employable, and thus may paint too sanguine a picture of drug abuse trends. Data from emergency room visits and drug treatment facility admissions are also biased, in the opposite direction from household surveys.

The Drug Abuse Warning Network (DAWN) statistical series reported here comes from the twenty-four largest metropolitan areas in the country, including New York, Los Angeles, Chicago, Detroit, Dallas, Atlanta, Miami, St. Louis, San Francisco, and the District of Columbia. Covering the years 1976 through 1985, this series reports trends from a consistent panel of 420 hospital emergency rooms. The total 1980 population covered was 66.1 million, or about 37 percent of all people residing in metropolitan areas. As Table 6-1 shows, the number of emergency room episodes involving heroin or its derivatives declined from 1976 through 1979 but has been rising steadily ever since, whether measured by the absolute number of episodes for all facilities (top panel of Table 6-1) or as a rate per 1,000 emergency room visits in the central cities (second panel). Cocaine-involved episodes show a steady and dramatic increase over the entire period but with larger jumps beginning in the early 1980s. The pattern for illicit drugs as a whole, in contrast, shows a steady decline from 1976 through 1984.

Over this period, an increasing proportion of drug-related emergency room episodes were attributed to dependency. (Other reasons cited for drug use include psychic effect and intent to commit suicide.) Overall, dependence as a reason for using illicit drugs increased in two steps during the early 1980s: between 1979 and 1980, and again from 1982 onward (third panel). Dependence on heroin or morphine fluctuated in a fairly steady range. Dependence on cocaine increased sharply between the 1970s and the 1980s.

The 1976 to 1985 data series does not cover the years of the crack epidemic. However, a second panel involving 382 emergency rooms in twenty-one metropolitan areas covers the critical years for crack, 1985 through 1989. Except in Miami, Table 6-2 shows, emergency room episodes involving cocaine increased dramatically during these years. Many areas experienced very large increases in every year of the period. Overall, the increase in cocaine-involved emergency room episodes over the previous year was 81 percent in 1986, 73 percent in 1987, and 33 percent in 1988. Between 1985 and 1988 the cumulative increase was 315 percent.

Drug treatment statistics also reflect striking increases in cocaine abuse during the 1980s. Between 1979 and 1984 the National Institute of Drug Abuse (1987b) required drug treatment centers that received some federal funding to report annual admissions data. These facilities, numbering almost 600, reported steady client loads of approximately 100,000 per year, but the proportion of admissions that involved cocaine addiction rose dramatically, from 4 to 15 percent of admissions in these six years. Admissions for heroin and other opiates declined over the period (from 53 to 46 percent), as did admissions for

Table 6-1 Emergency Room Episodes Involving Selected Illicit Drugs, 1976-1985

	1976	1977	1978	1979	1980	1981	1982	1983	1984	1985
All Episodes in Reporting MSAs (in 1000s)										
Heroin/morphine	11.6	7.3	5.7	4.9	5.5	6.1	7.9	8.5	8.9	10.6
Cocaine	1.0	1.1	1.4	1.9	2.8	3.1	4.2	4.9	7.9	9.4
All drugs	98.9	94.2	89.3	85.8	83.5	82.3	81.4	77.8	79.8	82.3
Episodes in Central City (per 1000 ER visits)										
Heroin/morphine	1.42	0.89	0.71	0.61	0.68	0.75	0.96	1.07	1.06	1.24
Cocaine	0.12	0.13	0.15	0.21	0.32	0.35	0.52	0.60	0.93	1.06
All drugs	8.83	8.02	7.58	7.32	7.19	7.28	7.60	7.54	7.48	7.64
Episodes with Drug Dependence as Reason for Use (% of total)										
Heroin/Morphine	68%	73%	74%	72%	76%	73%	76%	79%	73%	73%
Cocaine	30	33	34	35	47	44	50	46	41	46
All drugs	16	13	12	12	16	16	20	22	23	24

Source: National Institute on Drug Abuse, *Trends in Drug Abuse Related Hospital Emergency Room Episodes and Medical Examiner Cases for Selected Drugs: DAWN 1976-1985*. Series H, Number 3, 1987, Tables 2.ER1, 2.ER5, 2.ER9, 3.ER1, 3.ER5, 3.ER9, A.ER1, A.ER5, A.ER9.

Table 6-2 Emergency Room Episodes Involving Cocaine, 1985-1989, by SMSA

SMSA	1985	1986	1987	1988	1989	Change 1985–1989 (%)
Atlanta	125	306	466	873	1,643	1,214%
Baltimore	169	324	730	1,604	1,539	811
Boston	292	520	974	1,292	1,347	374
Buffalo	17	59	187	205	217	286
Chicago	703	1,591	2,772	3,842	4,135	488
Dallas	98	451	902	1,270	1,071	993
Denver	222	429	470	736	717	65
Detroit	933	2,487	453	4,295	4,000	329
Los Angeles	1,586	2,283	2,181	2,896	2,984	88
Miami	119	239	181	188	155	30
Minneapolis	131	253	391	500	423	223
Newark	104	313	651	698	1,073	932
New Orleans	495	408	1,865	3,164	3,101	526
New York	2,996	4,601	6,623	6,662	5,615	87
Philadelphia	475	1,135	2,906	4,586	4,639	877
Phoenix	114	363	768	1,200	790	593
St. Louis	60	144	267	339	705	1,075
San Diego	116	218	266	292	359	209
San Francisco	398	446	507	593	1,160	191
Seattle	206	386	768	1,098	1,088	428
Washington, D.C.	838	1,314	3,058	5,020	4,508	438
Total DAWN	10,248	18,580	32,052	42,512	42,144	311

Source: National Institute on Drug Abuse, unpublished data from the DAWN System. The year-by-year city figures are for a consistent panel of reporting hospitals. The "Total DAWN" figures include additional hospitals reporting in each year.

most other drugs. Approximately half of all persons admitted to these facilities had not completed high school. This level of educational attainment is comparable to most homeless populations.

Drug-related admissions to state-funded facilities have also increased. Member agencies of the National Association of State Alcohol and Drug Abuse Directors (NASADAD) report that drug abuse admissions rose from 253,400 in 1984 to 518,900 in 1988. Alcohol admissions increased only 29 percent during the same period (NASADAD, 1984 to 1988).

The evidence suggests that drug abuse, particularly cocaine abuse, rose enough in the later years of the 1980s to affect the risk of homelessness among poor and less educated people. If so, the homeless population of the later 1980s may have changed to include higher proportions of addiction to crack cocaine or to multiple drugs including crack. Anecdotes from New York and other cities (e.g., Washington, D.C., and New Orleans) suggest that abuse of crack cocaine among young single homeless people may have been as high as 40 percent in 1989.

The crack epidemic has had a devastating effect on networks and support systems in the most vulnerable neighborhoods. Violent struggles over drug turf have not only led to the murder of innocent bystanders, but have made people afraid to go outside, to church, or to other neighborhood events, thus eroding kin and friendship networks. Crack cocaine abuse has produced an increase in child abuse and neglect cases, including addicted newborns and the "boarder baby" phenomenon (addicted newborns retained by hospitals when the mother's addiction and behavior suggest a high risk of abuse or neglect). Compounding the general effects of severe poverty and housing problems, these indirect effects of cocaine abuse may increase the risks of homelessness for abusers and nonusers alike.

Data on current drug use and abuse among the homeless are difficult to interpret for several reasons. First, many studies report "substance abuse" without differentiating among alcohol and other drugs. Second, even when drug abuse is identified separately, studies often fail to differentiate among occasional use, regular use, and abuse, or among types of drugs (e.g., tranquilizers, sleeping or "stay-awake" pills, diet pills, marijuana, and other street drugs). Third, data collection methods make a very large difference; self-report, institutional records, and physiological (laboratory) evidence yield widely different rates of use and abuse. Fourth, very different frequencies of drug use have been reported, from "ever used" to "used at least once a week" to "used daily." Studies that include more types of drugs tend to report higher rates of drug abuse. Higher rates are also reported when researchers have broader definitions of "abuse."

Wright et al. (1987) report the only national-level data for rates of drug abuse among the homeless. They found that 11 percent of males and 8 percent of females who used Health Care for the Homeless clinics currently abused drugs other than alcohol. Vernez et al. (1988) found that 48 percent of a sample drawn from three California counties had abused drugs other than alcohol at some time during their lives.

Mulkern and Spence (1984) summarize the results of eight local studies of drug abuse conducted in the early 1980s, and attempt to derive reasonable estimates of "serious" drug use, which they defined as "regular and frequent." Milburn (1990) did the same for fourteen additional studies conducted later in the decade. Mulkern and Spence concluded that 3 to 20 percent of shelter users and 25 percent of the street homeless were current serious drug users, according to their definition. Milburn found:

> Prevalence estimates for current drug use among sheltered homeless people ranged from 20.8 to 58 percent; for current drug abuse, estimates ranged from 3 to 48 percent; and for current drug dependence, the estimates were less than 1 to 10.1 percent. The data on current drug dependence are probably the most precise, given the assessment techniques that were used. (p. 72)

In comparison with research conducted in the 1980s, earlier studies were less likely to report differentiations in drug type and degree of abuse or dependence. We therefore cannot make any definitive comparisons of drug abuse among the homeless of today and earlier skid row and transient populations. On the basis of trends in the general population (examined earlier), however, we would not expect substantial jumps in the prevalence of drug abuse among the homeless until late in the 1980s. Thus the growth in homelessness in the early part of the decade must have other explanations. Rising drug use, however, may help explain why the size of the homeless population did not decline in the later 1980s although the economic situation improved for many.

Drugs and alcohol often go together. Among Health Care for the Homeless clinic users across the country, 57 percent of male and 41 percent of female drug abusers were also alcoholic. Conversely, 18 percent of male alcoholics and 26 percent of female alcoholics also abused other drugs (Wright et al., 1987). Similarly, Farr et al. (1986) report that 31 percent of their sample of homeless people on Los Angeles' skid row had current substance abuse disorders, including 27 percent with alcohol abuse or dependence and 10 percent with drug abuse or dependence. (Significantly higher proportions had lifetime prevalence rates for both types of abuse.)

People with Multiple Conditions

When a person suffers from both chemical dependency and mental illness, the problems of each condition are compounded, and it becomes more difficult to obtain treatment for either condition. Facilities that treat the mentally ill will not take someone who is also alcoholic, and facilities that treat chemical dependency will not take clients if they are also mentally ill. Five of the NIMH-funded studies reviewed by Tessler and Dennis (1989) report data on dual diagnoses. Between 8 and 22 percent of their homeless samples had an active mental illness and were also abusing substances (alcohol, drugs, or both). Persons with dual conditions represent 17 to 52 percent of those with mental illness.

National comparisons are provided by Wright et al. (1987) and by Burt and Cohen (1989a, 1989b). Among men using the Health Care for the Homeless clinics in sixteen cities, 24 percent had a mental illness and 10 percent had both a diagnosable mental illness and a problem with alcohol. These dual-diagnosis clients represented 42 percent of mentally ill men. Among female clinic users, 37 percent were mentally ill and 7 percent had dual diagnoses. Because rates of alcohol abuse are much lower among female clinic users, only 17 percent of all women with mental disorders had dual diagnoses.

In Burt and Cohen's national data on urban service users, 8 percent of both single men and single women, and 3 percent of women with children, had histories of institutionalization for both mental illness and chemical dependency. (Such histories do not necessarily mean that people were both mentally ill and chemically dependent at the same time, which would be the criterion for true "dual diagnosis.") In each of the twenty cities sampled in their national study, Burt and Cohen also interviewed a small nonrandom sample of "street homeless"—people who did not use either soup kitchens or shelters.[3] These people may well represent the segment of the homeless population that is sickest and least able to cope. They were significantly more likely than service users to have experienced mental hospitalization, either alone (27 versus 19 percent) or in combination with chemical dependency treatment (16 versus 8 percent). These data suggest that the most vulnerable homeless are the hardest to reach through the usual service offerings.

WHAT HAS REALLY HAPPENED, AND WHY?

Despite limitations in available data, we can find answers—with varying degrees of confidence—to some important questions:

---

[3]This small sample (of 142) was interviewed in an effort to learn what biases resulted from excluding the street population from our larger random sample of homeless service users. Street locations were identified by police and local homeless activists as places where we were likely to find homeless people. Interviewers surveyed the people found at these locations with the goal of identifying approximately five homeless people per location. This effort yielded 445 individuals identified as homeless (out of 999 people approached on a random basis and screened). Of these 445, 142 had not used either a shelter or soup kitchen in the past week, and were retained in the sample of non-service users.

1. Has the prevalence of mental illness or chemical dependency increased in the general population?

2. Has the proportion of the homeless who have either or both of these problems risen?

3. Has the absolute number of homeless people who have a chronic mental illness or a substance abuse problem risen, independent of the proportions?

4. Has the proportion of the chronically mentally ill who are homeless risen?

5. Has the proportion of the chemically dependent who are homeless risen?

The first question is a relatively easy one. The proportion of the general population who are chronically mentally ill has not changed over the years, or in the 1980s. Further, the proportion of the general population who abuse alcohol or are alcoholics has been declining slowly but steadily, both in the 1980s and earlier. Thus any increase in the presence of these two groups among the homeless cannot be attributed to changes in their presence in the general population. This is an important point, since the mentally ill and alcohol abusers make up about half of the homeless population at any given time. Alcoholics represent an even higher proportion of the long-term homeless.

Abuse of heroin and cocaine, on the other hand, has increased during the 1980s. Data from high school seniors and high school graduates in their twenties show a gradual decline in the 1980s in use of most illegal drugs, with the exception of cocaine and crack cocaine. Data from urban hospitals show that emergency room episodes involving heroin and its derivatives dropped in the late 1970s, then began to increase in the 1980s. More than twice as many episodes were reported in 1985 as in 1979. However, different cities reported very different patterns, with about as many cities reporting decreases as reported increases. Episodes involving cocaine, or cocaine and heroin together, showed a ninefold increase over the 1976 to 1985 period, and the pattern of increase was consistent across reporting areas. Emergency room visits involving cocaine grew even more rapidly in the late 1980s. Admissions to federally supported drug treatment programs between 1979 and 1984 show a fourfold increase in cocaine as the primary drug of abuse, against a slight drop in heroin as the primary drug, and a fairly constant level of admissions.

The emergency room and treatment program data are presumably more relevant to issues of homelessness than the data from high school graduates or general household surveys, since the potential users of these facilities resemble more closely the poor urban population at greatest risk of homelessness. (Of course, these data are also biased by the self-selection involved in using hospital emergency rooms.) In major urban areas, it appears, serious drug abuse had begun to increase by the early 1980s, and reached epidemic proportions in the latter part of the decade.

The second question can also be answered, although with considerably less confidence. The proportion of homeless people who have serious problems with alcohol has probably not changed very much in the last decade. Although the range of prevalence statistics reported for the 1980s is rather wide, it is about the same as has been reported in earlier studies covering many decades.

The proportion of homeless people who are chronically mentally ill may truly have risen. Rates from 1980s studies vary, but a consensus has developed placing the probable proportion at about one-third of the homeless. For mental illness, the historical data are considerably sparser than for alcohol problems. The few studies available report rates of around one-fifth of skid row residents, substantially less than the apparent prevalence of mental illness among the homeless in the 1980s. These studies did not use any systematic methods to determine the presence of mental illness, so conclusions about increases of mentally ill persons among the homeless must be tentative.

No reliable figures exist on abuse of illegal drugs among homeless or skid row populations before 1980, and even data for the 1980s are not very reliable. As a result, no data-based conclusions can be drawn about whether drug abusers have become a larger proportion of the homeless. Anecdotal evidence suggests that the crack epidemic of the late 1980s increased the proportion of drug-dependent persons among clients of emergency food and shelter providers.

The answer to the third question follows from the first two. If the proportion of people with chronic mental illness or chemical dependency has remained stable or increased, the total number of homeless people has increased, and the proportion of the homeless with mental illness or chemical dependency has remained constant, then the numbers of homeless people with these conditions must have increased—probably at least doubling, as has the population of homeless people.

There are no answers to the last two questions, unless we make some critical assumptions and proceed by arithmetic inference. Even if the results of such an analysis are off by a factor of two or more, they are highly instructive. To begin, one must estimate the numbers of homeless people at the beginning and end of the 1980s. Assume for the purpose of calculation that there were 100,000 people homeless on any given night in 1980,[4] and 600,000 on any given night in

---

[4]This figure represents one-third of the HUD figure for 1983 (Department of Housing and Urban Development, 1984). Although much criticized, the HUD figure provides at least a lower-bound population estimate for 1983; since all agree that the visible homeless population exploded during the 1981–1982 recession, any number for 1980 should be much lower than a 1983 figure. My research shows that in 1981 about 30,000 shelter beds were available in cities of 100,000 or more. Assuming that there were one and one-half to two unsheltered homeless persons for every sheltered homeless person in these cities and that these cities contained 75 to 90 percent of all homeless people produces an estimate of approximately 100,000 homeless in the country in 1981.

1987 (Burt and Cohen, 1989). Taking figures presented earlier and using NIMH's estimate that there were 1.7 million chronically mentally ill people in the United States in 1980, one reaches the estimate of 1.9 million in 1987 (1 percent of the population sixteen and older).

Assuming (as discussed earlier) that one-fifth of the homeless were mentally ill in 1980 and one-third in 1987, then one can calculate that 1.2 percent of the chronically mentally ill were homeless in 1980 ($(0.2 \times 100,000)/1,700,000 = 1.2$ percent). By 1987, the proportion had risen to 10.4 percent ($(0.33 \times 600,000)/1,900,000 = 10.4$ percent). In other words, there seems to have been an almost ninefold increase between 1980 and 1987 in the proportion of chronically mentally ill persons in this country who were homeless. Even if one assumes, more conservatively, that the proportion of mentally ill among the homeless did not increase from 20 percent, or that only 500,000 people were homeless in 1987, homelessness among the chronically mentally ill has still increased drastically—to 6.3 percent or 8.7 percent of the total, respectively. If conservative assumptions are made for both variables, 5.3 percent of the chronically mentally ill were homeless in 1987—still more than four times the proportion of 1980.

The same type of calculation for the alcohol dependent yields equally striking results. Assume that one-third of the homeless were alcohol dependent in each year. One can estimate that 8.6 million people were alcohol dependent in 1980 and 9.4 million in 1987 (5 percent of the population sixteen and older). Then 2.1 percent ($(0.33 \times 600,000)/9,400,000 = 2.1$ percent) of the alcohol dependent were homeless in 1987, compared with 0.38 percent in 1980 ($(0.33 \times 100,000)/8,600,000 = 0.38$ percent). This is more than a fivefold increase in the rate of homelessness among alcohol-dependent people in the United States. It is not unreasonable to surmise that comparable data for the drug-dependent would show the same increases.

These increases are so large, even when assumptions are changed substantially, that one can conclude with some confidence that more people who are mentally ill or chemically dependent became and remained homeless in the 1980s than was ever the case in American history since the Depression. Research by Appleby and Desai (1987, 1985) documents this trend for people admitted to state mental hospitals in Illinois during the late 1970s and early 1980s. It is clear that factors other than trends in the general population are at work. Changes in housing, and in factors that apply specifically to the mentally ill and chemically dependent, all played a part.

Housing Changes

The loss of single-room-occupancy hotels (SROs), cubicle hotels, boarding and lodging houses, and other very cheap accommodations is the most significant housing issue for the populations of concern in this chapter. Conditions in some of these accommodations were only marginally better than today's shelters, but the rooms were available, and affordable (Hoch and Slayton, 1989). As we saw in Chapter 3, many cities lost a very large number of SRO and SRO-type rooms between the 1960s and 1980. Although most of the reports are for single cities, one study estimates a national loss of approximately 1.1 million SRO units (Green, cited in Baxter and Hopper, 1984). Among other factors, the loss reflects urban renewal, conversion to more profitable uses, and abandonment as skid rows shrank (Lee, 1980). Since 20 to 25 percent of chronically mentally ill individuals lived in such housing in the late 1970s, along with large numbers of alcohol abusers, losses of this magnitude make it far more difficult for those populations to remain housed in the community.

Changes in the System of Care for the Mentally Ill

The drastic reductions in state mental hospital beds between 1955 and 1980 (from 559,000 to 150,000) have been well documented. Most of this reduction took place between 1963, when there were 504,000 beds, and 1974, when there were 216,000 beds. The change was prompted by the advent of Medicaid and other federal support programs, which enabled states to shift costs of treatment for the chronically mentally ill to the federal government (Burt and Pittman, 1985; Shern, Surles, and Waizer, 1989).

Although the "deinstitutionalization" of mental patients is often blamed for the current plight of the homeless mentally ill, the reduction of state hospital capacity was essentially complete by the mid-1970s. As many have noted, the failure of deinstitutionalization was not so much that it moved patients out of long-term residence in state hospitals as that it failed to provide any alternate system of care and support in the community (Bachrach, 1979; Bassuk and Lamb, 1986; Burt and Pittman, 1985; Lamb, 1984; Warner, 1989). Without such support, many chronically mentally ill people cannot sustain themselves. With support, they often can. Evaluations of community support programs demonstrate increased community tenure and better quality of life for people with a chronic mental illness, if they have appropriate supports (Levine, Lezak, and Goldman, 1986; Morrissey and Goldman, 1984; Tessler and Goldman, 1982; Stein and Test, 1980). However, because appropriate housing is difficult to find and to finance for this population, institutions have often discharged patients to "address unknown." For example, Baxter and Hopper (1984) report that 23 percent of patients released from New York mental hospitals in the 1979–1980 fiscal year went to "unknown" living arrangements. Appleby and Desai (1987) document increasing homelessness at both admission and discharge among mental hospital patients in Cook County, Illinois. Some mental hospitals refer patients directly to shelters when they have no other possible address, rather than defer release until appropriate housing is available.

Other factors have also affected the probability of institutionalization. Admissions criteria have been tightened so that to gain admission even for a short-term stay, people must be sicker in the late 1970s and 1980s than they needed to be in earlier times. Today younger people who have never been hospitalized may show symptoms that would have led to institutionalization in the 1960s and early 1970s. Patients' rights litigation and advocacy have led to changes in commitment laws that substantially reduce the option of involuntary commitment. With their right to choose protected, many individuals choose autonomy over institutionalization even when autonomy means homelessness (Lamb, 1984). Whatever the abuses of involuntary commitment in the past, many observers are beginning to question the humanity as well as the legality of "free choice" for people whose illness impairs their ability to make choices in their own best interest (Kanter, 1989).

Many younger people with severe mental illness are currently homeless (Pepper et al., 1981). These young adults are more likely than older cohorts to exhibit overtly disturbed behavior and to be "management problems" in many living situations. They also are more likely to abuse alcohol and other drugs, placing them in the no-man's-land of the dually diagnosed. Given these problems, their detachment from support networks, their tendency to drift from town to town, and their rejection of assistance from the usual helping agencies, they are at greater risk of homelessness than are the older chronically mentally ill, or than they themselves would have been in earlier decades.

Demographic patterns have also contributed to the increased risk of homelessness among these young chronically ill people. The baby boom generation entered its late teens and twenties—the years of highest risk for developing severe mental illness—at the same time that hospitalization practices were changing and experimentation with illegal substances was increasing. This cohort as a whole has a higher likelihood of combining mental illness with chemical dependency and a lower likelihood of institutionalization (Bachrach, 1982; Pepper and Ryglewicz, 1984).

Some nonhospitalized mentally ill homeless people suffer institutionalization of another sort: criminalization (Lamb and Grant, 1982; Lamb, 1984; Lurigio and Lewis, 1989; Snow et al., 1989). A jail term can result from behavior that is a part of one's illness (disorderly conduct, creating a nuisance, trespass) or a means of survival (petty theft, shoplifting), as well as from serious felonies including violent crimes against persons. The last category is the least prevalent, but contributes to a 6 to 10 percent prevalence rate of mental illness among prison populations (Lamb and Grant, 1982).

The financial resources of the chronically mentally ill have also suffered, especially in the early 1980s. The rules governing SSI/SSDI eligibility and retention changed in March 1981. Even those who retained SSI benefits often found their value reduced, as we saw in Chapter 5. Barrow and Lovell (1982) reported that by the end of 1981, every mentally ill client referred to SSI by one New York City outreach team was turned down, no matter how disabling his or her condition. Michel (1983) reports similar trends in the Midwest; Burt and Pittman (1985) summarize the results nationwide. The loss of SSI or SSDI income, coupled with the loss or increased cost of SRO and similar housing, is very likely to have contributed to homelessness in the early 1980s for the chronically mentally ill.

Other financial resources for this population were shrinking as well. State resources spent for mental health (including federal resources administered by state agencies) dropped between 1981 and 1987. On average, inflation-adjusted mental health spending per capita declined 10 percent in these years, although states varied widely (from a 41 percent reduction to a 32 percent increase) (National Association of State Mental Health Program Directors and NASMHPD Research Institute, Inc., 1990). In 1981 states spent, on average, $27 per capita on all mental health services; by 1987 that figure was down to $24 (both in 1987 dollars).

The spending of greatest importance to the chronically mentally ill at risk of homelessness is directed to residential services outside psychiatric facilities (Table 6-3). Per capita spending in this category increased, on average, 90 percent between 1981 and 1987, in real terms. However, the absolute amounts were minuscule: $1.51 in 1981 and $2.86 in 1987. Thus only 6 percent of state mental health resources in 1981, and 12 percent in 1987, were being spent to maintain needy clients in stable community residences with appropriate mental health services.

Changes Affecting the Chemically Dependent

In addition to the changes in SRO-type housing and cocaine use described above, two other changes are of particular relevance to the chemically dependent. The first is the decriminalization of public drunkenness, vagrancy, and loitering that occurred in the late 1960s (Lamb, 1984; Rossi, 1989). The drunk tank at the local jail was often a shelter of last resort. Police used it as such, not just to clean up the streets, but to protect drunks on very cold nights. Decriminalization has reduced the use of the local jail as a housing resource, and detoxification centers have not taken over this housing function.

The loss of many day labor or pick-up jobs has also hurt skid row residents. Lee (1980) finds that an important factor in the demise of skid rows, which shrank by almost half from 1950 to 1970, was the dependence of their residents on day labor types of jobs, which disappeared in large numbers over the period.

Table 6-3 Trends in State Spending for Mental Health (1981-1987) and Chemical Dependency (1984-1988)

	Mental Health[a]		Chemical Dependency[b]	
	1981	1987	1984	1988
Alabama	$NA	$ NA	$ 1.60	$ 2.45
Alaska	0.00	NA	46.61	48.00
Arizona	0.00	1.96	9.58	7.05
Arkansas	1.05	0.00	2.65	3.36
California	1.58	1.76	9.94	9.45
Colorado	1.29	0.77	9.93	8.35
Connecticut	0.00	3.28	10.85	18.05
Delaware	0.64	1.27	7.45	7.02
District of Columbia	0.38	1.18	26.12	49.47
Florida	0.35	1.73	5.62	6.25
Georgia	0.08	0.89	4.35	6.32
Hawaii	0.41	0.77	5.26	4.72
Idaho	0.24	1.74	3.80	3.56
Illinois	0.58	1.26	6.74	5.88
Indiana	1.18	1.90	3.79	4.00
Iowa	0.00	0.06	4.54	6.24
Kansas	0.00	0.20	3.70	5.70
Kentucky	0.00	0.51	2.61	3.84
Louisiana	NA	NA	4.14	2.74
Maine	3.34	3.36	14.52	7.85
Maryland	0.46	6.61	7.59	10.48
Massachusetts	5.40	8.88	7.16	8.63
Michigan	3.25	6.54	8.57	8.85
Minnesota	0.00	11.06	2.43	10.85
Mississippi	NA	NA	3.31	2.45
Missouri	2.68	2.87	2.86	3.32
Montana	1.18	1.54	11.50	15.31
Nebraska	0.17	0.49	5.28	5.43
Nevada	0.19	1.13	9.71	7.54
New Hampshire	0.25	4.59	2.91	2.90
New Jersey	0.64	1.53	4.09	5.91
New Mexico	6.45	2.65	20.79	NA
New York	2.07	3.63	21.40	28.29
North Carolina	NA	NA	7.10	6.26
North Dakota	2.07	1.46	3.36	3.78
Ohio	0.00	1.86	3.21	5.91
Oklahoma	0.91	1.35	2.38	2.91
Oregon	1.47	1.14	6.04	22.25
Pennsylvania	3.95	2.41	6.96	7.23
Rhode Island	1.02	5.37	9.29	11.46
South Carolina	2.65	8.34	2.71	8.60
South Dakota	0.17	0.73	3.04	5.80
Tennessee	8.27	4.50	3.39	4.33

Table 6-3 Continued

	Mental Health[a]		Chemical Dependency[b]	
	1981	1987	1984	1988
Texas	0.16	1.37	1.74	1.48
Utah	0.00	0.49	11.58	9.81
Vermont	3.83	6.76	11.03	8.06
Virginia	0.35	10.07	5.57	6.22
Washington	1.88	3.18	6.14	8.06
West Virginia	0.00	3.40	4.56	4.49
Wisconsin	2.40	1.98	12.46	14.73
Wyoming	0.00	0.00	5.96	NA
Average	1.51	2.86	7.40	8.76

Source: Mental health data: National Association of State Mental Health Program Directors/NASMHPD Institute (1990). Chemical dependency data: National Association of State Alcohol and Drug Abuse Directors (1984, 1988), "State Alcohol and Drug Abuse Profiles, 1984 and 1988."
[a]Per capita spending in constant 1987 dollars. Spending for residential services only.
[b]Per capita spending in constant 1988 dollars. Spending for all services.

Peterson and Weigand (1985) and Weigand (1990) describe the types of work performed by Nashville's skid row residents. Of particular interest is their analysis of the deskilling process, whereby men who were once stably employed lost their jobs and began drifting from town to town, getting what work they could. Alcohol abuse appears in the stories of many of these men.

Finally, treatment resources have not kept up with the demand in the 1980s. Between 1984 and 1988 (the years for which data are available from the National Association of State Alcohol and Drug Abuse Directors), per capita expenditures rose 18 percent in real terms, from $7.40 to $8.76 (Table 6-3). Total spending by states for alcohol and drug treatment rose 21 percent, from $1.7 billion in 1984 and $2.1 billion in 1988 (both in 1988 dollars). But alcohol admissions were up 29 percent during the same period, rising from 942,000 to 1,218,000. Drug admissions, as reported earlier, increased 105 percent. Spending per admission thus dropped 17 percent, from $1,463 in 1984 to $1,218 in 1988 (all in 1988 dollars). More people needed services, but fewer real resources were available to assist them.

SUMMARY AND CONCLUSIONS

As we have seen, the prevalence of severe mental illness and alcohol dependency has not increased in the general population. The growing abuse of crack cocaine has probably affected homelessness, but only toward the end of the 1980s. It cannot explain the increase in homelessness that began early in the decade.

Resources for the severely mentally ill and chemically dependent have been reduced, however. Access to SSI/SSDI declined at the beginning of the decade, and the value of these benefits shrank for those who could get them. So did the value of General Assistance. In addition, many of the day labor jobs that sustained skid row populations in the past have disappeared. These changes, coupled with reductions in the supply of appropriate and affordable housing (SROs, lodging houses), have made it dramatically more difficult for people with these severe problems to remain housed.

In the 1950s, 1960s, and even the 1970s, people with these special problems could and did maintain themselves in housing, even if their shelter was the bare minimum, such as cubicle hotels. The descriptions of life on skid row suggest that even extraordinarily poor people, including alcoholics who might stereotypically be expected to spend all their money on drink, chose to take themselves off the streets when they could afford to do so. Most of the time, they could. Assuming the preferences of mentally ill and chemically dependent people have not changed (and there is no reason to think that they have), changes in resources and in housing options appear to have been the proximal causes of their increasing homelessness in the 1980s. If people supported by public benefits or day labor could find housing they could afford, we can assume they would purchase that shelter, as their predecessors did in past decades. Whether or not they desire a middle class lifestyle, or can maintain a steady job, they almost certainly would not "choose" the streets if a minimal roof were available. Their past behavior is the best guide to their preferences.

PART TWO

Impact on Homelessness

CHAPTER SEVEN

Shelter Bed Counts
and Homelessness Rates

■ The analysis of national trends reported in Part One of this book identified a number of factors that appeared likely to have influenced the growth of homelessness in the 1980s. Part Two will assess the association of these factors with changes in homelessness in a sample of American cities. This task required me to select a sample of cities and find a measure of homelessness that would be consistent across cities and over time. I also needed to define appropriate measures of the hypothesized causal factors, measures that would be available for all the cities at both the beginning and end of the 1980s. This chapter describes the measure of homelessness I used—shelter bed rates—and the patterns of growth of shelter bed capacity during the 1980s. Chapter 8 sets forth the variables representing the potential causal factors. Chapter 9 analyzes the causal structure hypothesized in Chapter 1 to affect homelessness. Chapter 10 explains which variables and variable combinations account for the most variance in homelessness rates, an important consideration for planning and policy development.

THE CITIES

My inquiry focused on U.S. cities with populations of 100,000 or more. Most of the nation's homeless are found in these cities, as are most of the shelters, soup kitchens, and other facilities that serve them. Partly because these cities made up the sampling frame for the Urban Institute's 1987 national study of the homeless (Burt and Cohen, 1988, 1989a), I was familiar with the scope of their homeless populations and services, and had reliable data to describe them.

In 1986 there were 182 cities of this size, including 35 suburbs of major cities.[1] These suburbs, although legally cities in their own right with populations

---

[1]For example: Hialeah for Miami; Scottsdale for Phoenix; Inglewood for Los Angeles; Chula Vista for San Diego; Plano for Dallas; Lakewood for Denver.

of 100,000 or more, differed in important ways from their major cities and were omitted from some analyses. The resulting set of 147 "primary" cities is the basis of analyses in Chapters 9 and 10. Appendix A lists the 147 primary cities and the 35 suburbs.

THE DEPENDENT VARIABLE

To develop a rate of homelessness, one needs first to know how many homeless people there are in a given jurisdiction. For my purposes, it was also necessary to have a count that was obtained using a *consistent methodology* across 182 cities at two points in time: 1981 (before the rise in homelessness was widely noted) and 1989.

No attempt yet made to count the homeless is without controversy, and some studies have severe methodological flaws. Even the studies that used defensible counting methodologies still have biases that reduce their utility in a multicity analysis. Further, with the exception of the Urban Institute's 1987 study (twenty cities representative of all cities over 100,000; Burt and Cohen, 1988, 1989a), the Rand Corporation's California study (three counties; Vernez et al., 1988), and the Census Bureau's 1990 efforts to count the homeless (not available), no single methodology has been applied to more than one location.

Pros and Cons of the Measure Chosen

No statistics on numbers of homeless people or homelessness rates were easily available to serve as the basis for this study's dependent variable. The only figures that would meet the criteria of consistent methodology for two years and many cities were counts of shelter beds within a clearly defined geographical area for which the population was known (so a rate could be calculated). Like any other measure of homelessness, this one has numerous flaws. First, we cannot be certain how the number of shelter beds relates to the true number of homeless people in a given jurisdiction. Second, the measure confounds local responsiveness to the homeless problem (the building of shelters) with the problem itself. Third, shelters that existed earlier in the decade but had closed their doors by 1989 may have gone uncounted. This last problem will be discussed later, in conjunction with the details of data collection.

Because many homeless people do not use shelters on any given night, a count of shelter beds will underestimate the true number of homeless people. A corollary problem is that different communities have developed shelters at different rates, so the ratio of shelter beds to the true number of homeless people almost certainly differs from city to city, by an unknown (and, pragmatically, unknowable) amount.[2] If the only issue were to estimate the number of homeless nationwide, the number of shelter beds could be multiplied by some factor to account for the unsheltered. But I wanted to analyze the intercity associations of homelessness rates with other variables. Lacking accurate correction factors for each city, I did not apply any multiplier to the shelter bed counts obtained, since the use of a constant would have made no difference for the analysis.

A further problem is that the official bed count for a given facility will not capture the precise number of homeless individuals it serves. The official count of beds may be too high (if the shelter operates at less than 100 percent capacity most of the time), or too low (if the shelter operates at overflow capacity most of the time). The overflow part of this problem was handled by recording separately the excess number of people sheltered at peak times, if a shelter accepted people beyond its official capacity. Rates were calculated with and without these overflow capacities, but the issue was dropped when no differences emerged in the results of regression analyses based on the two sets of rates. If a given facility was an "overflow shelter," operating only at peak demand, its entire capacity was included as a regular shelter. The same was true for shelters that operated only in the winter. No attempt was made to correct for underutilization of shelters (shelters operating below capacity). Because any count of shelter beds underrepresents the city's total homeless population, it seemed unnecessary to reduce the estimate still further to correct for underutilization.

Any measure based on shelter bed counts is partly a reflection of the jurisdiction's response to the problem, rather than of homelessness. There is plenty of evidence that some jurisdictions have been reluctant to open shelters, preferring to ignore any local homeless people or send them elsewhere.[3] Some

---

[2]The 1990 Census figures will not solve the problem of street-to-shelter ratios directly, because of the methods used by the Census Bureau for its March 20 S-night (S for "street and shelter") counts. Special shelters were opened for the S-night counts, and a major effort was made to attract as many homeless people as possible to these and other shelters, where counting would be easier than on the streets. Many of the people counted "in shelters" by the census on that night thus would not normally be in shelters. The size of this group and its relationship to the size of the normally sheltered homeless population will vary by an unknown amount for each community. Therefore a researcher would have to take the total census homeless count, obtain an indicator of the "usually sheltered" from some other source, and subtract to determine a rough street-to-shelter ratio. Even then, the ratio would still be quite rough because the S-night procedures were applied only to locations previously identified as likely to contain homeless people. Census takers did not enter abandoned buildings or count people sleeping in vehicles, and they did not do a complete, or even a random, street sweep. It would be hard to feel confident in a street-to-shelter ratio based on Census results.

[3]Certain communities that customarily sent homeless people to shelters in neighboring towns dispatched buses to get "their homeless" back for the 1990 Census count.

cities responded only after lawsuits were brought against them. As a result, shelter counts from early in the decade are probably a more highly variable reflection of the true underlying rate of homelessness than are later shelter counts.

Despite these complications, one may have reasonable confidence that homelessness rates based on shelter bed counts accurately reflect the *relative* degree of homelessness from city to city, and that is enough for the purposes of this study. This confidence stems from a comparison of two sets of independent readings on numbers of shelter beds and homeless people. First, the Urban Institute's 1987 study obtained readings on the number of shelter beds from interviews with providers, and on the number of homeless individuals from interviews with homeless people. These two readings were strongly associated ($r = .934$). The second strong association is based on forty-two cities that were examined in both the Department of Housing and Urban Development's 1984 study and the present study. Using the midpoint of HUD's "most reasonable range" of estimates of the homeless population for these cities and the 1983 shelter bed counts obtained for the present study, their zero-order correlation was .827.[4] These two very strong correlations suggest we are unlikely to be misled by using homelessness rates based on shelter bed counts.

Getting the Data

To get accurate counts of shelter and voucher-subsidized beds, the research team called virtually every shelter provider in all 182 cities.[5] Usually we spoke first with the person responsible for the local Comprehensive Homeless Assistance Plan (CHAP) submitted to the Department of Housing and Urban Development in order to qualify for HUD's Stewart B. McKinney Homeless Assistance Act funding. Lists of shelters operating in 1989 were obtained from the CHAPs and were supplemented in most instances with lists from local coalitions or coordinators of services for the homeless. Contacts were also obtained for any public or private voucher or payment systems available to the homeless (e.g., for welfare hotels or motels). In most cities we asked each provider three questions:

- What is your current bed capacity (or the number of people who get vouchers)?

---

[4]When a regression formulation is used rather than simple zero-order correlations, the *beta*s are identical to the r's and the second intercept is marginally significant.

[5]The enormous volume of telephone calls was supported by grants from the Federal National Mortgage Association and from the Rockefeller Foundation. Christopher Vaz and Garth Green made most of the calls, with help from Laura Bonanomi and Jennifer Parker.

- When did you open (or when did you first offer shelter services, if the facility had an earlier history of offering different services)?
- What was your bed capacity in 1981?

In several cities (e.g., Boston, Detroit, Washington, D.C.) the person supplying the list was able to answer all three questions for many facilities. In such cases we directly contacted only those shelters for which we still lacked certain information.

We were able to get complete information on shelter bed capacities. The first official answering the phone at each shelter usually could supply the shelter bed capacity for its current operations (1989). If not, we were referred to the program director, who supplied the data. For those shelters (37 percent of the total) that were already operating in 1981, the program director was asked about bed capacity in that year. In answering the question directors often referred to the fact that they were still operating in the same building, and therefore their capacity was the same. They could date program expansion or reduction to a move from one building to another, or to renovations on a building that expanded its capacity, or to new licensing or regulatory activity that changed the shelter's official capacity. Some directors consulted official records or referred us to a predecessor when they did not know the shelter's history.

All shelters were able to report whether they had been operating in 1981 or had opened only later. However, for 12 percent of the shelters that opened after 1981 (8 percent of all shelters counted), we could not learn the opening year. Working with the known opening dates of the large majority of post-1981 shelters, we interpolated shelter bed counts for 1983 and 1986 for that 12 percent group. Otherwise, a shelter that first opened, for example, in 1984 was counted as adding all of its 1989 shelter beds to the city's total bed count in 1984, and was assumed to have maintained those beds in subsequent years. We also determined whether or not a facility was a battered women's shelter. Many cities include such shelters in their roster of resources for the homeless, but because many other cities do *not* consider them homeless facilities, such facilities were *excluded* from the counts used in this book.

It is likely that some shelters in existence before 1989 had closed their doors by early 1990, when the data for this study were collected. They would therefore not have been included on the lists we used to contact shelters, and would have been omitted from our counts in the years during which they did operate. However, the number of shelter closings and the consequent undercount of shelter beds in earlier years are probably very small in comparison with the overall growth in shelter capacity. Virtually every city in the country was straining to supply shelter beds during the 1980s; the story is overwhelmingly one of growth, both of shelter facilities and of the capacity of existing facilities.

Thus while our methods pose a clear risk, the actual undercount of shelter beds in earlier years due to shelter closings is likely to be small.

THE GROWTH OF SHELTERS AND BED CAPACITY

The information gathered from shelters around the country gives a good picture of the growth in the number of shelters and in shelter bed capacity during the 1980s. The results are highly consistent with the findings of the Department of Housing and Urban Development (1989), although HUD's data apply to the country as a whole whereas the present data are limited to cities of 100,000 or more. Table 7-1 shows the year-by-year additions of shelters and bed capacity.

Slightly more than one-third (37 percent) of the shelters operating in 1989 had opened their doors in 1981 or earlier (a few went as far back as the 1870s). Increases were gradual until about mid-decade; passage of the McKinney Act, which made federal money available for the first time in 1987, is reflected in the expansion of capacity that occurred in 1987 and 1988. Twenty-nine percent of the shelters opened in 1987 or later.[6]

The right-hand columns of Table 7-1 report the changes in bed capacity over the decade. Again, slightly more than one-third of the beds available in 1989 were also available in 1981 or earlier. Whereas the number of shelters increased gradually, shelter bed capacity took a major leap in 1985, when New York City came under court order to provide shelter for homeless families (right-to-shelter for individuals had come earlier). Welfare hotels then came into use, and many of the 30,000 or so new beds in 1985 resulted from this change.

Shelter bed capacity did not grow uniformly throughout the country, as Table 7-2 shows. By 1983, for example, only 21 percent of the Northeast's 1989 capacity was in place, whereas the Midwest and the South already had about half their 1989 capacity available. Ultimately, however, the Northeast produced a greater number of beds (and higher rates as well, as will be seen below), so the 1983 and 1986 percentages reflect not only the speed of response but the ultimate extent of expansion beyond the 1981 baseline. City size also made a difference, with the larger cities (500,000 and over) expanding beyond their 1981 base far more than the smaller cities.

---

[6]Shelters in New York City were handled differently from shelters everywhere else. A total bed capacity for city-run or city-paid-for shelter beds was obtained for each of the years 1981, 1983, 1986, and 1989, to which were added Partnership for the Homeless and other privately supported beds in the city. However, the actual physical locations were not counted, since there are so many and they keep changing. Thus the total number of shelter *facilities* reported in Table 7-1 does not include New York City shelters and voucher arrangements. The total number of *shelter beds*, however, does include New York City shelter and vouchered beds.

Table 7-1 Growth of Shelters and Shelter Bed Capacity, 1981-1989

	Shelters		Bed Capacity	
	Number	Percentage of 1989 Shelters	Number of Beds in 1989	Percentage of 1989 Beds
Year Opened				
1981 or earlier	549	37.1%	40,723	34.9%
1982	72	4.9	3,968	3.4
1983	96	6.5	6,630	5.7
1984	82	5.5	6,470	5.5
1985	129	8.7	30,476	26.1
1986	122	8.2	5,098	4.4
1987	172	11.6	8,928	7.6
1988	154	10.4	10,513	9.0
1989	105	7.1	3,927	3.4
	1,481	100%	116,733	100%

Note: To be included, shelters had to be within the city limits of the 182 cities with 1986 populations of 100,000 or more. All domestic violence shelters are *excluded;* all public and private voucher programs and similar pay arrangements (e.g., welfare hotels) are *included.* New York City is treated as a special case, as explained in note 6 in the text. Figures for bed capacity include New York, but the numbers of shelter facilities do not.

Our data also reveal stability over the decade in the distribution of shelters by size (Table 7-3). The public has been repelled by the image of mass shelters housing 500 or 1,000 people, which suggests an unacceptably inhumane shelter environment. However, the cavernous and overcrowded shelter is the exception rather than the rule. Throughout the decade, only about 33 to 37 percent of shelters accommodated more than fifty people; only 13 to 15 percent accommodated more than 100; and only 1 percent had more than 500 beds. Even as pressure increased to shelter the homeless, most providers appear to have kept their facilities down to a size that would make personal contacts possible and prevent people from getting lost in the crowd. In particular, shelters created for family households usually had eight to twenty-four beds, accommodating as few as two and rarely more than five or six families at a time.

Creating Rates from Counts

The number of shelter beds in a community is obviously related to the sheer size of the community. No one would expect Reno, Nevada, with a population of 110,000, to have as many shelter beds as New Orleans, with a population of

555,000. To be meaningful in cross-city comparisons, the number of shelter beds must be measured against population. Rates of homelessness have customarily been expressed as the number of homeless persons for every 10,000 people in the city, and I follow that convention.

Our data on shelter bed availability represents the numerator in this ratio, while the denominator is the city population. (All the beds are within the city

Table 7-2 Growth in Shelter Bed Capacity, 1981-1989, by Region and City Size

	Number of Shelter Beds Available			
	1981 and Earlier	By 1983	By 1986	By 1989
Region[a]				
Northeast (22)	5,670	8,860	34,430	43,050
Midwest (39)	8,000	11,340	15,660	20,270
South (66)	9,580	12,440	18,790	27,110
West (55)	7,600	10,840	18,890	26,300
	30,850	43,480	87,770	116,730
Share of 1989 Capacity (%)				
Northeast (22)	13%	21%	80%	100%
Midwest (39)	39	56	77	100
South (66)	35	46	69	100
West (55)	29	41	72	100
City Size[a] *(000)*				
100–249 (122)	7,620	10,320	15,620	22,710
250–499 (37)	10,410	13,470	20,000	26,670
500–999 (15)	4,280	8,080	13,620	19,640
1,000+ (8)	8,540	11,610	38,530	47,710
	30,850	43,480	87,530	116,730
Share of 1989 Capacity (%)				
100–249 (122)	34%	45%	69%	100%
250–499 (37)	39	51	75	100
500–999 (15)	22	41	69	100
1,000+ (8)	18	24	81	100

Note: This table reports shelter bed *capacity* (not 1986 occupancy) in all shelters serving the homeless within the city limits of the 182 cities with populations of 100,000 or more. All domestic violence shelters are *excluded;* all public and private voucher programs and similar pay arrangements are *included* (e.g., welfare hotels).
[a]Number of cities is shown in parentheses.

Table 7-3 Shelter Size in 1989

	Maximum Capacity (Including Children) of Each Shelter or Voucher Program						
	1-10	11-25	26-50	51-100	101-500	501+	Total
Number of Shelters							
1981	90	145	138	109	64	3	549
1983	96	178	194	147	97	5	717
1986	133	266	273	225	145	8	1,050
1989	208	401	373	287	201	11	1,481
Share of Total (%)							
1981	16%	26%	25%	20%	12%	1%	100%
1983	13	25	27	21	13	1	100
1986	13	25	26	21	14	1	100
1989	14	27	25	19	14	1	100

Note: This table reports shelter bed capacity (not occupancy) in all shelters serving the homeless within the city limits of the 182 cities with 1986 populations of 100,000 or more. All domestic violence shelters are *excluded*; all public and private voucher programs and similar pay arrangements (e.g., welfare hotels) are *included*.

limits and clearly serve city residents.) Nineteen eighty-one and 1983 shelter bed counts were divided by the city's 1980 population; 1986 and 1989 counts were divided by the 1986 population. Table 7-4 gives the homelessness rates (shelter bed rates) for 1981, 1983, 1986, and 1989.

For the entire group of 182 cities, homelessness rates tripled between 1981 and 1989, from 5.0 per 10,000 to 15.0 per 10,000. The primary cities have substantially higher rates than the suburbs. In fact, the 1989 rate for the suburbs is less than the 1981 rate for the primary cities, and the suburban cities did not undertake any major expansion of shelter capacity until around 1986.

Table 7-4 also shows regional and city-size differences in homelessness rates for the 147 primary cities in the data base. Cities in the Northeast and West clearly have higher rates from mid-decade onward, although the Northeast began the decade with the lowest rates of any region. The significance of city size is less apparent. It appears that the cities of moderate size (250,000 to 1 million) have led in developing shelters for their citizens, and hence have the highest homelessness rates according to the measure used here.

Table 7-4 Shelter Bed Rates per 10,000 Population, by Region and City Size, for 1981, 1983, 1986, and 1989

	Homelessness Rates[a]			
	1981	1983	1986	1989
Totals				
All 182 Cities	5.0	7.0	10.6	15.0
147 Primary Cities	6.1	8.4	12.6	17.6
35 Suburbs	0.7	1.0	2.2	4.5
147 Primary Cities Only[b]				
Region				
Northeast (22)	4.2	8.8	15.3	20.5
Midwest (35)	6.1	7.9	12.3	15.6
South (59)	5.9	7.5	10.2	15.3
West (31)	7.6	10.7	15.4	22.2
City Size (000)				
100–249 (89)	5.7	7.7	11.3	16.2
250–499 (35)	7.9	10.2	14.9	20.1
500–999 (15)	4.6	8.9	14.0	20.3
1,000+ (8)	4.4	7.5	13.3	18.0

[a]The "homelessness rate" is the number of shelter beds in the city divided by the city population (in 10,000s).
[b]Number of cities is shown in parentheses.

To make this picture more concrete, it may help to focus on cities with extremely low or high rates at different times during the decade. Nineteen cities had shelter bed rates of zero in 1981, and another thirty-one had rates of less than 3 per 10,000. Thus slightly more than one-third of the primary cities had very low homelessness rates in 1981. The number of cities with rates of zero shrank to thirteen in 1983, six in 1986, and none in 1989. The number of cities with rates of less than 3 per 10,000 (including zero) decreased from fifty in 1981 to thirty-one in 1983, eleven in 1986, and three in 1989.

At the high end, only five cities had rates of homelessness exceeding 20 per 10,000 in 1981: Atlanta; Grand Rapids, Michigan; Eugene, Oregon; Salt Lake City; and Seattle. By 1983 these five had been joined by another six—Birmingham, Alabama; Boston; Minneapolis; St. Louis; Reno, Nevada; and Yonkers, New York—two of which had rates over 30 per 10,000. In addition, four other cities had rates between 18 and 20 per 10,000.

The real growth in shelter capacity came between 1983 and 1986. In 1986 there were twenty-four cities with rates over 20 per 10,000, more than double the number in 1983. Eleven of these twenty-four cities had rates higher than 30 per 10,000; two of the eleven exceeded 40 per 10,000. Nine additional cities had rates between 18 and 20 per 10,000.

The final year of our inquiry, 1989, had the largest number of cities with very high rates, as one would expect. Forty-five had rates over 20 per 10,000, of which nineteen exceeded 30 per 10,000 and seven were over 40 per 10,000: Washington, D.C.; Atlanta; Boston; Reno, Nevada; New York City; Eugene, Oregon; and Seattle. An additional eight cities had rates between 18 and 20 per 10,000. Thus the decade saw these 147 largest cities in the country shift from having 34 percent with homelessness rates under 3 per 10,000 in 1981 to having 31 percent with rates over 20 per 10,000 in 1989—a dramatic increase by any standard.

SUMMARY AND CONCLUSIONS

The data gathered for this study clearly indicate an impressive growth in the number of shelter beds, and in homelessness rates based on shelter bed counts, between 1981 and 1989. These increases occurred in every region of the country, in cities from 100,000 to over 1 million in population, and even in relatively prosperous suburbs of primary cities. Both numbers and rates increased almost threefold over the period.

The rates created for this study are based on the number of shelter beds in U.S. cities over 100,000. Because many homeless people do not use shelters on any given night, and because some shelters that were open in 1981 but had closed by 1989 may have been missed, the reader may wonder whether any rate based on shelter counts seriously misestimates the relationship of one city's homelessness rate to another's, or the true growth of homelessness. (It is axiomatic that any rates based only on shelter bed counts will underestimate the true number of homeless people, unless all homeless people in town use shelters.)

Two independent assessments of the relationship of homelessness counts to shelter bed counts in different cities yielded correlations of .934 and .827, effectively settling the issue for intercity comparisons. There are few sources of data available to examine the relationship of growth in shelter beds to growth of the total homeless population. The best estimates of the total homeless population are HUD's 1984 figure of 250,000 to 350,000 (Department of Housing and Urban Development, 1984), and the Urban Institute's 1987 figure of 500,000 to 600,000. Comparing the midpoints of these two ranges to each other (550/300) suggests that the homeless population in early 1987 was 1.8 times larger than it was in early 1984. A similar comparison of numbers of shelter beds identified in this study as available in large cities indicates that bed capacity doubled from late 1983 to late 1986 (87,770/43,480 = 2.0, see Table 7-2). Comparing HUD shelter bed figures from early 1984 and early 1988 shows an even greater increase in shelter beds (275,000/100,000 = 2.75; Department of Housing and Urban Development, 1984, 1989). These figures suggest that the number of shelter beds probably grew proportionally more in the mid-1980s than the total number of homeless people, implying that the proportion of homeless people who were sheltered increased over the period. This conclusion is not surprising, but it does mean that any estimates based on shelter bed counts will exaggerate the growth of the total homeless population.

CHAPTER EIGHT

Constructing
the Data Set

■ Because my goal was to examine changes in the 1980s that might have contributed to homelessness, I sought data sources that could supply parallel indicators for early and late in the decade. With one exception the data were all assembled from published sources, federal government statistical agencies, or other researchers' analyses of publicly available data (e.g., the 1980 Census, the American Housing Survey). The exception is information about county General Assistance programs in 1981 and 1989, which was obtained by a telephone survey. Where possible the data are at the city level. When city-specific data were not available, county-level data were sought. In some instances state-level data are used, either because there is no within-state variation (e.g., AFDC benefit levels) or because no pertinent data could be found for local jurisdictions. More complete and precise data are available for the early part of the decade because city-level data could be taken from the 1980 Census.

The need to find measures that would be available for each of 182 cities and for the beginning and end of the decade was a severe constraint. In some instances the variables chosen to represent characteristics of interest are less than ideal—but they are the best available, given the requirements of the data set. Numerous suggestions of potentially useful variables and data sources had to be rejected because they were not available for both the early and the later 1980s, or were available only for a much smaller number of cities, or both. Even so, only 1980 values could be found for some important variables—a problem that will be discussed later in this chapter.

The variables are presented here in groups that roughly correspond to the potential causal factors they are intended to measure. I include both variables that did and did *not* turn out to have important associations with homelessness. This will give the reader a chance to see the range of variables tested, as well as the subset of variables selected for the final analyses.

HOUSING-RELATED VARIABLES

The model of homelessness that guided this research (Figure 1-1) included several levels on the housing side. The "higher" levels reflecting national policy—interest rates and monetary, fiscal, and tax policy—are not represented in the data set. Of these factors, only interest rates would have shown any local variation, and that would be slight. Otherwise federal macroeconomic policy sets the context for local housing markets and is a constant as far as intercity analysis is concerned. All of the housing variables in the data set index characteristics of the local housing market.

Most of the housing variables come from the 1980 Census; no parallels that covered all or even most of the 182 cities were available for later in the decade. Table 8-1 gives the name of each housing variable, its source, and the method used to construct it (if it did not come directly from a source). Unless otherwise stated, all variables apply to the city level.

Four housing-related variables based on 1980 Census data measure characteristics of the housing market. They come directly from the *County and City Data Book: 1988* published by the U.S. Bureau of the Census (1988). They are:

• Percentage of occupied dwelling units in the city that are occupied by their owners.

• Percentage of occupied units in the city in buildings with five or more units.

• Percentage change in the number of dwelling units in the city between 1970 and 1980.

• Number of units for which building permits were issued in 1980 through 1986, expressed as a percentage of all 1980 dwelling units in the city.

Since most homeless people were renters immediately before becoming homeless, cities with higher proportions of renters would be likely also to have higher rates of homelessness. The measure of owner-occupancy (and its inverse, renter-occupancy) provides a reading on this dimension. The density of dwelling units is indexed by the proportion of units in medium and large multiunit buildings. The two measures of change in the number of dwelling units were included because they reflect the degree to which the city is prosperous and expanding, rather than losing jobs and people. The variable for change between 1970 and 1980 is a measure of *net change*—some cities have negative readings. Since the next decennial Census had not yet been taken, such a measure of net change was not available for the late 1980s. Instead, we recorded the number of building permits issued between 1980 and 1986 as a percentage of units existing in 1980, a measure that will distinguish between fast- and slow-growing cities, but cannot be negative. The 1970–1980 unit change figures and the 1980–1986 permit change figures are highly correlated with one another ($r = .722$), and with population change between 1980 and 1986 ($r = .712$ and $.803$, respectively).

Rental vacancy rates are assumed to reflect the tightness of the housing market; a rate under 5 percent is usually taken to mean a local market in which

Table 8-1 Housing Variables[a]

Variable	Year(s) Data Represents	Source
Percentage Owner-occupied	1980	CCDB—City item-48
Percentage in Structure with Five or More Units	1980	CCDB—City item-46
Percentage Change in Number of Units, 1970–1980	1980	CCDB—City item-43
Permits Issued 1980–1986 as Percentage of 1980 Units	1986	CCDB—City item-53
Rental Vacancy Rate, 1980[b]	1980	HC—Tables 9 and 12
Rental Vacancy Rate, 1988 (MSA)	1988	Estimates of National Association of Home Builders, based on 1987 American Housing Survey
Percentage of Renter-occupied Units with Rents Under $150 in 1980 (1980 $)	1980	HC—Table 9
Fair Market Rent *for the* MSA—2 Bedroom	1980, 1989	*Federal Register*
1 Bedroom	1981, 1989	*Federal Register*
Public Housing Units per 100 Population	1981, 1989	HUD—special runs
Section 8 Certificates or Vouchers per 100 Population	1981, 1989	HUD—special runs
Excess of Very-low-income Renters Over Units They Can Afford *in the State* (%)	1980	Low Income Housing Information Service, 1985

Sources: CCDB = *County and City Data Book: 1988*; HC = *Census of Housing, 1980*, HC80-2-58/380; Low Income Housing Information Service, *The Rental Housing Crisis Index,* Washington D.C.: Low Income Housing Information Service, 1985.
[a]All variables are for the city, unless specifically noted.
[b]Vacant rental units divided by the sum of vacant and renter-occupied units.

rental housing is scarce and demand for housing may force prices higher. Most cities with any form of rent control law use 5 percent as the trigger point at which rent control should take effect. Our rental vacancy rate for 1980 was calculated using data from the 1980 Census of Housing for each of the 182 cities (U.S. Bureau of the Census, HC80-2). The number of vacant-for-rent units was obtained from Table 12 for each city, while the number of units currently occupied by renters was obtained from Table 9. The vacancy rate was calculated as the number of vacant-for-rent units divided by the sum of that quantity plus the number of renter-occupied units. No such calculation was possible for each city for 1988. However, the Census Bureau estimates vacancy rates for the fifty largest metropolitan areas (MSAs) based on the American Housing Survey.[1] These MSAs include a very large proportion of all cities over 100,000, and I used geographical proximity to these MSAs as the basis for assigning rental vacancy rates to the remaining cities. Thus the 1988 vacancy rate data are not as precise as those for 1980.

The remaining housing-related variables pertain to the cost of housing, enabling us to test the extent to which homelessness is due to an increase in the price of housing, or a decline in the ability of many people to pay that price. The percentage of occupied rental units with rents lower than $150 in 1980 was derived from data in Table 9 of the 1980 Census of Housing for each city. The number of units with rents under $150 was divided by the number of renter-occupied units with rents specified.

Fair market rents (FMRs) for two- and one-bedroom apartments for each city were obtained from the *Federal Register,* where they are routinely published. The FMR is a figure developed by the Department of Housing and Urban Development. It establishes the maximum rent that the federal government will accept for recipients of Section 8 housing assistance certificates and vouchers. It is generally significantly higher than housing allowances available through the welfare system (Newman and Schnare, 1988), but still is sometimes too low to enable some eligible households to find appropriate housing. The FMRs apply to entire MSAs, but they have the advantage of being available for every year during the decade. They are thus a fairly good measure of the relative cost of rental housing across cities.

The rates, per 100 population, of HUD-assisted public housing units and Section 8 certificates and vouchers in each city were calculated using data from special computer runs supplied by the Department of Housing and Urban Development. HUD assistance of this sort—intended to make housing affordable for its beneficiaries—could have been considered a public benefits variable. Instead, I grouped these measures with the housing variables, since they define a characteristic of the city's housing stock: the relative availability of publicly subsidized housing.

The final housing variable is the most direct reflection of the mismatch between rental housing costs and the ability of poor people to pay those costs. The percentage by which the number of very-low-income renters in a state exceeds the number of rental units they could afford is based on 1980 Census figures. It was published as *The Rental Housing Crisis Index* (Low Income

---

[1]A Metropolitan Statistical Area covers more land area than its central city. At a minimum it includes suburbs, smaller cities, and incorporated areas. Often an MSA will include more than one large city (over 100,000); Minneapolis and St. Paul are in one MSA, as are Tampa and St. Petersburg, Dallas and Fort Worth, and Raleigh and Durham. The Los Angeles MSA includes seven cities over 100,000.

Housing Information Services, 1985). For the purpose of this study it is a very rough measure since it is available only at the *state* level. Nevertheless, it proved to be useful in subsequent analyses. It was derived by first estimating the incomes of households that qualify as "very-low-income renters" according to HUD standards—those with incomes less than 50 percent of the median renter household income for the MSA. Based on the average income of these renters, the amount they could afford for housing was calculated using HUD's standard that a household should only spend 30 percent of its income for this purpose.[2] Rents were then examined to determine how many units were available for less than 30 percent of the average very-low-income renter household's income. The figures are given in terms of *excess* percentage, so "12 percent" means there are 112 very-low-income renter households for every 100 rental units they can afford at 30 percent of their income.

POPULATION VARIABLES

Population characteristics are not directly represented in my model of homelessness. Yet the homeless population clearly differs from the housed population in several obvious ways, as described in Chapter 2. Their demographic characteristics may not be causal in themselves, but they may be strongly related to causal factors—for example, the percentage of families with female heads will be related to the percentage of people or families in poverty. In addition to the more substantive predictor variables, such as poverty, it seemed important to include indicators of the obvious demographic differences between the homeless and the housed populations (Table 8-2).

Each city is characterized in the data set by its current population and its recent population change, in 1980 and 1986. Conceivably there are significant differences in the nature of homelessness in the nation's largest cities, and those with populations of less than 250,000. For example, the service systems in these smaller cities may be more cooperative and less chaotic, allowing them to respond more appropriately to people's crises and to some extent avert homelessness altogether. The data set also includes the population of the county in which the city is located, for 1980 and 1986. This measure was needed to convert some variables, such as county tax revenues, into per capita rates.

Other demographic characteristics were included because they are over- or underrepresented in the homeless population, or because the characteristic may influence the risk of homelessness in some other way. If the characteristics of the present homeless population are any guide, the proportion of a city's

---

[2]In its publication, the Low Income Housing Information Service adjusted 1980 Census figures by a series of constants to update them to 1985, but the underlying data reflect 1980 conditions.

Table 8-2 Population Variables[a]

Variable	Year(s) Data Represents	Source
City Population	1980, 1986	CCDB—City items-6;3
Percentage Change in City Population, 1970-1980; 1980-1986	1980, 1986	1970 and 1980 Census; CCDB—City item-8
Percentage Black	1980	CCDB—City item-10
Percentage Hispanic	1980	CCDB—City item-13
Percentage Female-headed Households	1980	CCDB—City item-17
Percentage One-person Households	1980	CCDB—City item-18
Mean Persons per Household	1980	CCDB—City item-16
Percentage 65+	1980	CCDB—City item-14
County Population	1980, 1986	CCDB—County items-5;2

Sources: CCDB = *County and City Data Book: 1988.*
[a] All variables are for the city, unless specifically noted.

population that is black is correlated with the risk of homelessness, as are the proportions of households that are headed by women or consist of only one person. Old people are underrepresented among the homeless, as are multiperson households; variables indexing these characteristics were also included in the data set. All values for these variables come from the *County and City Data Book: 1988,* and are based on the 1980 Census; with the exception of city and county population, all are available only for 1980.

POVERTY AND INCOME VARIABLES

Study after study of the homeless emphasizes not only their current poverty, but also their tenuous economic status before they became homeless. Next to housing, poverty is most frequently cited as an antecedent of homelessness by both advocates and researchers. Since my model of homelessness hypothesizes that a household's lack of financial resources contributes to its inability to afford housing, a variety of measures of income and poverty were included in the data set (Table 8-3).

The percentage of individuals in poverty in each city (based on the federal poverty level) was taken from the *County and City Data Book: 1988* (U.S. Bureau of the Census, 1988). These figures are available only for 1980. Per capita incomes for each city for 1979 and 1985 were taken from the same source.

Table 8-3 Poverty and Income Variables[a]

Variable	Year(s) Data Represent	Source
Percentage of Persons in Poverty	1980	CCDB—City item-40
Per Capita Income	1979, 1985	CCDB—City items-38;36
Median Renter Income *for the MSA*	1980, 1989	HC—Table 9; Dolbeare, 1989
Mean Household Income *for the MSA*	1980	Jargowsky, 1990, unpublished data based on 1980 Census
Standard Deviation of Household Income *for the MSA*	1980	Jargowsky, 1990, unpublished data based on 1980 Census
Inequality *for the MSA* {SD Income/Mean Income}	1980	
Percentage of Blacks Living in Census Tracts with 40% or More Poverty Households *in the MSA*	1980	Jargowsky and Bane, 1990
Cost of Living	1985-1987	ACCRA

Sources: ACCRA = American Chambers of Commerce Researchers Association, quarterly *Cost of Living Index;* CCDB = *County and City Data Book: 1988;* HC = *Census of Housing, 1980,* HC80-2-58/380; Dolbeare, *Out of Reach,* Washington, D.C.: Low Income Housing Information Service, 1989; Jargowsky and Bane, "Urban Poverty: Basic Questions." Cambridge, Mass.: Center for Health and Human Resources Policy, John F. Kennedy School of Government, Harvard University, 1990.
[a]All variables are for the city, unless specifically noted.

Median renter household income for MSAs, available for both 1980 and 1989, were obtained from Cushing Dolbeare.[3]

For each MSA, I obtained mean household income, standard deviation of household income, and inequality (standard deviation of household income/mean household income) from Paul Jargowsky; their values are also based on Census data for 1980[4] and are only available for that year. Paul Jargowsky also supplied a statistic assessing ghetto poverty in each MSA. This index, defined as the

---

[3]The 1979 median renter incomes come from the 1980 Census. Dolbeare (1989) includes figures for median renter income in 1989, which are projections of 1979 data for each MSA based on 1980 Census data. The projections are based on the same correction factor for each MSA that HUD uses to update its median family income figures (from which they set income limits) in lieu of new survey data. I obtained both from Dolbeare.

[4]Paul Jargowsky, Kennedy School of Government, Harvard University, 1990, personal communication.

percentage of blacks in an MSA who live in census tracts in which 40 percent or more of the households have incomes below the federal poverty line, reflects the extremity of poverty among the black population, in locations that would certainly be considered "underclass" and characterized by many social problems. Highly concentrated poverty might be expected to produce more homelessness than lower concentrations; the variable was included to test this hypothesis.

Although it was considered essential, from a theoretical standpoint, to have some measure of cost of living in the data set, no highly reliable measure exists that would differentiate all of the cities in our sample. The only data available come from the *Cost of Living Index* published quarterly by the American Chambers of Commerce Researchers Association (ACCRA). Every quarter, members of chambers of commerce in more than 200 cities price a consistent "shopping bag" of goods and services (including housing). Cities of all sizes participate, including many not covered by this study. The ACCRA index is based on however many cities participate in a particular quarter—a number that varies from quarter to quarter. The index is calculated by assigning a value of 100 to the average cost of the shopping bag for all participating cities, and showing the deviations from that average. It thus measures the relative cost levels for consumer goods and services in participating areas. A city with a very high relative cost of living might have an index of 130, for example, while a city with low living costs might have an index of 94.

The ACCRA index figures are not strictly comparable across quarters, since the average depends on which cities are included for the quarter. It would thus have been preferable to take all the data from a single quarter's reports. This, however, was not possible since some of the cities in our sample did not report in every quarter, or even in every year. The base period used for the index was the fourth quarter of 1985, when the ACCRA report contained information for about 75 percent of the 147 primary cities in our sample. Some data had to be taken from other quarterly reports, as close to the fourth quarter of 1985 as possible. Although methodologically undesirable, this combining of ACCRA data from different quarters was the only way to include a cost of living indicator in the data base. My hope was that the cities' standing *relative to each other* would not vary very much from quarter to quarter, so that distortion would be minimal. As will be seen, this cost of living indicator, however rough, does relate to other variables as one would expect.

EDUCATION AND EMPLOYMENT VARIABLES

Educational attainment and job-related skills appear in my model of homelessness as part of each household's human capital resources. Table 8-4 displays the variables that measure these potential risk factors for homelessness. To capture

Table 8-4 Education and Employment Variables[a]

Variable	Year(s) Data Represent	Source
Percentage of Adults 25+ with 12+ Years of Education	1980	CCDB—City item-34
Percentage of Adults 25+ with 16+ Years of Education	1980	CCDB—City item-35
Professional Specialty and Technical (Percentage of Employment)	1980	CCDB—City item-59
Precision Production, Craft and Operators (Percentage of Employment)	1980	CCDB—City item-60
Unemployment Rate	1980, 1989	PC—Table 120; DOL/BLS unpublished data
Employment to Population Ratio		
{ # Employed }	1980, 1989	PC—Table 120; DOL/BLS
{ # 16 and Older }	1980, 1989	unpublished data
Number Employed and Total Payroll for Week of March 12, by Sector, for *County* Employment:	1980, 1987	CBP:1980; 1987—Table 2
Total, Mining, Construction, Manufacturing, Transportation/ Communications/ Utilities, Wholesale Trade, Retail Trade, Financial/ Insurance/Real Estate, Services		

Sources: CCDB = *County and City Data Book: 1988;* PC = *Census of Population, 1980, PC80-1, General Social and Economic Characteristics;* CBP = *County Business Patterns, 1980* and *1987,* U.S. Bureau of the Census, 1982 and 1989; DOL/BLS = Department of Labor, Bureau of Labor Statistics.
[a]All variables are for the city, unless specifically noted.

educational barriers to employment, the data set includes the percentages of adults twenty-five or older with at least twelve, and at least sixteen, years of education. Both figures are based on the 1980 Census and were taken from the *County and City Data Book: 1988.*

Like education, skill levels can facilitate or hinder employment. Two variables taken from the *County and City Data Book: 1988* reflect the proportion of a city's employed population whose jobs have relatively high skill requirements. Presumably their jobs are also higher-paying and more stable, and thus would provide a greater hedge against homelessness than jobs requiring fewer skills. Accordingly, the data set includes the proportions of employed city residents with (1) professional specialty and technical, and (2) precision production, craft, and operator jobs. These figures are based on 1980 Census data.

The number of workers, or potential workers, in each household is hypothesized to affect its ability to earn enough to avoid homelessness. The data set contains two measures of employment, although neither is at the household level. Each city's unemployment rate for 1980 was taken from the *Census of Population: 1980* for each state (U.S. Bureau of the Census, 1982, Table 57). The standard definition of unemployment rate was used for this study, namely the number of people who are out of work but looking for work as a proportion of the labor force (those working plus those looking). Parallel data for 1989 were obtained from computer printouts provided by the Bureau of Labor Statistics, U.S. Department of Labor.

A common criticism of the standard unemployment rate is that it overlooks discouraged workers: those who are no longer looking for work or never began to look, although they are of working age. An alternative measure of employment is the ratio of workers to all those who could be working (i.e., adults of working age). This measure registers both discouraged workers and those who for whatever reason are not interested in working. This employment-to-population ratio for each city for 1980 was calculated from data in the *Census of Population: 1980* (U.S. Bureau of the Census, 1982, state volumes, Table 57); the number employed was divided by city population aged 16 and older. Since employment-to-population ratios are more commonly calculated with the entire population (not just the working-age population) in the denominator, the figures in this study are somewhat higher than usual. Parallel data on number employed in each city for 1989 were obtained from computer printouts supplied by the Bureau of Labor Statistics, U.S. Department of Labor.

I also wanted to include some indication of employment structure: the way jobs are distributed among economic sectors. The "professional specialty and technical" and "precision production, craft, and operators" variables reflect the work that people do, regardless of which sector they work in. The employment sector variables reflect where people work, regardless of what they do. Thus one could be an engineer (a professional) employed in mining, or in construction, or in manufacturing, or by a utility company.

Recently there has been much discussion and debate, summarized in Chapter 4, about the shifting nature of employment in the United States. Many analysts have maintained that the increase in service sector jobs and the decrease in goods-producing jobs, with the accompanying drop in average wages and loss of job security and benefits, have contributed to homelessness by reducing people's earning potential. To examine the validity of this argument, I included variables that measure the distribution of employment and pay among the sectors of the economy as customarily defined: mining, construction, manufacturing, transportation/communications/utilities (TCU), wholesale trade, retail trade, financial/insurance/real estate (FIRE), and services. These are county-level data, assembled and published annually for each state by the Bureau of the Census in *County Business Patterns* (U.S. Bureau of the Census, 1982; 1987, Table 2). Data are for 1980 and 1987 (the latest year available when the data set was constructed). In the analyses described in later chapters these variables were converted to proportions (e.g., manufacturing employment as a percentage of total county employment), because the raw numbers reflected the size of the county rather than the sectoral distribution. Mining was dropped, since very few cities had any employees in this sector.

PUBLIC BENEFITS AND PROGRAMS VARIABLES

In our model of homelessness, the supports available through public benefit programs represent one source of income that may help a household avoid homelessness. As we saw in Chapter 5, the erosion in the real value of public benefits could easily have put recipients at risk of homelessness if they had no other income. Most public programs determine benefits at the state, rather than the city, level. This is true for all benefits variables in the data set except General Assistance, which is specific to the county level. Table 8-5 shows the benefits variables in the data set. I excluded benefits such as food stamps or the federal component of SSI, because they are set at the federal level and do not vary in different jurisdictions.

General Assistance (also called General Relief, Public Relief, Home Relief, Public Aid, and other variations) is probably the public benefit program most relevant to the people at risk of homelessness. It is the only cash assistance program that serves single nondisabled people, the group to which most homeless individuals belong. General Assistance is usually offered by counties, each of which sets its own eligibility criteria and benefit levels; in a few states, it is a state program. The General Assistance grant amount for a single individual living independently was obtained for 1981 and 1989 through a telephone survey of General Assistance offices in the counties serving all 182 cities in the sample (or the independent cities, when they functioned as counties for this purpose).

The maximum AFDC grant for a family of three, and SSI state supplement grant for an individual living independently, were obtained for 1980 and 1989 from *The 1990 Green Book* (U.S. House of Representatives, Committee on Ways and Means, 1990). I used the SSI state supplement rather than the total SSI grant amount because the latter is set by the federal government and is uniform throughout the country. The state supplement, on the other hand,

Table 8-5 Public Benefits and Programs Variables[a]

Variable	Year(s) Data Represent	Source
AFDC-Maximum State Benefit for a Family of Three	1980, 1989	*1990 Green Book*
Supplemental Security Income (SSI), State Supplement for One Person Living Alone	1980, 1989	*1990 Green Book*
County General Assistance Maximum for One Person Living Independently	1981, 1989	Telephone survey done for this research
Percentage of Unemployment Covered by Insurance	1979, 1986	Shapiro and Greenstein, 1989
State Per Capita Mental Health Expenditures	1981, 1987	NASMHPD/NASMHPD Institute, 1990
State Per Capita Spending for Alcohol and Drug Abuse Programs	1984, 1988	NASADAD, 1984, 1988

Sources: U.S. House of Representatives, Committee on Ways and Means, *The 1990 Green Book,* Washington, D.C.: USGPO, 1990; Shapiro and Greenstein, *Holes in the Safety Net,* Washington, D.C.: Center for Budget and Policy Priorities, 1989; National Association of State Mental Health Program Directors/NASMHPD Institute, 1990, *Funding Sources and Expenditures of State Mental Health Agencies: Revenue/Expenditure Study Results FY 1987;* National Association of State Alcohol and Drug Abuse Directors (NASADAD), "State Alcohol and Drug Abuse Profiles, 1984-1988."
[a] All variables are for the state, unless specifically noted.

varies widely; many states offer no supplement at all to individuals living independently. The percentage of unemployed persons covered by unemployment insurance for 1979 and 1986 was taken from Shapiro and Greenstein (1988, Table A13). In the late 1980s, as we saw in Chapter 5, unemployment insurance covered far fewer of the unemployed than it had in 1980. The change may have contributed to some workers' risk of homelessness.

It would be desirable to have direct measures of the extent of mental illness, alcoholism, and drug addiction in each city, since these problems are found extensively among homeless populations. However, no such measures exist for the city, county, or state level. The most relevant available information pertains to expenditures by state agencies that serve the mentally ill and chemically dependent. The two national organizations of state directors of these programs have been compiling this information for some years. The National Association of State Mental Health Program Directors (NASMHPD) conducts a biannual survey of state agencies, and our data set includes its figures for state-level per capita expenditures for mental health services for 1981 and 1987 (NASMHPD and NASMHPD Institute, 1990). State-level expenditures for alcohol and drug abuse treatment services for 1984 and 1988 were obtained from publications of the National Association of State Alcohol and Drug Abuse Directors (NASADAD, 1984, 1988), as were the number of alcohol and drug admissions paid for in whole or in part by state funds. Per capita rates were calculated from these data and state population figures.

OTHER VARIABLES

Table 8-6 presents several variables that were not easily classified, but seemed potentially important in explaining the rise in homelessness. The five variables related to local resources and expenditures were obtained from *Local Govern-*

Table 8-6 Other Variables

Variable	Year(s) Data Represent	Source
Total Per Capita *County* Revenues—All Sources	FY1986	GF—Table 6
Per Capita *County* Revenues from Property Taxes	FY1986	GF—Table 6
Per Capita Expenditures, by Any Public Entity within *County* Boundaries, for Education, Public Welfare, Housing/Urban Renewal	FY1986 FY1986	GF—Table 8 GF—Table 8
Average January Temperature	1980	CCDB—City item-125
Average July Temperature	1980	CCDB—City item-126
Per Capita Alcohol Admissions in *State*	1984, 1988	NASADAD, 1984, 1988
Per Capita Drug Abuse Admissions in *State*	1984, 1988	NASADAD, 1984, 1988
Percentage Increase in Per Capita Alcohol Admissions, 1984–1988	1988	
Percentage Increase in Per Capita Drug-related Admissions, 1984–1988	1988	

Sources: CCDB = *County and City Data Book: 1988;* GF = *Local Government Finances in Major County Areas: 1985-1986,* GF-86-6, Washington, D.C.: U.S. Bureau of the Census; National Association of State Alcohol and Drug Abuse Directors (NASADAD), "State Alcohol and Drug Abuse Profiles, 1984-1988."

ment Finances in Major County Areas: 1985-1986 (Bureau of the Census, 1988, Tables 6 and 8). They are available only for FY 1986; so many data were missing from the parallel publication for FY 1980 that the series was unusable. Per capita county revenues from all sources, and specifically from property taxes, index the relative ability of local jurisdictions to provide services and supports that might help people avoid homelessness. In a jurisdiction already facing an obvious homeless population, moreover, available resources may have a bearing on the local government's willingness to fund shelters and other services. Thus per capita county revenues might be related to the number of shelter beds per 10,000 population because it reflects local responsiveness to the problem, independent of the number of homeless people in the jurisdiction.

Variables in the data set measuring local government per capita *expenditures* for education, public welfare functions, and housing, community development, and urban renewal include all public expenditures for these functions that occur within the boundaries of the county, regardless of the jurisdiction involved (e.g., county, city, school district, water district) or the source of the money (federal, state, local, special taxing district). Expenditures may reflect local government willingness to spend for these functions; or they might reflect a poorer population with greater eligibility for federal programs, the money for which would flow through local governments. If the former, it would be reasonable to expect that increases in the value of these variables (other things equal) should be associated with lower rates of homelessness. If, however, local government expenditures are swollen by federal payments for welfare, housing subsidies, and the like, higher expenditures should be associated with more poverty, and hence more homelessness.

Officials and the public in cities with warm climates have often expressed the view that their homeless problem stems from the attractiveness of their area for outdoor living. To test the accuracy of the perception, our data set includes the average January and July temperatures in each city.

Finally, some crude indicators of addiction problems are included, because the latter part of the 1980s has seen such a large increase in the number of homeless people affected by chemical dependency, especially abuse of crack cocaine. Unfortunately the city-level emergency room data presented in Chapter 6 are available only for a small fraction of the sample. Instead, our data set includes the per capita number of alcohol and drug abuse admissions in the state that were paid for at least partly with state-controlled resources. The basic information on number of admissions was available for 1984 through 1988 from the National Association of State Alcohol and Drug Abuse Directors (NASADAD, 1984, 1988). From those data we calculated per capita rates for 1984 and 1988, along with a measure of change in the per capita rate between 1984 and 1988 for both alcohol and drug admissions.

PRELIMINARY ANALYSES

Once the data set was assembled, basic descriptive data were calculated and examined for each variable. These preliminary analyses are reported in Appendix B, which presents the mean, standard deviation, minimum, and maximum values for each variable, distinguishing the 147 primary cities from the thirty-five suburbs. (The income, benefits, and expenditures data in Appendix B are all in current dollars.)

We found a very broad range of values for each variable. Our sample includes some cities that are very prosperous, others that are economically depressed. On average, however, residents of the primary cities are poorer than the nation as a whole (15.8 percent versus 12.4 percent below the poverty line in 1980). Households in the primary cities are less likely to own their housing (53.2 percent versus 64.4 percent in 1980), more likely to consist of one person alone (27.6 percent versus 22.7 percent), and more likely to be headed by a woman (13.7 percent versus 10.5 percent). All of these differences would seem likely to increase the risk of homelessness for residents of these cities.

Appendix B also shows significant differences between the primary cities and the suburbs. Residents of the suburbs are better educated and more fully employed, with higher per capita and household incomes. They are more likely to own their own homes, which are more expensive and less affordable than those in the primary cities. The suburbs have also grown faster than the primary cities, in both the 1970s and the 1980–1986 period. They have fewer black people and fewer female-headed families, proportionally, and far fewer public housing units per capita. None of these differences is particularly surprising. The suburbs also have higher proportions of Hispanic residents and are warmer in winter, but these differences are explained primarily by their location—twenty-nine of the thirty-five are in the four states of Arizona (four), California (eighteen), Florida (two), or Texas (five).

Our preliminary analysis also suggests the degree to which cities have changed on certain dimensions during the 1980s. Some developments are hardly surprising, such as the growth in population and housing units that occurred in most cities. More interesting are the changes in variables that seem related to the risk of homelessness, shown in Table 8-7. Variables expressed in dollars were adjusted for inflation before mean changes were computed.

Except for the variables for per capita income, General Assistance, and SSI, all changes shown in Table 8-7 are significantly different from zero at the 5 percent level. Renter households had higher real incomes at the end of the decade than at its beginning. City residents faced a somewhat higher average rent and a smaller AFDC benefit; they were more likely to be involved in the labor force. The sectoral shifts so frequently mentioned as a hallmark of this

Table 8-7 Changes in Risk Variables for Primary Cities (N = 147)

Change in Risk Variables	Mean Change	S.D. Change	Minimum Change	Maximum Change
Per Capita Income— 1985/1979[a]	$−105	$ 702	$−2781	$2372
Median Renter Income— 1989/1980[b]	$ 3060	$1551	$ −726	$8993
Fair Market Rent for a 2-Bedroom Apartment— 1989/1980[b]	$ 51	$ 73	$ −139	$ 320
AFDC Maximum, Family of 3—1989/1980[b]	$ −59	$ 54	$ −197	$ 121
General Assistance— 1989/1981[b]	$ −4	$ 70	$ −132	$ 309
SSI State Supplement— 1989/1980[b]	$ 3	$ 74	$ −83	$ 384
HUD-supported Housing Units, per 100 Population—1989/1981	.37	.44	−.87	3.04
Rental Vacancy Rate— 1988/1980	1.49	3.70	−15.84	11.08
Unemployment Rate— 1989/1980	−1.25%	2.3%	−7.7%	5.4%
Employment to Population Ratio—1989/1980	7.72	6.65	−15.96	27.24
Sectoral Employment as a Percentage of All Employment—1987/1980				
Construction	−1%	2%	−8%	7%
Manufacturing	−5%	4%	−16%	5%
TCU	0%	1%	−7%	6%
Wholesale Trade	0%	1%	−3%	7%
Retail Trade	1%	2%	−3%	9%
FIRE	1%	1%	−3%	10%
Services	5%	2%	−1%	11%

[a]In constant 1985 dollars.
[b]In constant 1989 dollars.

decade are evident in these cities as well. Manufacturing showed an average decline, while services (very low-paying, on average) increased the most.

The next step was to examine the correlations of each independent variable with homelessness rates in 1989, 1986, 1983, and 1981. (Chapter 7 explains how these rates were created.) As Table 8-8 shows, homelessness rates in the late 1980s, and particularly the 1989 rates, are more strongly related to the potential

Table 8-8 Correlations of Risk Variables with Homelessness Rates, for Primary Cities (N = 147)

	1989	1986	1983	1981
Housing Variables				
% Owner-occupied, 1980	−.329**	−.290**	−.181	−.001
% 5+ Units, 1980	.387**	.374**	.246*	.047
% Units Change, 1970–80	−.081	−.111	−.027	−.093
% Units Change, 1980–86	−.184	−.195	−.099	−.103
Rental Vacancy Rate, 1980	−.070	−.087	−.045	−.046
Rental Vacancy Rate, 1988	−.297**	−.268*	−.168	−.036
% w. Rents LT $150, 1980	.031	−.003	.026	.073
FMR, 2-br, 1980	.241*	.257*	.196	−.015
FMR, 1-br, 1980	.232*	.245*	.193	−.019
FMR, 2-br, 1989	.288**	.212*	.121	−.021
FMR, 1-br, 1989	.293**	.220*	.130	−.010
P.C. Pub. Hsg. Units, 1981	.279**	.230*	.176	.099
P.C. Sec. 8 Units, 1981	.263*	.214*	.139	.131
P.C. Pub. Hsg. Units, 1989	.291**	.242*	.161	.084
P.C. Sec. 8 Units, 1989	.249*	.205	.124	.103
VLI Renters/Units, 1980	.118	.108	.029	−.032
Population Variables				
City Population, 1980	.146	.176	.029	−.037
County Population, 1980	.090	.136	.032	−.019
City Population, 1986	.138	.167	.022	−.042
County Population, 1986	.081	.126	.027	−.018
1970–1980 Pop. Change	−.103	−.128	−.039	−.099
1980–1986 Pop. Change	−.185	−.218*	−.123	−.134
% Black, 1980	.032	.007	−.000	.001
% Hispanic, 1980	−.092	−.123	−.092	−.085
% Female-headed, 1980	.059	.024	−.025	−.053
% One-person, 1980	.459**	.458**	.370**	.297**
Persons/Household, 1980	−.339**	−.379**	−.309**	−.254*
% 65 or Older, 1980	.207	.205	.155	.125
Poverty and Income Variables				
% in Poverty, 1980	.051	−.003	−.020	.005
P.C. Income, 1979	.133	.170	.163	.072
P.C. Income, 1985	.147	.159	.140	.053
Median Renter Inc., 1980	.199	.244*	.151	.042
Median Renter Inc., 1989	.240*	.253*	.167	.037
Mean Hshld. Inc., 1980	.192	.208	.120	.022
Std. Dev. Hshld. Inc., 1980	.217*	.213*	.136	−.010
Inequality, 1980	−.054	−.096	−.033	−.074
% Blacks in 40%+ Poverty Areas, 1980	−.036	.023	.029	−.062
Cost of Living, 1985–86	.304**	.269**	.153	−.054

Table 8-8 Continued

	1989	1986	1983	1981
Education and Employment Variables				
% 12+ Yrs. Education, 1980	.092	.081	.110	.103
% 16+ Yrs. Education, 1980	.138	.091	.088	.084
% w. Prof. Employ., 1980	.166	.085	.077	.070
% w. Craft Employ., 1980	−.261*	−.199	−.210	−.159
Unemployment Rate, 1980	.054	.044	−.019	−.007
Unemployment Rate, 1989	−.080	−.053	−.038	−.015
Empl./Pop. Ratio, 1980	−.007	.006	.060	.029
Empl./Pop. Ratio, 1989	.069	.073	.096	.163
% of 1980 Employment that is:				
Construction	−.222*	−.235*	−.144	−.098
Manufacturing	−.144	−.103	−.168	−.118
TCU	.169	.186	.151	.102
Wholesale	−.031	.018	.098	.092
Retail	−.270**	−.262*	−.167	−.048
FIRE	.343**	.313**	.221*	.133
Services	.320**	.230*	.177	.099
% of 1987 Employment that is:				
Construction	−.272**	−.279**	−.192	−.188
Manufacturing	−.109	−.071	−.112	−.043
TCU	.195	.183	.192	.130
Wholesale	−.028	.039	.108	.079
Retail	−.349**	−.358**	−.276**	−.143
FIRE	.358**	.370**	.278**	.163
Services	.375**	.286**	.221*	.110
Benefits Variables				
AFDC Max, 3 pers., 1980	.182	.179	.093	.003
AFDC Max, 3 pers., 1989	.198	.177	.112	.003
SSI State Supp., 1980	.152	.078	.116	.003
SSI State Supp., 1989	.127	.117	.023	−.064
GA, Single Person, 1981	.290**	.270**	.238*	.161
GA, Single Person, 1989	.326**	.295**	.193	.089
% Unemploy. Covered, 1979	.205	.230*	.183	.038
% Unemploy. Covered, 1986	.271**	.209	.196	.037
P.C. Mental Health $, 1987	.171	.199	.153	−.038
P.C. Alch./Drug $, 1984	.204	.217*	.160	−.019
P.C. Alch./Drug $, 1988	.232*	.257*	.219*	.030
P.C. Alch./Drug $, 1988	.348**	.361**	.290**	.105
Other Variables				
P.C. County Revenues, FY86:				
Total	.428**	.339**	.285**	.141
From Property Taxes	.173	.177	.158	−.030
P.C. County Expenditures, FY86, for:				
Public Welfare	.206	.159	.038	−.087

Table 8-8 Continued

	1989	1986	1983	1981
Education	.005	−.004	.076	−.088
Housing/Cmty. Devel.	.464**	.284**	.198	.123
Average January Temp.	−.098	−.159	−.089	.005
Average July Temp.	−.227*	−.271**	−.179	−.103
P.C. Alcohol Adms., 1984	.121	.043	.099	.060
P.C. Drug Adms., 1984	.005	−.028	−.015	−.011
P.C. Alcohol Adms., 1988	.135	.069	.118	.076
P.C. Drug Adms., 1988	.093	.029	.052	.033
Incr. Alch. Adms., 1984–88	.042	.080	.056	.049
Incr. Drug Adms., 1984–1988	.215*	.115	.149	.096

Notes: "P.C." means "per capita." * = $p < .01$; ** = $p < .001$, two-tailed.

predictor variables than are rates for earlier in the decade. To some extent shelter bed counts may gradually have become a more accurate indicator of the size of a city's homeless population. However, it is equally likely that the phenomenon of homelessness only "settled down" in response to underlying structural factors as the decade progressed. The problem did not become a public issue—indeed, had not even been identified as "homelessness"—until the middle or end of the 1981–1982 recession. Thus the 1981 rates probably should not be expected to respond to the same factors that seem to influence homelessness later in the decade. Many of the variables that have strong associations to 1989 and 1986 homelessness rates show a reduced and perhaps only marginal relationship to the 1983 rates, and no relationship at all to the 1981 rates, almost as if homelessness was "getting into gear" starting in 1982 or 1983. Certainly the build-up of shelter beds was only beginning in these years, and that build-up was driven by the level of perceived need in cities across the nation.

Almost all of the housing variables shown in Table 8-8 bear significant relationships to 1989 and 1986 homelessness rates. Higher proportions of renters, and of units in multiunit buildings, lower vacancy rates, and higher rental costs all are associated with more homelessness. The only surprise is that higher per capita availability of subsidized housing, whether public housing or Section 8 units, is also associated with higher homelessness—probably because of the strong association between the availability of subsidized housing and the community's poverty rate.

In contrast, very few of the population variables show any relationship to homelessness, in any year. City size is only marginally related in later years of the decade, and the variables representing minority presence and female-headed households are insignificant. The proportion of one-person households and its inverse, the average number of persons per household, do show a significant relationship to homelessness rates in every year.

A surprising finding is that the poverty rate does not appear to bear a significant relationship to homelessness—at least, not on its own. The same is true for the prevalence of ghetto poverty among blacks. And homelessness appears to be higher in cities that have higher mean incomes (in 1980) and higher median renter incomes in both 1980 and 1989. More readily understood is the significant relationship of homelessness to the cost of living (which reflects rental costs).

Education and employment levels are not strongly correlated with homelessness, but the structure of the employment market does show strong associations. Chapter 9 will describe the analyses undertaken to sort out the effects of employment sector structure.

Benefits variables, where they are significant, are positively correlated with homelessness—another surprising finding. However, the association makes more sense when one realizes that benefit levels follow the cost of living. Higher cost-of-living states and counties tend to have higher benefit levels, but the benefits still are not adequate for the expenses that households encounter in these jurisdictions. Higher expenditures for drug and alcohol treatment and higher homelessness rates go together across the decade, suggesting that the higher levels of drug and alcohol problems in certain jurisdictions stimulate both state spending on the problem and homelessness. The association of increases in drug admissions between 1984 and 1988 supports this interpretation.

The only other variables showing important associations with homelessness rates are per capita total county revenues and per capita county expenditures on housing and community development. The latter result parallels the positive correlations between per capita public housing units and homelessness. Total county revenues appear to be significant because they reflect the county's position as a pass-through for various federal programs aimed at the poor. It is essentially a measure of need, not generosity. This interpretation is supported by the much smaller (and insignificant) association between homelessness and the level of county revenues generated from local resources (property taxes).

Ideally, in a data set used to determine the causes of homelessness, the hypothesized causal variables would represent years preceding the one in which homelessness is measured, or at least the same year. Presumably the more remote in time the causal condition is from the dependent condition, the less precise the results; at worst the results could be misleading. This is a particularly difficult issue for the present endeavor, since many important variables are available only for 1980, and others are available only for a single mid-decade year. If predictions are very sensitive to temporal ordering, this could be a problem. On the other hand, it is not unreasonable to expect considerable stability, over a decade, in the ordinal relationship of cities on variables such as poverty, minority representation, cost of living, and educational level; then a 1980 reading would not grossly mislead the researcher as to the cities' relative standing in 1986 or 1989. And for the analyses to be performed in this study, the relative ordering of cities is the important factor.

Happily, Table 8-8 can lay some of these concerns to rest. With two exceptions (rental vacancy rate and population growth), all the variables for which two different years are available show the two years having very similar relationships to all four homelessness rates. Apparently the variables for income, housing cost, benefits, employment, and population are all relatively insensitive to the year in which the data were collected, at least in regard to their association with homelessness rates. In fact, in most instances 1980 values bear stronger relationships to 1986 and 1989 homelessness rates than they do to 1981 or 1983 rates. This stability is good for researchers, but probably reflects a reality that is unfortunate for policymakers: the basic characteristics of cities that are presumed to affect homelessness are persistent and difficult to change.

CHAPTER NINE

Causes of Homelessness

■ Now we may begin to address the question of how our causal model of homelessness predicts differences between U.S. cities in 1989, and changes in homelessness rates within each city from 1981 to 1989. The major hypotheses are diagrammed in Figure 9-1, which translates the general causal model outlined in Chapter 1 into blocks of variables in the data set. (As explained below, the regression analyses used to test this model include only a subset of the variables described in Chapter 8.) Each arrow represents a causal association that has been hypothesized in the literature on homelessness, as reviewed in Part I of this book.

At the extreme left of Figure 9-1 is the dependent variable, a city's homelessness rate. It is most immediately affected by housing and income variables. (The housing and income variables also formed the two sides of the housing affordability (in)equality at the core of the more abstract causal model depicted in Chapter 1 (Figure 1-1)). The analysis uses two housing variables: the city's 1988 rental vacancy rate, which is expected to affect homelessness negatively (the lower the vacancy rate, the more homelessness); and the ratio of very-low-income renters to units they can afford, which is expected to affect homelessness positively (the higher the ratio, the more homelessness).[1] The analysis also uses two income variables: the city's 1980 poverty rate and its 1985

---

[1]Three other housing variables—proportion of units with rents under $150 in 1980, per capita public housing units (1981 and 1989), and per capita Section 8 units (1981 and 1989)—were excluded from the analysis because of their strong associations with a city's poverty rate, and the resulting problems of multicollinearity. Fair market rents were strongly associated with the cost of living variable, which was selected for its greater generality.

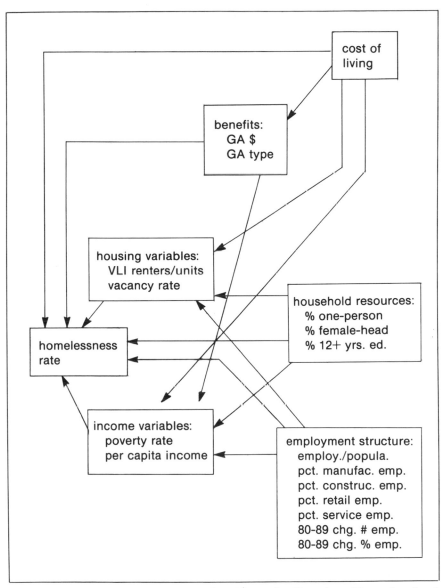

Figure 9-1 Causal Model to Be Tested, Showing Hypothesized Relationships of Variables in the Data Set

per capita income.[2] More poverty and a lower per capita income are commonly hypothesized to increase homelessness.

Moving to the right-hand side of Figure 9-1, the hypothesized relationships become more complex. Benefits are expected to affect homelessness both directly and through their effects on the income variables. Greater benefit availability and higher payment levels should both reduce homelessness. All of the benefits variables (AFDC, General Assistance, SSI state supplement, unemployment coverage, mental health and chemical dependency spending) are strongly interrelated and behave in similar ways. General Assistance (GA) was selected to represent this block of variables because it is the most directly relevant to homelessness; GA is often the only possible source of support for single individuals, who make up the bulk of the homeless population. Two variables are included: *GA type* indicates whether General Assistance is available to employables as well as the disabled (coded 2), to the disabled only (coded 1), or is not available at all (coded 0). *GA $* is the maximum benefit amount for a single individual living independently (including zero if no GA is available).

The household resources variables describe the ability of households to make a living, through the number of workers they can potentially send into the work force (represented here by the proportion of one-person and female-headed households), and through their human capital, represented here by years of education. More potential workers and greater educational attainment are expected to help people avoid homelessness, both directly and through their effects on income variables. More one-person households are also expected to affect homelessness through their influence on the availability of housing (consuming more housing units per person).

Employment structure has been hypothesized to cause homelessness through a number of mechanisms, some of which may appear contradictory. Both increases and decreases in employment have sometimes been implicated in increased homelessness, although in general the literature leans toward predicting that higher unemployment and a shrinking work force will produce more homelessness. This analysis provides the opportunity to sort out some of these effects. Employment structure variables are expected to affect homelessness directly, and also through their effects on housing and income variables. In addition to the unemployment rate and the employment-to-population ratio, I include several sectoral employment variables. These include the percentages of a city's employment that are accounted for by the construction, manufacturing, retail trade, and services sectors. Construction was included because of its

---

[2]All of the income variables in the data set were very highly interrelated. Per capita income was selected because it was available for two time periods (unlike mean income), reflected the cash available to households from all sources (unlike average payroll dollars), and covered all households while accounting for household size (unlike median renter income).

relationship to both housing availability and a city's economic health, although it accounts for only 6.5 percent of employment, on average.[3] The other three sectors were chosen because they are typically the largest, with services accounting for 30 percent of employment, on average, retail trade for 22 percent, and manufacturing for 19 percent.

The final independent variable is the city's cost of living, which affects homelessness directly and through its effects on benefits, housing, and income variables.

Each of the blocks shown in Figure 9-1 (e.g., housing costs) was represented by a number of variables (presented in Chapter 8), which were very highly interrelated. A single representative variable had to be selected for the analysis, since including more than one resulted in unacceptable levels of multicollinearity. Preliminary analyses were conducted to determine which variable in a set would make the most meaningful contribution to the overall analysis.[4]

This chapter presents the results of estimating the hypothesized model, first for all the primary cities in the analysis (N = 147) and then for two important breakouts: (1) cities with high and low proportions of manufacturing employment (N = 71 and 76, respectively), and (2) cities whose population did and did not grow in the 1980s (N = 68 and 79, respectively).

Although our model of homelessness is complex and the analysis fairly sophisticated, I should emphasize that this entire enterprise should be regarded as an exploratory endeavor. The data available to represent many of the key concepts in the analysis are not ideal. While every effort was made to obtain city-level data, we sometimes had to settle for county-level, MSA-level, or state-level data because nothing else could be found at all, or the available data did not cover the relevant cities. In addition, some 1980 measurements are treated as predictors of 1989 homelessness rates because no later data were

---

[3]The employment type variables (professional and craft/production/operator employment) were available only for 1980 and were highly interrelated to variables already in the model.

[4]There is one other group of variables, including city size, proportion black, proportion Hispanic, proportion of units in multiunit buildings, and region of the country, that I think of as antecedent to the entire set of variables included in the model in Figure 9-1. Thus minority proportions might predict poverty or education levels, and region might predict income and benefit levels. One might include these variables in a model if one did not have more precise measures of the factors they are expected to predict. Since our data set did include direct measures of poverty, income levels, and so on, it was considered unnecessary to include these antecedent variables.

One final set of variables was dropped: those describing per capita revenues and expenditures. Although these variables might appear to reflect the resources a jurisdiction could tap to address social problems, they are very highly associated with levels of poverty and public benefits. They indicate a need for assistance rather than a high level of resources. Because other measures of this need were already in the model, the revenue and expenditure variables were excluded.

available, and some 1989 measures are treated as predictors of 1980 or 1985 measures. As noted in Chapter 8, the consistency of effects of earlier and later measurements of the same concept suggests that the results of our analysis will not be seriously distorted by the violations of real temporal order necessitated by data availability.

A further limitation is that our measure of homelessness, because it depends on counts of shelter beds, certainly is influenced by factors other than the size of a city's homeless population, yet these factors are not included in the model. Finally, no effort was made to account for the relationships among variables *within* blocks (e. g., one-person households with female-headed households or education levels), although such relationships clearly exist. The analysis reported here was conducted in the spirit of doing the best possible with available materials. The results are quite informative, although conclusions must remain tentative.

ZERO-ORDER CORRELATIONS OF PREDICTORS AND RATES

The simplest way to examine the relationship between potential causal factors and homelessness rates is to look at their zero-order correlations, which show strength of association without accounting for the influence of any other predictor variables. Table 9-1 gives these correlations for each block of variables in the analysis. Many of the variables in Table 9-1 also appear in Table 8-8. However, Table 9-1 excludes those variables that were not used in the regression analyses, includes new variables representing the change in values of some variables between early and late in the 1980s, and shows associations with change in homelessness rates as well as with rates for each year.

The columns of Table 9-1 represent the homelessness rates for four years during the 1980s, based on the availability of shelter beds per 10,000 city population, as explained in Chapter 7. The final column represents the change in these rates between 1981 and 1989. In the analyses to follow, the 1989 homelessness rates will be used in between-city analyses, which try to explain why some cities have more homelessness than others. The change in homelessness over the decade will be used as the dependent variable in analyses of within-city increases in homelessness. Table 9-1 contains all of the predictor variables involved in both sets of analyses.

The middle panel of the table contains the variables used in the between-city analyses of 1989 rates. These include the most recent data available for each variable, which is 1980 in several cases. The final panel contains earlier values of each variable (usually from 1980), plus (when two readings on the variable are available) measures of change over the decade.

Table 9-1 Zero-Order Correlations of Predictor Variables with 1981, 1983, 1986 and 1989 Homelessness Rates and 1981-1989 Change in Rates

Independent Variables	Homelessness Rates				1981-1989 Change in Rates
	1981	1983	1986	1989	
1981 HL RATE	—				
1983 HL RATE	.827**	—			
1986 HL RATE	.698**	.853**	—		
1989 HL RATE	.676**	.805**	.921**	—	
1981-1989 CHANGE	.216*	.504**	.746**	.865**	—
COST/LIVING	−.054	.152	.269**	.304**	.440**
1989 GA $	.089	.193	.395**	.299**	.336**
GA TYPE	−.017	.090	.174	.123	.174
% ONE-80	.297**	.370**	.458**	.471**	.422**
% FH-80	−.053	−.025	.024	.040	.088
% 12+ YRS-80	.103	.110	.080	.100	.062
E/P-89	.163	.096	.073	.094	.014
UE-89	−.015	−.038	−.053	−.066	−.078
% MFG-87	−.043	−.112	−.071	−.109	−.115
% CNS-87	−.188	−.192	−.279**	−.272**	−.233*
% RTL-87	−.143	−.276**	−.358**	−.349**	−.365**
% SRV-87	.110	.221*	.286**	.375**	.423**
1980-89 CHG # EMP	−.029	−.029	.040	.022	.049
1980-89 CHG % EMP	.040	−.043	−.090	−.051	−.095
VLI R/U-85	−.032	.029	.108	.132	.196
VAC RATE-88	−.036	−.168	−.268*	−.278**	−.344**
% POV-80	.005	−.020	−.003	.021	.024
P.C. INC-85	.053	.193	.159	.167	.185
1981 GA $	.161	.238*	.270**	.274**	.254*
CHG GA $	−.131	−.075	.061	.063	.172
E/P-80	.029	.060	.006	.005	−.013
CHG E/P	.194	.078	.092	.121	.029
UE-80	−.007	−.019	.044	.064	.090
CHG UE	−.004	−.009	−.098	−.134	−.175
% MFG-80	−.114	−.157	−.097	−.142	−.111
CHG MFG	.077	.008	−.021	−.135	−.007
% CNS-80	−.093	−.123	−.223*	−.216*	−.224*
CHG CNS	.005	.007	−.042	−.020	−.030
% RTL-80	−.080	−.204	−.291**	−.275**	−.310**
CHG RTL	−.102	−.129	−.131	−.094	−.055
% SRV-80	.132	.234**	.293**	.378**	.411**
CHG SRV	−.075	−.114	−.139	−.103	−.085
# EMP-80	−.033	.035	.180	.150	.221*
VAC RATE-80	−.045	−.045	−.087	−.053	−.038
CHG VAC. RATE	−.002	−.127	−.192	−.225*	−.296**
P.C. INC-79	.072	.163	.170	.173	.180

Table 9-1 Continued

Independent Variables	Homelessness Rates				1981–1989 Change in Rates
	1981	1983	1986	1989	
CHG P.C. INC.	−.037	−.037	−.002	.014	.044
CITY POP-70	−.023	.047	.199	.172	.243*
POP CHG 70-80	−.099	−.034	−.128	−.098	−.063
HSG UNIT CHG 70-80	−.093	−.027	−.111	−.074	−.036
CITY POP-80	−.037	.029	.176	.148	.222
POP CHG 80-86	−.136	−.123	−.218*	−.196	−.168
HSG UNIT CHG 80-86	−.103	−.099	−.195	−.183	−.172
CITY POP-86	−.042	.022	.167	.139	.213*

*$P < 0.01$; **$P < 0.001$, two-tailed. N = 147.

Note: COST/LIVING = Cost of living; 1989 GA $ = maximum GA payment for one person living independently, 1989; GA TYPE = none/disabled only/also employables; % ONE-80 = % one-person households, 1980; % FH-80 = % female-headed households, 1980; % 12+ YRS-80 = % with twelve or more years of education, 1980; E/P-89 = employment/population ratio, 1989; UE-89 = unemployment rate, 1989; % MFG-87 = % of employment in manufacturing sector, 1987; % CNS-87 = % of employment in construction sector, 1987; % RTL-87 = % of employment in retail sales sector, 1987; % SRV-87 = % of employment in services sector, 1987; 1980-89 CHG # EMP = change in the number of people employed in the city between 1980 and 1989; 1980-89 CHG % EMP = change in employment between 1980 and 1989, as a percent of 1980 employment; VLI R/U-85 = ratio of very-low-income renters to units they can afford, 1985; VAC RATE-88 = 1988 rental vacancy rate; % POV-80 = % individuals below poverty line, 1980; P.C. INC.-85 = per capita income, 1985; 1981 GA $ = maximum GA payment for one person living independently, 1981; CHG GA $ = 1981-1989 change in GA $; E/P-80 = employment/population ratio, 1980; CHG E/P = 1980-1989 change in E/P; UE-80 = unemployment rate, 1980; CHG UE = 1980-1989 change in UE; % MFG-80 = % of employment in manufacturing, 1980; CHG MFG = 1980-1987 change in MFG as percent of 1980 MFG; % CNS-80 = % of employment in construction, 1980; CHG CNS = 1980-1987 change in CNS as percent of 1980 CNS; % RTL-80 = % of employment in retail, 1980; CHG RTL = 1980-1987 change in RTL as percent of 1980 RTL; % SRV-80 = % of employment in services, 1980; CHG SRV = 1980-1987 change in SRV as percent of 1980 SRV; # EMP-80 = number employed, 1980; VAC RATE-80 = rental vacancy rate, 1980; CHG VAC. RATE = 1980-1988 change in rental vacancy rate; P.C. INC-79 = per capita income, 1979; CHG P.C. INC = 1979-1985 change in per capita income; CITY POP-70 = 1970 city population; POP CHG 70-80 = 1970-1980 change in city population; HSG UNIT CHG 70-80 = 1970-1980 change in number of dwelling units in city; CITY POP-80 = 1980 city population; POP CHG 80-86 = 1980-1986 change in city population; HSG UNIT CHG 80-86 = 1980-1986 change in number of dwelling units in city; CITY POP-86 = 1986 city population.

Patterns over the Decade

As the top panel of Table 9-1 shows, homelessness rates for each year are generally quite highly correlated with rates for other years; not surprisingly, the closest associations are with years closer in time. The 1981 rates do not appear to be very good indicators of the change in a city's homelessness level over the decade (r = .216). This low correlation suggests that there may have been some significant changes between the 1970s and the 1980s in the factors affecting homelessness. It is also possible that the pattern observed is partly a consequence of the measure of homelessness used, since it took some time for communities to develop shelter bed capacity in response to the increase in homelessness. As the decade progresses, the point-in-time rates become more closely associated with the change in rates, which may suggest that those cities that had the most homeless also increased their capacity the most.

Data in the second and third panels of Table 9-1 indicate that the strength of association between homelessness rates and many of the hypothesized independent variables also increased as the decade progressed, and that the same variables influenced the 1981–1989 change in rates. This pattern, already noted in Chapter 8, could reflect an increase in the importance of the factors hypothesized to cause homelessness. If earlier homelessness was the product of quite different factors, the model tested here would become increasingly relevant only as the conditions of the 1980s assumed more causal importance. The significant associations between our predictor variables and the 1981–1989 change in homelessness suggest that these factors did play an increasing role in generating homelessness after about 1983. Alternatively, the causal factors influencing actual homelessness might have remained the same, while shelter bed availability became an increasingly accurate indicator of actual levels of homelessness as the decade progressed. Probably both explanations are true to some degree, but the data available cannot differentiate between the two.

Consistency of Effects Across Time

The correlations shown in Table 9-1 are relatively insensitive to the dates of the predictor variables. That is, earlier and later versions of the same variable show similar associations with homelessness rates. For example, although GA payment levels changed between 1981 and 1989, the two GA $ variables bear much the same relationship to 1981, 1983, 1986, and 1989 homelessness rates and the 1981–1989 change in rates.

From a researcher's point of view, this is a very important observation. It is difficult, sometimes impossible, to obtain data for the precise years one would like to have. As a result, the analyses reported here have some undoubted technical flaws: data may be taken from the "wrong" years, and certain variables with data gathered late in the decade are used to "predict" variables representing an earlier period. Pragmatically, however, cities appear to remain quite stable on many of the variables critical to this analysis. That is, cities may change on these dimensions, but they move in parallel, so that their rank order with relation to each other remains much the same. The poverty rate and size of the manufacturing sector may change in each city, but in general high-poverty cities will still be high compared with low-poverty cities, high-manufacturing cities will still have proportionally more manufacturing than low-manufacturing cities, and so on. As a result, the associations revealed by correlational or regression analysis remain valid.

This persistence is good news for researchers, since it means available data can be used to explore associations among cities. I was obliged to rely on 1980 readings on some critical variables because no later data were available; the correlations in Table 9-1 give some reassurance that these procedures do not distort the results a great deal.

Unexpected Associations

Some variables hypothesized to bear strong relationships to homelessness levels and growth do not appear to do so, at least at the level of zero-order correlations. This category includes levels of education, proportion of female-headed families, the employment-to-population ratio, the unemployment rate, employment growth or change, and—most surprising—the poverty rate for different cities. Further, some variables show associations that go in the opposite direction from theoretical predictions. Both per capita income and General Assistance payment levels are positively, not negatively, correlated with homelessness rates. In addition, the zero-order correlations show only weak associations for city size and for the severity of the shortage of affordable housing (VLI R/U-85). The latter result is especially noteworthy, since such shortages figure in all hypotheses about the rise in homelessness. Regression analysis was used to explore these associations further and to determine how they are affected by the presence of other causal factors.

REGRESSION RESULTS

The regression analyses presented in Tables 9-2 through 9-7 test the adequacy of the causal model presented in Figure 9-1.[5] In these tables, independent

---

[5]Regression analysis tests the association of an independent variable with a dependent variable when the effects of all other independent variables in the model are held constant. The results reported in Tables 9-2 through 9-7 are expressed as *beta* coefficients, which show the effect of a change of one standard deviation unit of an independent variable on the dependent variable (also expressed in standard deviation units) when all other independent variables are controlled.

variables are arrayed in columns arranged from left to right in the same order as the variables are displayed in Figure 9-1. Thus the first columns in Table 9-2 give housing and income variables, then benefits variables, then household resources and employment structure variables, and finally cost of living. Each row in Table 9-2 represents a predictive equation for a variable that has arrows pointing to it in Figure 9-1 (symbolizing that other variables in the model are expected to affect it). Rows 1 to 6 of Table 9-2 represent these equations for the two benefits variables, two housing variables, and two income variables. Rows 7 to 11 of Table 9-2 represent predictive equations for homelessness rates, each of which includes only one group of predictor variables (i.e., row 7: housing and income variables; row 8: benefits variables; row 9: household resources variables; row 10: employment variables; row 11: cost of living).

Row 12 presents all the potential predictors of homelessness in the full model. Row 13 eliminates those variables that do little to predict homelessness. In deciding which variables to drop for this "best" model, two criteria were used: explained variance (R^2) and significance level. If deletion of the variable reduced R^2 by 2 percent or more, the variable was retained. In general variables were retained if their significance was $p < .30$ (that is, if there was less than a 30 percent probability that the observed relationship would have happened by chance rather than reflecting a true causal relationship). This is obviously a much more forgiving standard than the usual $p < .05$. However, a significance level of $p < .30$ still means that the odds are 7 to 3 that the variable is a significant predictor of homelessness. In this exploratory work, it seemed wise to retain possible predictors and try to understand their action, rather than risk rejecting potentially important factors. In Table 9-2 coefficients that meet the conventional significance level of $p < .05$ are underlined.

The final two columns of these tables show the predictive power of each equation, both as R^2, the proportion of variance in the dependent variable that is explained by the model, and as AR^2, which is R^2 adjusted for the degrees of freedom absorbed by the number of variables in the equation. The adjusted R^2 is a more accurate reflection of the true amount of variance explained by the equation, because without the adjustment R^2 overestimates the variance explained as more variables are included in the equation. R^2 is underlined if the set of independent variables in an equation predicts the dependent variable at a significance level of $p < .05$.

All Cities

Testing our model of homelessness for all cities in the analysis ($N = 147$) produced the results shown in Table 9-2. Let us look first at the five equations that use individual groups of variables to predict homelessness. The housing and income variables together predict 10.6 percent of the variance (AR^2) in

Table 9-2 Antecedents of 1989 Homelessness Rates*
All Cities (N = 147)

	INDEPENDENT VARIABLES							
DEPENDENT VARIABLE	VLI RENTERS/ UNITS	VACANCY RATE	PCT. POVERTY	PER CAP. INCOME	GA $	GA TYPE	PCT. ONE	PCT. FH
1. GA $	—	—	—	—	—	—	—	—
2. GA TYPE	—	—	—	—	—	—	—	—
3. VAC. RATE	—	—	—	—	—	—	−.186	−.372
4. VLI R/U	—	—	—	—	—	—	.449	−.512
5. POVERTY	—	—	—	—	−.018	−.107	.174	.533
6. PCINC	—	—	—	—	−.132	−.025	.143	−.077
7. HLRATE	.089	−.231	.236	.296	—	—	—	—
8. HLRATE	—	—	—	—	.647	−.417	—	—
9. HLRATE	—	—	—	—	—	—	.451	−.085
10. HLRATE	—	—	—	—	—	—	—	—
11. HLRATE	—	—	—	—	—	—	—	—
12. HLRATE	−.209	−.124	.052	−.102	.570	−.413	.235	−.178
13. HLRATE	−.213	−.118	—	−.119	.569	−.417	.248	−.151

Notes: HLRATE = 1989 homelessness rate per 10,000 city population; VLI RENTERS/UNIT = degree of shortage of affordable housing; VACANCY RATE = 1988 rental vacancy rate; PCT. POVERTY = 1980 percent of individuals below poverty line; PERCAP INCOME = 1985 per capita income; GA $ = 1989 maximum benefit for single individual living independently; GATYPE = none/disabled only/also employables; PCT. ONE = percent of one-person households in 1980; PCT. FH = percent of households that are female headed in 1980; PCT. 12 YRS+ = percent of population twenty-five or older who have twelve or more years of education in 1980; EMPL/POPULA = ratio of employed to population sixteen and older, 1989; PCT. UE = percent unemployed, 1989; PCT. MFG, PCT. CNS, PCT. RTL, PCT. SRV = proportion of employment in county that is in the manufacturing/construction/ retail/services sector; CHA# EMP, CHA% EMP = 1980-1989 change in people employed in the city, expressed as a number, and as a percent of 1980 employment; COST/LIVING = cost of living. See Chapter 8 for full description of variables.
*An underlined coefficient is significant at p = .05 or better; an underlined R² indicates an F significant at p = .05 or better.

homelessness (row 7), and the rental vacancy and poverty rate variables behave as expected, having negative and positive signs, respectively (tighter rental markets and higher poverty rates associated with more homelessness). The equation contains some surprises, however. First, the effect of affordable housing shortages (VLI Renters/Units) is small and insignificant, contrary to expectation. Second, per capita income has a positive and significant effect, meaning that higher per capita incomes and higher homelessness appear to go together. This result is contrary to expectation; in fact, since poverty rates and per capita income are negatively related to each other, it is quite surprising to

				INDEPENDENT VARIABLES							
PCT. 12 YRS+	EMPL/ POPULA	PCT UE	PCT. MFG	PCT. CNS	PCT. RTL	PCT. SRV	CHA# EMP	CHA% EMP	COST/ LIVING	R^2	AR^2
—	—	—	—	—	—	—	—	—	.512	.262	.257
—	—	—	—	—	—	—	—	—	.400	.160	.154
−.220	.093	.329	−.224	.138	−.089	.052	.115	−.038	−.363	.433	.382
−.632	−.090	.007	.347	.202	.511	.128	.321	−.095	.152	.366	.261
−.292	−.255	.077	−.164	−.147	.093	.087	−.012	.301	−.011	.789	.767
.455	.267	−.155	.044	.078	−.052	.018	−.007	−.192	.300	.690	.657
—	—	—	—	—	—	—	—	—	—	.130	.106
—	—	—	—	—	—	—	—	—	—	.143	.131
.109	—	—	—	—	—	—	—	—	—	.226	.210
—	.148	.112	−.243	−.226	−.388	.188	−.113	.072	—	.294	.253
—	—	—	—	—	—	—	—	—	.304	.093	.086
.119	.138	.339	−.189	−.113	−.360	.115	−.133	.147	.113	.461	.385
.112	.129	.340	−.196	−.120	−.357	.111	−.133	.161	.119	.461	.390

find they both have the same sign in this equation.[6] Yet in this analysis and in those to follow, poverty rates and per capita income usually display the same sign. Once all the results have been presented, we will take a closer look at this anomaly.

General Assistance payment levels (GA $) also behave in an unexpected manner (row 8). Both GA $ and type of General Assistance (GA TYPE) are significant, and together they explain 13.1 percent of the variance in homelessness. Higher payment levels do not seem to prevent homelessness, but are associated with higher rates of homelessness—presumably because the local cost of living drives GA payment levels.[7] Even the highest payment levels do not provide enough resources to meet these living costs. In an equation that takes account of GA payment levels, GA type has the expected negative effect on homelessness. Cities with no GA appear to have higher homelessness rates than those with some type of GA, and cities whose GA program includes

---

[6]Were individuals or households the unit of analysis, this would not happen. But the unit of analysis here is cities. It is quite possible for some people in cities to be poor while the higher incomes of others have the effect of raising the average per capita income.

[7]Besides cost of living, region is the most important other factor affecting GA payment levels (including zero for counties that have no GA program). Payment levels are higher in the Northeast and West, and lower in the South. Together, cost of living and region produce an adjusted R^2 of .628 for 1989 GA payment levels. These regional differences themselves are proxies for the political philosophy and history of local governments.

Table 9-3 Antecedents of 1989 Homelessness Rates High-Manufacturing Cities (N = 71)

| | INDEPENDENT VARIABLES | | | | | | | |
DEPENDENT VARIABLE	VLI RENTERS/ UNITS	VACANCY RATE	PCT. POVERTY	PER CAP. INCOME	GA$	GA TYPE	PCT. ONE	PCT. FH
1. GA $	—	—	—	—	—	—	—	—
2. GA TYPE	—	—	—	—	—	—	—	—
3. VAC. RATE	—	—	—	—	—	—	−.179	−.296
4. VLI R/U	—	—	—	—	—	—	.018	−.455
5. POVERTY	—	—	—	—	−.124	.108	.221	.703
6. PCINC	—	—	—	—	.168	−.275	.087	−.067
7. HLRATE	.100	−.028	−.005	.093	—	—	—	—
8. HLRATE	—	—	—	—	.505	−.310	—	—
9. HLRATE	—	—	—	—	—	—	.328	−.032
10. HLRATE	—	—	—	—	—	—	—	—
11. HLRATE	—	—	—	—	—	—	—	—
12. HLRATE	−.047	−.023	−.061	−.066	.526	−.503	.481	.023
13. HLRATE	.086	—	—	—	.554	−.505	.422	—

Notes: See Notes, Table 9-2.
*An underlined coefficient is significant at p = .10 or better; an underlined R^2 indicates an F significant at p = .05 or better.

Table 9-4 Antecedents of 1989 Homelessness Rates Low-Manufacturing Cities (N = 76)

| | INDEPENDENT VARIABLES | | | | | | | |
DEPENDENT VARIABLE	VLI RENTERS/ UNITS	VACANCY RATE	PCT. POVERTY	PER CAP. INCOME	GA$	GA TYPE	PCT. ONE	PCT. FH
1. GA $	—	—	—	—	—	—	—	—
2. GA TYPE	—	—	—	—	—	—	—	—
3. VAC. RATE	—	—	—	—	—	—	−.067	−.416
4. VLI R/U	—	—	—	—	—	—	.421	−.353
5. POVERTY	—	—	—	—	−.024	−.160	.184	.531
6. PCINC	—	—	—	—	−.391	.203	.250	−.091
7. HLRATE	.121	−.349	.367	.345	—	—	—	—
8. HLRATE	—	—	—	—	.647	−.417	—	—
9. HLRATE	—	—	—	—	—	—	.552	.195
10. HLRATE	—	—	—	—	—	—	—	—
11. HLRATE	—	—	—	—	—	—	—	—
12. HLRATE	−.244	−.107	−.036	−.092	.392	−.162	.260	.037
13. HLRATE	−.228	−.112	—	—	.422	−.195	.234	—

Notes: See Notes, Table 9-2.
*An underlined coefficient is significant at p = .10 or better; an underlined R^2 indicates an F significant at p = .05 or better.

INDEPENDENT VARIABLES

PCT. 12 YRS+	EMPL/ POPULA	PCT UE	PCT. MFG	PCT. CNS	PCT. RTL	PCT. SRV	CHA# EMP	CHA% EMP	COST/ LIVING	R²	AR²
—	—	—	—	—	—	—	—	—	.558	.312	.302
—	—	—	—	—	—	—	—	—	.514	.265	.254
−.053	.045	.296	−.092	.323	.056	−.021	−.031	.080	−.278	.463	.352
−.085	−.342	.146	−.205	−.263	.163	−.106	.035	.312	.786	.641	.567
−.108	−.331	−.101	−.079	.078	.082	.064	−.011	.282	.059	.838	.797
.553	.267	−.089	.157	.047	−.148	−.011	.077	.212	.164	.666	.583
—	—	—	—	—	—	—	—	—	—	.021	.000
—	—	—	—	—	—	—	—	—	—	.096	.070
.210	—	—	—	—	—	—	—	—	—	.151	.113
—	.123	.052	−.247	−.224	.065	.063	−.157	.098	—	.158	.050
—	—	—	—	—	—	—	—	—	.078	.000	.000
.252	.067	.234	−.150	−.142	.070	−.005	−.228	.423	.104	.412	.208
.264	—	.268	−.180	−.138	—	—	−.237	.378	—	.405	.306

INDEPENDENT VARIABLES

PCT. 12 YRS+	EMPL/ POPULA	PCT UE	PCT. MFG	PCT. CNS	PCT. RTL	PCT. SRV	CHA# EMP	CHA% EMP	COST/ LIVING	R²	AR²
—	—	—	—	—	—	—	—	—	.517	.268	.258
—	—	—	—	—	—	—	—	—	.363	.131	.120
−.036	.093	.297	−.111	.124	−.098	.106	.243	−.055	−.495	.453	.349
−.123	−.334	.322	.143	.206	−.022	.388	−.027	.544	.168	.454	.350
−.235	−.182	.216	−.054	−.149	.134	−.112	.003	.269	.032	.832	.794
.275	.290	−.219	−.152	.073	−.040	−.038	−.013	−.182	.320	.768	.715
—	—	—	—	—	—	—	—	—	—	.259	.217
—	—	—	—	—	—	—	—	—	—	.143	.131
−.011	—	—	—	—	—	—	—	—	—	.356	.329
—	.079	.122	−.086	−.201	−.547	.181	−.091	.050	—	.482	.420
—	—	—	—	—	—	—	—	—	.478	.228	.217
−.047	.202	.318	−.061	−.074	−.407	.107	−.125	.061	.175	.617	.496
—	.214	.370	—	—	−.368	.150	−.109	—	.164	.611	.544

Table 9-5 Antecedents of 1989 Homelessness Rates
High-Growth Cities (N = 68)

DEPENDENT VARIABLE	VLI RENTERS/ UNITS	VACANCY RATE	PCT. POVERTY	PER CAP. INCOME	GA$	GA TYPE	PCT. ONE	PCT. FH
				INDEPENDENT VARIABLES				
1. GA $	—	—	—	—	—	—	—	—
2. GA TYPE	—	—	—	—	—	—	—	—
3. VAC. RATE	—	—	—	—	—	—	−.058	−.244
4. VLI R/U	—	—	—	—	—	—	.320	−.255
5. POVERTY	—	—	—	—	−.072	−.015	.254	.327
6. PCINC	—	—	—	—	−.259	−.017	.074	.130
7. HLRATE	.217	−.194	−.107	.075	—	—	—	—
8. HLRATE	—	—	—	—	.675	−.436	—	—
9. HLRATE	—	—	—	—	—	—	.379	−.184
10. HLRATE	—	—	—	—	—	—	—	—
11. HLRATE	—	—	—	—	—	—	—	—
12. HLRATE	−.130	−.580	−.765	−.592	.131	−.475	.438	.054
13. HLRATE	—	−.601	−.641	−.572	—	−.420	.349	—

Notes: See Notes, Table 9-2.
*An underlined coefficient is significant at p = .10 or better; an underlined R^2 indicates an F significant at p = .05 or better.

Table 9-6 Antecedents of 1989 Homelessness Rates
Low-Growth Cities (N = 79)

DEPENDENT VARIABLE	VLI RENTERS/ UNITS	VACANCY RATE	PCT. POVERTY	PER CAP. INCOME	GA$	GA TYPE	PCT. ONE	PCT. FH
				INDEPENDENT VARIABLES				
1. GA $	—	—	—	—	—	—	—	—
2. GA TYPE	—	—	—	—	—	—	—	—
3. VAC. RATE	—	—	—	—	—	—	−.019	−.067
4. VLI R/U	—	—	—	—	—	—	.189	−.212
5. POVERTY	—	—	—	—	−.202	.077	.251	.997
6. PCINC	—	—	—	—	.147	−.139	.160	−.217
7. HLRATE	−.122	−.222	.465	.527	—	—	—	—
8. HLRATE	—	—	—	—	.549	−.391	—	—
9. HLRATE	—	—	—	—	—	—	.516	.417
10. HLRATE	—	—	—	—	—	—	—	—
11. HLRATE	—	—	—	—	—	—	—	—
12. HLRATE	−.213	−.045	.330	−.070	.576	−.406	.166	−.326
13. HLRATE	−.123	—	.105	—	.507	−.391	.270	—

Notes: See Notes, Table 9-2.
*An underlined coefficient is significant at p = .10 or better; an underlined R^2 indicates an F significant at p = .05 or better.

176

INDEPENDENT VARIABLES

PCT. 12 YRS+	EMPL/ POPULA	PCT UE	PCT. MFG	PCT. CNS	PCT. RTL	PCT. SRV	CHA# EMP	CHA% EMP	COST/ LIVING	R²	AR²
—	—	—	—	—	—	—	—	—	.575	.330	.320
—	—	—	—	—	—	—	—	—	.578	.334	.324
−.253	.220	.436	.031	.167	.138	.216	.214	−.320	−.430	.520	.416
−.138	−.220	.315	.367	.197	−.051	.248	.051	.296	.437	.465	.349
−.457	−.168	.133	.032	.084	.291	.075	.062	.148	−.071	.831	.786
.564	.223	−.224	−.009	−.020	−.019	.014	.007	−.259	.442	.830	.784
—	—	—	—	—	—	—	—	—	—	.160	.107
—	—	—	—	—	—	—	—	—	—	.093	.065
−.069	—	—	—	—	—	—	—	—	—	.156	.117
—	.259	.281	−.090	−.160	−.403	.236	−.207	.042	—	.315	.222
—	—	—	—	—	—	—	—	—	.326	.106	.093
−.088	.302	.609	.237	−.024	.122	.410	−.090	−.160	.337	.547	.381
—	.293	.693	.175	—	—	.386	—	−.199	.269	.531	.438

INDEPENDENT VARIABLES

PCT. 12 YRS+	EMPL/ POPULA	PCT UE	PCT. MFG	PCT. CNS	PCT. RTL	PCT. SRV	CHA# EMP	CHA% EMP	COST/ LIVING	R²	AR²
—	—	—	—	—	—	—	—	—	.470	.221	.211
—	—	—	—	—	—	—	—	—	.267	.071	.059
.061	.025	.242	−.136	.408	−.119	.004	−.097	.098	−.292	.371	.257
−.563	.450	.210	.083	−.217	.233	.071	−.234	−.102	.665	.456	.357
.290	−.595	−.175	−.107	.045	−.070	−.222	−.029	.380	.022	.886	.861
.048	.878	.067	.178	.140	.096	.257	.030	−.469	.241	.666	.593
—	—	—	—	—	—	—	—	—	—	.197	.153
—	—	—	—	—	—	—	—	—	—	.141	.119
.460	—	—	—	—	—	—	—	—	—	.350	.324
—	.032	.046	−.291	−.188	−.323	.175	−.014	.203	—	.323	.245
—	—	—	—	—	—	—	—	—	.282	.080	.068
.105	.137	.348	−.232	−.173	−.311	−.115	−.035	.126	.058	.546	.410
.318	—	.195	−.274	−.138	−.309	—	—	—	—	.510	.438

Table 9-7 Comparing Antecedents of 1989 Homelessness Rates Across Subgroups of Cities

				INDEPENDENT VARIABLES				
DEPENDENT VARIABLE = HLRATE	VLI RENTERS/ UNITS	VACANCY RATE	PCT. POVERTY	PER CAP. INCOME	GA$	GA TYPE	PCT. ONE	PCT. FH
Proximate Variables Only								
ALL CITIES	.089	−.231	.236	.296	—	—	—	—
HIGH MFG	.100	−.028	−.005	.093	—	—	—	—
LOW MFG	.121	−.349	.367	.345	—	—	—	—
HIGH GROWTH	.217	−.194	−.107	.075	—	—	—	—
LOW GROWTH	−.122	−.222	.465	.527	—	—	—	—
Best Models								
ALL CITIES	−.213	−.118	—	−.119	.569	−.417	.248	−.151
HIGH MFG	.086	—	—	—	.554	−.505	.422	—
LOW MFG	−.228	−.112	—	—	.422	−.195	.234	—
HIGH GROWTH	—	−.601	−.641	−.572	—	−.420	.349	—
LOW GROWTH	−.123	—	.105	—	.507	−.391	.270	—

Notes: See Notes, Table 9–2.
*In the "ALL CITIES" models an underlined coefficient is significant at p = .05 or better; in the subgroup analyses an underlined coefficient is significant at p = .10 or better; an underlined R^2 indicates an F significant at p = .05 or better.

employables as eligibles have lower homelessness rates than those that serve only disabled people and families.

Leaving payment level out of the equation usually reduces the coefficient for GA program type to insignificance, whereas omitting program type merely reduces the size of the coefficient for payment level. These results suggest that payment levels supply the larger effect; the type of GA program has its influence only after payment levels have accounted for their share.

Among household resources variables, which together account for 21.0 percent of the variance in homelessness (row 9), the proportion of one-person households in a city is highly significant. The more one-person households, the higher the homelessness rate. Some one-person households (e.g., people living in SROs) are very vulnerable to homelessness. Given a fixed number of dwelling units, moreover, a larger share occupied by one-person households will mean a tighter housing market; more people will have to fit into the remaining units. Thus even if the one-person households are affluent and not at risk of homelessness, their presence may make others more vulnerable.

Among employment structure variables (row 10), lower proportions of manufacturing, construction, and retail employment are all associated with higher homelessness. Taken by itself, this set of variables accounts for 25.3 percent of the variance in homelessness. In this equation the unemployment

				INDEPENDENT VARIABLES							
PCT. 12 YRS+	EMPL/ POPULA	PCT UE	PCT. MFG	PCT. CNS	PCT. RTL	PCT. SRV	CHA# EMP	CHA% EMP	COST/ LIVING	R²	AR²
—	—	—	—	—	—	—	—	—	—	.130	.106
—	—	—	—	—	—	—	—	—	—	.021	.000
—	—	—	—	—	—	—	—	—	—	.259	.217
—	—	—	—	—	—	—	—	—	—	.160	.107
—	—	—	—	—	—	—	—	—	—	.197	.153
.112	.129	.340	−.196	−.120	−.357	.111	−.133	.161	.119	.461	.390
.264	—	.268	−.180	−.138	—	—	−.237	.378	—	.405	.306
—	.214	.370	—	—	−.368	.150	−.109	—	.164	.611	.544
—	.293	.693	.175	—	—	.386	—	−.199	.269	.531	.438
.318	—	.195	.274	−.138	−.309	—	—	—	—	.510	.438

rate and employment-to-population ratio are not significant. Remarkably, both have positive signs. Here again (as with poverty rates and per capita income) two variables with a negative relationship to each other operate in the same direction in a predictive equation. This anomaly too persists in subsequent analyses and will be discussed in more detail below. Finally, the higher a city's cost of living, the higher its homelessness; cost of living accounts for 8.6 percent of the variance in homelessness rates (row 11).

When all five sets of predictor variables are combined in an equation representing the full model (row 12), together they account for 38.5 percent of the variance in homelessness. The variables representing benefits, percentage of one-person households, and the size of the retail employment sector retain their influence and significance in this equation. Comparison with the partial models in rows 7 through 11 reveals several interesting and important changes, however. The coefficients of the three significant housing and income variables shrink in size and significance, suggesting that their apparent influence on homelessness is actually due to variables earlier (to the right) in the model. Also, the effect of affordable housing shortages becomes significant and *negative*, quite contrary to expectation. Finally, the unemployment rate becomes significant, and the effects of several other factors are reduced in size and significance. The "best" model, presented in row 13, explains 39 percent of the variance while dropping a single variable (the poverty rate) from the full model; the effects of other variables remain essentially what they were in the full model.

Most of the significant factors in the final equation work through other variables before exerting their ultimate influence on homelessness. These intermediate relationships can be seen in the first six rows of Table 9-2. Certain variables that are significant when only their block is included in the regression equation are reduced in the presence of a second, more proximate variable, suggesting that the first variable produces its effect on homelessness *through* the second variable. Cost of living, for example, significantly affects homelessness in the equation reported in row 11. It is also significantly related to both benefits variables (rows 1 and 2). But when the benefits variables and cost of living are all included in the equation for homelessness (rows 12 and 13), cost of living loses its direct impact, while the benefits variables retain their significance.

In a second pattern also clear in Table 9-2, the more proximate variable is significant by itself, but loses its significance in the presence of a second, more antecedent variable. This pattern can be seen in the effects of rental vacancy rates in the presence of the one-person household and unemployment variables. Both the unemployment rate and the proportion of one-person households significantly predict rental vacancy rates (row 3), and rental vacancy rates initially predicted homelessness (row 7). However, when all three variables are in the same equation (rows 12 and 13), the effect of rental vacancies is reduced in size and significance while the effects of unemployment are strengthened. This pattern suggests that the initial association of vacancies and homelessness was spurious in a causal sense, since both appear to be caused by their common antecedents: one-person households and unemployment.

Further analysis indicated that the causal antecedents of homelessness differ considerably among subgroups of cities. Several ways of dividing the sample were explored; the two breakouts ultimately selected were chosen because of the substantive importance of the differentiating variable, and because the subgroups of cities display quite different patterns of antecedents of homelessness.

Tables 9-3 and 9-4 show the results of dividing the original sample of 147 primary cities into two approximately equal groups based on manufacturing's share of 1987 employment (17 percent or more, $N = 71$; less than 17 percent, $N = 76$). In 1987, manufacturing employment ranged from 2.6 percent of employed persons to 42.3 percent. The second break, reported in Tables 9-5 and 9-6, divides the sample on the basis of the cities' 1980–1986 population change (3 percent increase or more, $N = 68$; less than 3 percent, $N = 79$). Population changes during these years ranged from an 11 percent decline to a gain of 47 percent. All but 12 of the 79 low-growth cities experienced population decline or stagnation.

The relationship between the two variables used to create subgroups—

proportion of manufacturing employment and a city's population change—is significant ($r = -.401$, $p < .001$). The chi-squared statistic, which assesses the presence of a nonchance association among categorical variables, is 14.10 ($p = .0002$) for the two-by-two association of high-low manufacturing with high-low growth, with most high-manufacturing cities being low growth and most low-manufacturing cities being high growth. Nevertheless, 30 percent of high-manufacturing cities grew enough during the first half of the 1980s to be categorized in this analysis as high growth, and 31 percent of high-growth cities are categorized as high manufacturing. Among low-manufacturing cities, 37 percent are low growth by the definitions used here, and about 38 percent of low-growth cities are low manufacturing. These differences are enough to make it worthwhile to examine both subgroup breakouts.

Comparing High- and Low-Manufacturing Cities

Overall, our model is less able to explain homelessness rates in high-manufacturing cities than in low-manufacturing cities. The adjusted R^2s shown in the last rows of Tables 9-3 and 9-4 are .306 and .544 respectively. Still, both are respectable levels of prediction for an exploratory endeavor. Because the sample sizes are smaller in analyses of sample subgroups, coefficients in Tables 9-3 through 9-6 are underlined as significant if $p < .10$ rather than the more conventional $p < .05$. Of course, many of the larger coefficients meet and exceed the .05 criterion.

A comparison with Table 9-2 reveals that many of the effects apparent in the full-sample analysis reflect the situation in low- rather than high-manufacturing cities. The housing and income variables are consistently insignificant in high-manufacturing cities, not only as individual coefficients but when taken as a group. In low-manufacturing cities, however, most of these variables are significant when that variable block is alone in the equation, and the shortage of affordable housing is significant even in the final models. The cost of living variable (by itself) exerts a significant influence only in low-manufacturing cities, where it retains a marginal influence even in the full model.

Unemployment levels are important in the final equations for both subgroups, but the employment-to-population ratio is significant only in low-manufacturing cities. There its association with homelessness is positive, as is the effect of unemployment rates. This pattern, also found in the all-cities analysis, suggests cities in which households with more potential workers are sending them to work, while other households are experiencing unemployment and its effects. Manufacturing and construction employment are important in high- but not in low-manufacturing cities. In cities with high proportions of manufacturing, it appears that more construction employment contributes to higher vacancy rates (more available housing), and that both construction and manufacturing employment contribute to reducing the shortage of affordable housing. Probably, construction employment's effect is due partly to its impact on supply, while both variables may exercise influence by increasing people's ability to pay for housing, since wage rates are generally higher in these sectors.

The differences between the predictive equations in Tables 9-3 and 9-4 suggest two potentially quite different ways in which homelessness may grow. One is the situation of a generally depressed economy, as in many cities that were once heavily dependent on manufacturing. In these cities, growth in employment (CHA % EMP) is actually associated with higher poverty and lower per capita incomes; its association with more severe shortages in affordable housing probably operates by reducing ability to pay (see Table 9-3). Strong effects of unemployment and of (un)availability of benefits add to the picture.

The second pattern might be described as a squeeze situation, which appears to be more characteristic of low-manufacturing cities. In these cities, it seems, many people are doing well, but their less successful neighbors are getting squeezed out of housing. This interpretation is supported by the positive associations between homelessness and both poverty rate and per capita income, both unemployment rate and the employment-to-population ratio, and the cost of living variable. A higher employment-to-population ratio (whose calculation is restricted to those sixteen and older) suggests that households with additional potential workers are sending them into the work force, thereby raising the household's per capita income and standard of living. Households that cannot send any more workers into the labor force, which might include a high proportion of poor households and those relying on fixed incomes or public benefits, may find themselves falling further and further behind. As the cost of living is pushed ever upward by city residents who are participating in the economy, those who cannot do so or cannot increase their effort may become increasingly at risk for homelessness. The ability of most households to cover housing costs may not help those whose incomes are not rising, even though these latter households may not be a large proportion of the population. The surprising *negative* effect of the affordable housing shortage variable (ratio of very-low-income renters to units they can afford) in low-manufacturing cities may reflect a situation in which most households can afford the housing available, but the people most at risk of homelessness increasingly cannot do so.

Comparing High- and Low-Growth Cities

As Tables 9-5 and 9-6 show, our model's ability to predict homelessness is about equal in high-growth and low-growth cities, with an adjusted R^2 of .438 in both subgroups. Patterns of association in the two groups are very different, however. In high-growth cities, rental vacancy rates have a strong effect on homelessness, suggesting a pattern very similar to the squeeze situation just described for low-manufacturing cities. The low-growth cities, on the other hand, seem closer to the depressed economy of the high-manufacturing subgroup, characterized by unemployment and poverty. In these low-growth cities, the association of homelessness with lower levels of manufacturing, construction, and retail employment also suggests a depressed economy.

Among the four subgroup analyses, the high-growth cities present the most anomalies and unexpected associations. Especially striking is the strong negative association of both poverty and per capita income with homelessness, and the fact that these variables become significant only in the full equation, which includes all the remaining variables in the model (row 12). Neither is significant or sizable in the first homeless equation (row 7), where the housing and income variables act alone. No additional variable or group of variables by itself can bring out these effects of poverty and per capita income; at least one variable in each other block must be present. The variables most influential in revealing the negative effects of poverty and per capita income are the household resources variables, unemployment, and the employment-to-population ratio.

Some idea of the dynamics of homelessness in these cities may be gleaned from the negative effects of both poverty and per capita income on homelessness, coupled with cost of living in these high-growth cities. Perhaps in these cities only a small proportion of the population falls below the official poverty line, but many low-income households have difficulty maintaining housing because of the high cost of living. And perhaps in cities with quite low poverty rates, the poor have little or no political clout, and their needs are more easily ignored. The squeeze situation created by the general prosperity of the city would leave these few poor and near-poor households with inadequate resources and little recourse, and thus a greater risk of homelessness.

To facilitate comparisons across subgroups, Table 9-7 displays two equations from each analysis: the effects on homelessness of the housing and income (proximate) variables acting alone, and the "best" model for each breakout. The top panel suggests that the effects of vacancy rates, poverty rates, and per capita income noted in the all-cities analysis derive predominantly from the low-manufacturing and low-growth subgroups. The subgroup effects of affordable housing shortages appear largely to cancel each other when subgroups are combined in the all-cities analysis.

The picture changes considerably, however, when the remaining variables are added to the model. Except in high-growth cities, the effects of vacancy rate, poverty rate, and per capita income largely disappear in the presence of the household resources and employment variables. The striking negative associations between poverty rates and per capita income and homelessness in high-growth cities have already been discussed. Another important change is the disappearance of the positive association between affordable housing shortages and homelessness noted in low-manufacturing and high-growth cities when only proximate variables were included in the equation. These two subgroup changes together produce a significant negative association of affordable housing shortages to homelessness in the all-cities analysis.

Why does the effect of proximate variables seem to change once the remaining variables are included in the equation? A careful interpretation is needed, rather than a quick conclusion that affordable housing shortages, poverty, and the other proximate variables are not "really" associated with homelessness.

A more judicious reading of the results might be as follows. Greater homelessness does seem to be associated with lower vacancy rates, higher poverty rates, and higher per capita income in low-manufacturing and low-growth cities, and with relatively extreme shortages of affordable housing in high-growth cities. In all but high-manufacturing cities (where they have no effect), these proximate variables explain between 11 and 22 percent of the variance in 1989 homelessness rates. However, much of this effect is actually due to the antecedent variables, working through the proximate variables, as the full equations reveal. Thus the proximate variables are important indicators of homelessness, but often are not causal in the context of this model.

The proportion of one-person households and the unemployment rate have consistently positive and significant effects in the best models shown in the second panel of Table 9-7. Even if these one-person households consist of elderly persons and young professionals, their presence appears to be strongly related to affordable housing shortages and to homelessness. By occupying units that might house more people, they contribute to tightening the housing market. In addition, some of these households, such as SRO residents, may be individually vulnerable to homelessness.

The unemployment and financial hardship experienced by many households during the recession of 1981–1982 occasioned the first public concern with homelessness as a social issue for the 1980s. Our best equations show that unemployment remains a significant factor contributing to homelessness in every subgroup examined. It is most important in high-growth cities, but its influence is felt everywhere.

Policymakers cannot do much to affect the proportion of one-person households, but they can influence levels of unemployment. More important for helping the unemployed overcome short-term crises, policymakers can create or enhance programs that temper the shocks of the transition period until new jobs can be secured. Unfortunately public policies have moved in the opposite direction during the 1980s, as we saw in Chapter 5. One result of this retrenchment in unemployment benefits and coverage may be to increase homelessness among people with work histories who would have been protected in previous decades.

The results of the final models suggest that short-term policy efforts to alleviate homelessness might best be directed toward protecting the poor and near-poor from the effects of both generally depressed economies and economic squeeze. Appropriate mechanisms include relieving the immediate impact of unemployment through improved benefits and coverage, providing General Assistance benefits to single employables, and raising assistance levels to match local costs of living. Long-term policy attention should be directed toward improving the ability of the disadvantaged to earn enough to achieve a decent standard of living. This effort will involve both improving their human capital (including the human capital of displaced workers) and developing and making accessible the types of jobs that pay a living wage.

Plotting the Results

Our regression results can be used to calculate how much of a difference in homelessness rates would result from a change in each predictor variable. Figure 9-2, based on the all-cities analysis, shows graphically the effect of varying the proportion of one-person households, unemployment and vacancy rates, manufacturing's share of employment, and cost of living. Changes in the independent variable are measured as percentage increases or decreases from the mean value in our data set.[8]

The most dramatic changes come from varying the proportion of one-person households, closely followed by the cost of living and the unemployment rate. A 5 percent difference between cities in the proportion of one-person households (e.g., from its mean of 27.6 to 29.0) predicts a 4 percent shift in homelessness, the equivalent of 0.73 more or fewer homeless persons per 10,000 city population. A 5 percent difference in the local cost of living has approximately the same effect (a shift of 3.8 percent). Likewise a 5 percent difference in city unemployment rates (equivalent to adding or subtracting .293 to the 5.86 mean unemployment rate for these cities) predicts a 3 percent difference in homelessness. Other variables have more modest effects. A 5 percent difference in either the rental vacancy rate or the proportion employed

---

[8]For variables with low mean values such as the unemployment rate (5.86) and the rental vacancy rate (9.06), a 5 percent difference is quite small (.293 and .453, respectively). For variables with higher mean values, such as the percentage of one-person households (mean of 27.6), a 5 percent difference is larger (1.38). Yet the meaning of a 5 percent difference is the same in both cases; thus we can compare the size of the effects of each variable in graphic form, using a more intuitively comprehensible metric than a standardized regression coefficient.

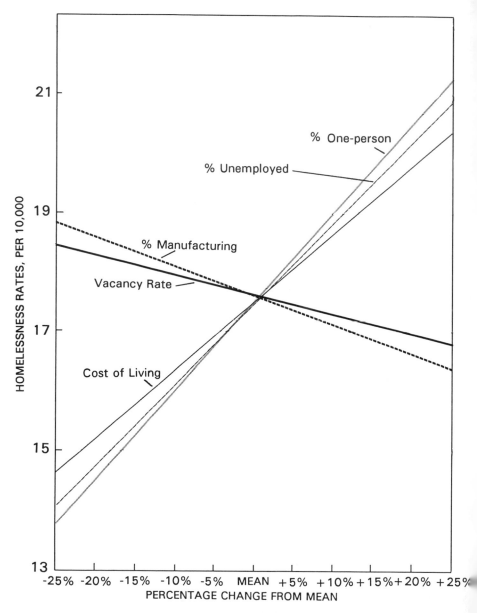

Figure 9-2 Predictors of 1989 Homelessness Rates: All Cities (N = 147)

in the manufacturing sector produces a 1 percent difference in the homelessness rate.

The next group of figures illustrate subgroup differences on four important predictor variables: the proportion of one-person households (Figure 9-3), the unemployment rate (Figure 9-4), manufacturing's share of employment (Figure 9-5), and the rental vacancy rate (Figure 9-6). In each figure, curves for the four subgroups show how their homelessness rates vary as the independent variable ranges from 25 percent below to 25 percent above its mean value. The slope of each line indicates the degree to which the predictor variable influences homelessness in that subgroup.

In Figure 9-3, for example, the lines for high- and low-growth cities have quite similar slopes, indicating that one-person households have similar effects in the two subgroups. The slopes of the lines for high- and low-manufacturing cities are much more different from one another, since (as Table 9-7 indicates) the proportion of one-person households has its strongest effect (steepest slope) in high-manufacturing cities.

Figure 9-4 makes it clear that unemployment influences homelessness somewhat more in high-growth and low-manufacturing cities than it does in low-growth or high-manufacturing cities. Evidently the slope of the unemployment effect displayed in the all-cities analysis (Figure 9-2) derives primarily from high-growth and low-manufacturing cities.

Figures 9-5 and 9-6 show the effects of manufacturing employment and rental vacancy rates for those subgroups for which these variables remained in the final equations. For high-manufacturing and low-growth cities, higher proportions of employment in the manufacturing sector produce lower homelessness rates. The opposite is true for high-growth cities. This reversal of effect poses a difficulty of interpretation that is probably due to the nature of the data available. The employment sector variables do not indicate the levels of employment in the city itself; they also cover the surrounding county. The counties of many high-growth cities have experienced considerable growth in their manufacturing sectors during the 1980s. But that growth has often occurred in the suburbs, far from the inner city populations most in need of well-paying jobs and most at risk of homelessness (Suro, 1991). Thus it is possible for a county to have a growing manufacturing sector that does not benefit inner city residents, and in fact may increase their vulnerability to homelessness by channeling employment growth in ways that reduce their access to good jobs.

The tightness of the rental housing market also contributes to homelessness in some subgroups. On average, high-growth cities have looser rental housing markets than do low-growth cities (vacancy rates of 10.78 percent versus 7.59 percent, $F = 33.38$, $p < .0004$). But in high-growth cities, Figure 9-6 shows, small variations in vacancy rates have dramatic effects on

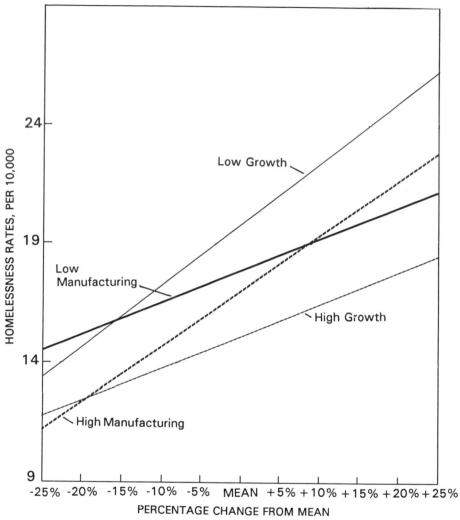

Figure 9-3 Effects of One-Person Households for All Subgroups

homelessness. These effects are much less pronounced in low-manufacturing cities, while vacancy rates do not even appear in the final equations for low-growth or high-manufacturing cities.

Predicting Change in Homelessness Rates

The final analyses of this chapter examine which factors predict the growth in homelessness during the 1980s, as measured by the difference between a

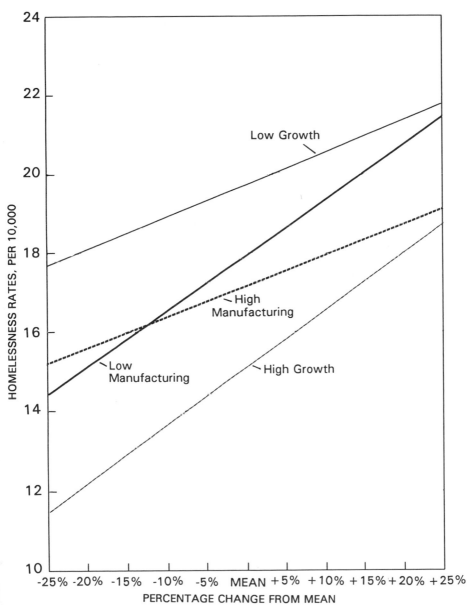

Figure 9-4 Effects of Unemployment Rate for All Subgroups

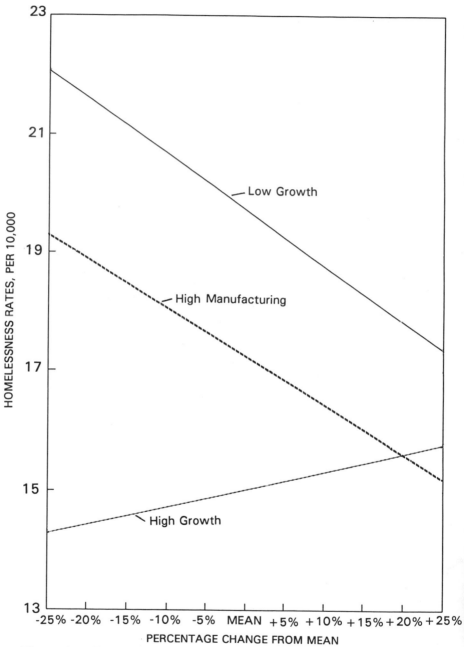

Figure 9-5 Effects of Manufacturing Employment: Selected Subgroups

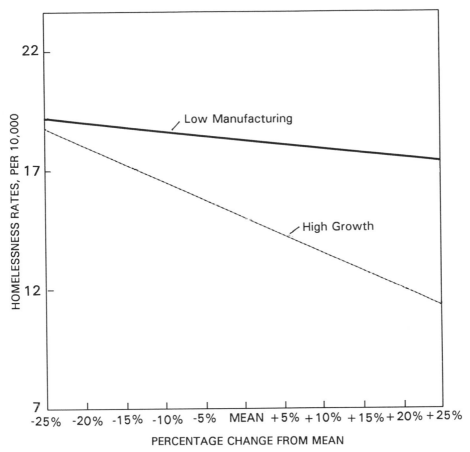

Figure 9-6 Effects of Vacancy Rates: Selected Subgroups

city's 1989 and 1981 homelessness rates (Table 9-8). The tables and figures discussed so far used the latest data available to predict *between*-city levels of 1989 homelessness. In contrast, these change analyses focus on the growth of homelessness *within* each city during the 1980s. The first step is to test the effect of the base condition in a city, using readings on all variables from 1980 or 1981 (1979 in the case of per capita income). The results of these analyses, for the entire sample and the four subgroups, are shown on the left side of Table 9-8. Thereafter variables are added representing the change in critical factors over the decade (right side of Table 9-8). In most analyses, the initial conditions explain a considerable amount of the variance in growth of homelessness. In all but high-manufacturing cities, the change in conditions over the decade also contributes to understanding the growth of homelessness.

Table 9-8 Predictors of 1981-1989 Growth in Homelessness

Break = N =	Base Conditions				
	All Cities (147)	High Manufacturing (71)	Low Manufacturing (76)	High Growth (68)	Low Growth (79)
Predictor Variables					
VLI R/U-85	−.060	.311	−.084	—	−.095
VAC. RATE-80	—	.186	—	—	−.047
% POV-80	.156	−.165	—	.181	.259
PCINC-79	—	—	—	.126	—
GA$-81	.113	—	.033	—	.040
GA TYPE	−.150	—	—	—	−.083
% ONE-80	—	.474	.159	.176	—
% FH-80	−.374	.258	—	−.327	−.484
% 12 + YRS-80	—	.230	—	—	—
E/P-80	—	−.183	.125	.305	—
UE-80	.273	—	.262	.662	.147
% MFG-80	−.216	—	−.158	−.240	−.461
% CNS-80	−.195	—	−.180	−.147	−.373
% RTL-80	−.354	—	−.290	−.286	−.287
% SRV-80	.238	—	—	—	—
COST/LIVING	.348	—	.390	—	.412
CITY POP-80	—	−.246	—	—	—
# EMP-80	—	—	—	—	—
POP CHG 70-80	—	.304	—	—	—
CHG VAC RATE	—	—	—	—	—
CHG P.C. INC	—	—	—	—	—
CHG GA $	—	—	—	—	—
CHG E/P	—	—	—	—	—
CHG UE	—	—	—	—	—
CHG MFG	—	—	—	—	—
CHG CNS	—	—	—	—	—
CHG RTL	—	—	—	—	—
CHG SRV	—	—	—	—	—
CHG # EMP	—	—	—	—	—
CHG % EMP	—	—	—	—	—
POP CHG 80-86	—	—	—	—	—
R^2	.414	.387	.591	.440	.470
AR^2	.366	.159	.535	.353	.382

Notes: VLI R/U-85 = ratio of very-low-income renters to units they can afford, 1985; VAC RATE-80 = 1980 rental vacancy rate; % POV-80 = % individuals below poverty line, 1980; P.C. INC-79 = per capita income, 1979; GA $-81 = maximum GA payment for one person living independently, 1981; GA TYPE = none/disabled only/also employables; % ONE-80 = % one-person households, 1980; % FH-80 = % female-headed households, 1980; % 12+ YRS-80 = % with 12 + yrs. education, 1980; E/P-80 = employment/population ratio, 1980; UE-80 = unemployment rate, 1980; % MFG-80 = % of employment in manufacturing, 1980; % CNS-80 = % of employment in construction, 1980; % RTL-80 = % of employment in retail, 1980; % SRV-80 = % of employment in services, 1980; COST/LIVING = cost of living; CITY POP-80 = 1980 city population; # EMP-80 = number of people employed in the county, 1980; POP CHG 70-80 = 1970-1980 change in city population; CHG VAC. RATE = 1980-1988

Base Conditions and Change Variables				
All Cities (147)	High Manufacturing (71)	Low Manufacturing (76)	High Growth (68)	Low Growth (79)
−.105	.271	−.195	—	−.230
—	.187	—	—	−.150
.194	−.286	—	.397	.361
—	—	—	.333	—
.310	—	.138	—	.236
−.281	—	—	—	−.236
—	.487	.134	.153	—
−.434	.379	—	−.368	−.665
—	.338	—	—	—
—	−.360	.290	.364	—
.454	—	.705	.965	.336
−.377	—	−.151	−.327	−.633
.239	—	−.183	−.328	−.412
−.412	—	−.242	−.281	−.337
.166	—	—	—	—
.272	—	.451	—	.362
—	−.179	—	—	—
—	—	—	—	—
—	.262	—	—	—
−.139	—	—	—	−.160
—	—	—	—	—
.256	.286	.217	—	.362
—	—	.453	.518	—
.273	.160	.474	.460	.248
.168	—	.457	.415	—
−.085	—	—	−.170	—
—	—	—	.364	—
.160	—	—	—	.190
—	—	—	—	—
—	—	—	—	—
−.269	.108	−.666	—	−.311
.498	.397	.686	.588	.605
.428	.272	.614	.470	.502

change in rental vacancy rate; CHG P.C. INC = 1979-1985 change in per capita income; CHG GA $ = 1981-1989 change in GA $; CHG E/P = 1980-1989 change in E/P; CHG UE = 1980-1989 change in UE; CHG MFG = 1980-1987 change in MFG as percent of 1980 MFG; CHG CNS = 1980-1987 change in CNS as percent of 1980 CNS; CHG RTL = 1980-1987 change in RTL as percent of 1980 RTL; CHG SRV = 1980-1987 change in SRV as percent of 1980 SRV; CHG # EMP = change in the number of people employed in the city between 1980 and 1989; CHG % EMP = change in employment between 1980 and 1989, as a percent of 1980 employment; POP CHG 80-86 = 1980-1986 change in city population.

*In the "ALL CITIES" models an underlined coefficient is significant at p < .05; in the subgroup analyses an underlined coefficient is significant at p < .10. An underlined R^2 indicates an F significant at p < .05.

As in the between-cities analyses, changes in homelessness in high-manufacturing cities prove most difficult to explain within our model. The adjusted R^2s in the last row of Table 9-8 indicate that, with the exception of high-manufacturing cities, 1980 conditions explained between 35 and 54 percent of the within-city growth in homelessness over the 1980s. In high-manufacturing cities these early conditions could explain only 16 percent of the variance. Including the change variables adds between 8 and 15 percent more explanatory power to the models, again with the exception of high-manufacturing cities.

Leaving aside the high-manufacturing cities for the moment, the models for the remaining subgroups and for the all-cities analysis indicate considerable consistency of effects. Lower 1980 levels of manufacturing, construction, and retail employment consistently predict greater growth in homelessness. So do 1980 unemployment levels and 1981–1989 increases in unemployment. Other variables are consistent where they remain in the model (which is not the case in all subgroups). The higher the 1980 poverty rate, the level of General Assistance payments in 1981, the increase in those payments by 1989, the cost of living, the change in the employment-to-population ratio, or the change in manufacturing employment, the greater the growth of homelessness. In addition, three variables are consistently associated with slower growth of homelessness in the 1980s: shortages of affordable housing, the proportion of female-headed households, and greater population growth between 1980 and 1986.

In high-manufacturing cities, on the other hand, the direction of many of these effects appears to be reversed. In addition, the proportion of one-person households plays a much more significant role in the growth of homelessness in this subgroup than in any other. Among these high-manufacturing cities, those that were still relatively small in 1980 but had experienced population growth in the 1970s appear vulnerable to the growth of homelessness. The results in high-manufacturing cities suggest cities where higher one-person occupancy rates and a lower employment-to-population ratio make housing less affordable. These are the only cities where the variable assessing the shortfall in affordable housing retains a positive association with homelessness. The simultaneous positive effect of female-headed households suggests that if these cities have many nonworking female householders, relatively small poverty populations, and growing general populations, it may be increasingly difficult for the poor to afford the available housing.

Taken as a whole, these change analyses suggest that a depressed economy with higher unemployment, coupled with higher living costs and more poverty, contributed to the growth in homelessness within individual cities during the 1980s.

SUMMARY AND IMPLICATIONS

The analyses presented in this chapter demonstrate that the predictive model developed in Chapter 1 can explain much of the variance in between-city homelessness rates and within-city changes in homelessness rates between 1981 and 1989. The most important variables in the model that tended to increase homelessness were:

- the unemployment rate and the employment structure faced by city residents;
- the city's population change (loss, stagnation, or growth), which is also a reflection of its economic fortunes;
- the city's proportion of one-person households;
- the absence of General Assistance;
- the cost of living for city residents;
- the failure of public benefit payment levels to keep up with the cost of living.

We also saw that, contrary to expectation, higher levels of public benefit payments were associated with higher rates of homelessness, and that poverty rates were largely ineffective in explaining between-city differences in homelessness rates. Further, the important factors accounted for considerably more of the variance in cities with low rather than high proportions of manufacturing employment. The division of the sample that produced the best level of explanation for both subgroups was based on population growth rates.

Before this research was undertaken, most of the factors in this model had already been suggested as causes of homelessness because they had changed for the country as a whole at the same time that homelessness increased. (The importance of one-person households is new to this analysis.) But this effort was the first to demonstrate how much each variable affected levels of homelessness in a multicity analysis based on a consistent method of determining homelessness rates across cities.

Another important finding is that homelessness may result from quite different urban conditions. Thus even cities with relatively favorable housing conditions and employment structures nevertheless had a homeless population, as a result of a squeeze situation in which the prosperity of the many hurt the welfare of the few. Because the range of factors contributing to the production of homelessness is so broad, policymakers have an equally broad range of potential avenues to ameliorate the problem. Even if we are not likely to achieve significant economic restructuring in the near future, we can do something about benefit levels in relation to the cost of living and housing subsidies. And we can make a greater effort to improve the human capital of those most vulnerable to homelessness.

Unfortunately, even a structural model such as the one analyzed here can go only so far toward illuminating causality, especially when cities, rather than individuals or households, are the unit of analysis. It is a matter of interpretation to decide which of the associations described in this chapter probably bear a causal relationship to homelessness rates, which may be reliable indicators of homelessness levels but could not be considered causal, and which are most likely artifacts of the analysis.

I believe that the effects of unemployment on homelessness are causal, as are the effects associated with the structure of a city's employment opportunities. Local economies dominated by low-paying service jobs have higher homelessness rates as a result, and shifts of a local economy toward services and away from manufacturing promote increased homelessness. These results underscore the link between homelessness and the quality of available jobs, as well as the ability of those searching for work to find any work at all.

I think it is also reasonable to conclude that higher living costs and a squeeze on poor and/or nonworking households affected homelessness levels later in the 1980s, and influenced the growth of homelessness throughout the decade in high-growth and low-manufacturing cities. By "squeeze" I mean that conditions in a city may be stable or improving for people with jobs and/or skills. But these very improvements may put more pressure on the housing market, forcing poorer or nonworking households to pay increasing proportions of their incomes for housing and perhaps exceeding the ability of some to cover these expenses. Evidence for this squeeze can be seen in the subgroup analyses for high-growth and low-manufacturing cities. A higher cost of living also predicted more homelessness in both the between-cities and within-cities comparisons.

The squeeze could not be countered by higher initial levels of public benefits, by increases in these benefits as the decade progressed, or by increases in the number of public housing units available per capita (a result not shown in the tables of this chapter). In short, compensatory mechanisms have failed to enable very poor people to maintain a viable position in the housing market. I interpret the positive association of public benefit levels and homelessness rates as an artifact of their common relationship to the cost of living.

Further, certain aspects of a city's housing market appear to be strongly associated with homelessness. Even so crude a measure as *statewide* shortages of affordable housing (VLI RENTERS/UNITS) showed a positive association with homelessness rates from 1983 onward. The mean homelessness rate for cities with two or more very-low-income renters per affordable unit was 20.59 per 10,000 population compared with a rate of 15.44 for cities with less severe shortages; the difference is highly significant ($F = 8.12$, $p = .005$). In addition, tighter rental housing markets were associated with higher homelessness and with increases in homelessness rates over the decade. However, these initial effects were substantially reduced by the inclusion of more antecedent variables in the predictive models. The antecedent variables provided some explanation of the reasons for housing unaffordability (less money, higher costs, or both).

Population change patterns appear to reflect the economic environment of the city, which probably influences both population shifts and homelessness. Low-growth cities have lost population because they have lost jobs, either to their own suburbs or to other parts of the country. As with the structure of the labor market, the influence of population growth suggests that a city's economic ill health will affect homelessness.

The proportion of one-person households may be either an indicator of homelessness or a direct cause. (As a social indicator, this variable is the best single predictor of homelessness rates, whether or not it has causal influence.) At the very least, a high proportion of single-person households in a city places a greater strain on existing housing resources than would higher-density occupancy of units, simply because more units are required to house the same number of people. As single people, perhaps with more money to spend, compete for housing with poorer families, the pressure on the housing market may lead to higher prices, reduced availability, and some consequent homelessness.

High rates of one-person households may also indicate a relatively high proportion of people with disabilities such as mental illness or physical handicap, who live in single-room-occupancy accommodations or the like. (The Census Bureau counts an SRO occupant as a one-person household.) Not only are such persons vulnerable to homelessness because of their limited resources, but the destruction or conversion of SROs may push them directly into homelessness. Such a change is clearly documented in Lee's (1989) counts of Nashville's homeless population before and after the destruction of the city's last three downtown SRO hotels in the mid-1980s; the same has probably happened in other cities as well.

Even if most one-person households consist of elderly persons or young professionals, this demographic distribution may indicate a city with a relatively isolated population; people who have few family ties or sources of support in times of trouble may be at higher risk of homelessness. There are thus a number of mechanisms through which a high rate of one-person households might have a causal influence on a city's homelessness rate.

The relatively mild or even negative effects of city poverty rates are puzzling, for it is clear that virtually all homeless people are very poor and were so before becoming homeless. These findings are reminiscent of our experience with the sampling and weighting process for the Urban Institute's national study of homelessness (Burt and Cohen, 1988). As part of that study, described in Chapter 2, we sampled cities in proportion to the size of their poverty population. This procedure was expected to reduce error variance in the population estimates because poverty was assumed to be related to homelessness. In fact the precision of our estimates was not improved by this procedure. Elliott and Krivo (1991) also find no effects of poverty rates in their analysis of factors affecting homelessness in cities included in the Department of Housing and Urban Development's 1984 study (HUD, 1984).

The pattern of nonintuitive effects suggests a need to rethink the relationship of poverty to homelessness. In the discussion to follow, the reader should remember two things. First, a vulnerable population need not increase in size in order for more of its members to become homeless. As we saw in Chapter 6 when looking at the situation for people with chronic mental illness or alcoholism, the population of people with these conditions in the country was stable or declining at the same time that more of them became homeless because of changes in other conditions that put pressure on their incomes and housing costs. Thus an increase in the number or proportion of poor people in the country does not *necessarily* mean that there will be more homelessness.

Second, our findings show a strong association between the proportion of a city's population that is poor (living in a household with income below the federal poverty line for a household of its size) and the proportion of a city's rental units with rents below $150 in 1980. In the full sample of 182 cities over 100,000, that correlation was .702. Even among the 147 primary cities, eliminating the suburbs (which had the lowest proportions of cheap housing), the correlation was .598. The implication is that many poor people live in cities that have a good deal of cheap housing. Further, many of the cities with very high poverty rates are in the South, which also has many more cities with only moderate low-cost housing shortages, and more cities in which the cost of living is lower. If half the city is poor and more than half the housing is cheap, even very high poverty rates would not be expected to lead to high homelessness rates. This characterization is accurate for at least some of the cities in the present sample.

The trouble begins when very poor people live in cities with very high living costs, and cannot earn enough or receive enough in benefits to cover expenses. In this sense poverty represents a vulnerability, a lower likelihood of being able to cope when the pressure gets too great. It thus resembles serious mental illness, physical handicaps, chemical dependency, or any other vulnerability that reduces one's resilience, and the resilience of one's family and friends. One would be reluctant to say that mental illness *causes* homelessness, but being mentally ill may well increase the probability that homelessness will result if the person faces a severe crisis. As noted earlier, there was no increase in the rate of serious mental illness in this country in the 1980s, yet a larger proportion of mentally ill persons are now homeless. This is the way I now think of poverty in relation to homelessness. Higher poverty rates certainly make more people vulnerable to homelessness. But without the structural pressures of poor-quality jobs, high living costs, pressure from the middle class, and tight housing markets, they would not be homeless. Even without any growth in poverty, increases in these contributing risk factors could easily make more poor people homeless. I think that is what happened in the 1980s.

CHAPTER TEN

Getting the Best Predictions

■   In Chapter 9 the task was to understand the causes and antecedents of homelessness in the 1980s, using a complex theoretical model. Consequently we included only variables with potential causal influence, and tested the same model for all cities and for several subgroup breaks. Although a slightly different model, or a different selection of variables to represent components of the model, might have resulted in somewhat higher overall levels of explanation (R^2s and AR^2s), the goal of examining causation made it important to maintain the consistency of the model throughout the analysis.

Policymakers also have an interest in developing the best possible predictive model of homelessness. In this endeavor it is less important to understand completely why a variable is highly related to homelessness than it is to recognize and quantify the association.

If a particular statistic is to be useful as a predictor, the necessary data should be relatively easy to find—for example, through routinely generated data sources, usually prepared by the government. The policymaker who must forecast future needs or distribute resources equitably cannot usually afford to collect original data.

Since virtually all of the data used in this study are available from public sources, they lend themselves to treatment as social indicators. This chapter explores the most useful combinations of variables for predicting levels of homelessness and changes in rates, without trying to understand why the variables act as they do. First, I present the combinations of variables that produce the highest adjusted R^2 in 1989 homelessness rates or in change in rates, for all cities and for each subgroup of cities (high- and low-manufacturing and high- and low-growth).

Also presented are the first four variables selected in the stepwise regression analyses that produced these "best prediction" equations.[1] These are the variables that account for the largest proportions of the explained variance in homelessness rates (or in changes in rates). For an analyst who wishes to use only a few variables to make predictions, these first few variables selected by the stepwise procedures will be the best choice.

ACCOUNTING FOR HOMELESSNESS RATES

Stepwise regression techniques were used to develop the maximum explanatory power for 1989 homelessness rates. To identify the best predictors of current rates, one would presumably want to use data that represented approximately the same point in time. However, one might also include variables representing the recent past, or recent changes, to see whether earlier conditions or changed conditions also contribute to prediction. Our data set (described in Chapter 8) contains each of these types of variable:

1. Variables representing the later years of the 1980s (usually 1987–1989). Examples include: 1988 rental vacancy rate; General Assistance $ for 1989; per capita alcohol and other drug abuse spending for 1988. Fifteen variables from this group were included in the analysis.
2. Variables representing changes in conditions during the decade. Examples include: 1980–1988 change in the rental vacancy rate; population change between 1980 and 1986; 1980–1989 change in the unemployment rate; 1980–1987 change in the proportion of employment in the services sector. Twenty variables from this group were included in the analysis.
3. Variables representing the earlier years of the 1980s (usually 1980). Examples include: 1980 percentage of one-person households; 1980 percentage of female-headed households; 1980 proportion of a city's dwelling units that were in buildings with five or more units; 1980 percentage of a city's rental stock with rents under $150. Nineteen variables from this group were included in the analysis.

Stepwise regression analyses were conducted using all fifty-four variables, for the entire sample of 147 cities and for each subgroup of interest (high- and low-manufacturing cities, and high- and low-growth cities). As Table 10-1

---

[1]Stepwise regression selects first the variable that can account for the most variance in the dependent variable; selects second the variable that can account for the most of the variance remaining; and so on.

Table 10-1 Accounting for the Most Variance in 1989 Homelessness Rates

	All Cities	High Manufacturing	Low Manufacturing	High Growth	Low Growth
Later Variables					
VLI R/U-85	−.218	—	—	−.325	−.237
VAC. RATE-88	—	—	—	−.332	—
P.C. INC-85	—	—	—	−.824	—
GA $-89	.654	.995	—	—	.633
GA TYPE	−.384	−.515	—	−.300	−.330
P.C. AODA $-88	.293	—	.321	—	.468
P.C. MH $-87	−.232	−.519	—	—	−.453
E/P-89	.287	.156	.163	.539	—
UE-89	.250	.270	—	.996	.248
HILOMFG-87	—	—	—	.149	−.236
% CNS-87	—	—	−.192	—	—
% RTL-87	−.203	.165	−.430	—	−.244
% SRV-87	.122	—	—	.433	—
FMR-89	—	—	.286	.336	—
COST/LIVING	.230	—	—	—	.314
Change Variables					
CHG AVG $	—	—	—	—	.145
CHG VAC. RATE	—	—	—	−.304	—
GROWTH 80-86	—	.194	−.246	—	—
CHG GA $	—	—	—	.146	—
CHG AFDC $	—	—	−.175	—	—
CHG E/P	—	—	—	—	.312
CHG UE	—	—	.369	−.355	—
CHG MFG	.229	—	.338	—	—
CHG CNS	—	—	−.218	—	—
CHG SRV	—	.216	—	.507	—
CHG WHL	−.217	−.220	—	—	−.228
CHG TCU	−.127	—	—	−.223	−.179
CHG FIRE	—	—	—	.142	—
CHG # EMP	−.104	−.270	—	—	—
CHG % EMP	—	—	—	−.737	—
Early Variables					
PCT. POV-80	—	—	—	−.757	—
PCT. ONE-80	.254	.548	—	.503	.249
% 12 + YRS-80	—	—	—	—	.328
% LOW RENT-80	.277	—	.221	—	.400
% CRAFT-80	—	−.197	—	—	—
UE-80	—	—	.252	—	—
% CNS-80	—	—	—	—	−.213
% SRV-80	—	—	—	—	−.230
R^2	.556	.572	.696	.697	.717
AR^2	.501	.483	.639	.585	.632
Chapter 9- Best Models					
R^2	.461	.405	.611	.531	.510
AR^2	.390	.306	.544	.438	.438

Note: a coefficient is underlined if $p < .05$.

shows, thirty-eight of the fifty-four variables were included in at least one of the five analyses.[2]

The Full Models

Table 10-1 presents the results of stepwise regression procedures to determine the set of variables that best predicts 1989 homelessness rates for all cities and for each subgroup. The variables are presented in three groups (late 1980s, change variables, and early 1980s). At the bottom of the table appear the R^2s and AR^2s showing the proportions of variance accounted for in each analysis by the selected variables. For comparison, the last two rows of the table also give the R^2s and AR^2s for all cities and subgroups that resulted from the final models in Chapter 9. The equations in Table 10-1 improve considerably on the Chapter 9 models, explaining 9 to 20 percent more of the variance, depending on the model. This is true both for the R^2s (before adjustment for degrees of freedom) and for the AR^2s. On an adjusted basis, the models of Table 10-1 explain between 48 and 63 percent of the variance in homelessness rates. This level of explanation is substantial enough to warrant use in many policy contexts.

The variables that had the most consistent effects in the causal analyses of Chapter 9 are also important in these best-prediction equations. These variables include the 1989 unemployment rate and employment-to-population ratio, the proportion of one-person households, and the type of General Assistance available to city residents.

Some of the variables included in the equations in Table 10-1 will not be familiar from the analyses in Chapter 9. HI-LO MFG-87 and GROWTH-80-86 are the variables used to split the sample into high and low-manufacturing cities, and high- and low-growth cities. Accordingly, HI-LO MFG-87 is not included in the analyses for high- and low-manufacturing cities, and GROWTH-80-86 is not included in the analyses for high- and low-growth cities. But as Table 10-1 shows, the proportion of employment in manufacturing plays a role in predicting homelessness levels in the analyses for high- and low-growth cities, and vice versa. Apparently in low-manufacturing cities, more rapid growth reduces homelessness, and in low-growth cities, more manufacturing

---

[2]Variables included in the regression procedures that were not selected for any of the five analyses were: employment-to-population ratio, 1980; percentage manufacturing and retail employment, 1980; General Assistance payment levels, 1981; per capita income, 1979; rental vacancy rates, 1980; percentage employed as professional specialty or technical workers, 1980; 1980 city population; percentage of female-headed households, 1980; percentage of dwelling units in buildings with five or more units, 1980; percentage ownership housing, 1980; 1979–1985 inflation-adjusted change in per capita income; 1980–1989 inflation-adjusted change in median renter income; 1980–1989 inflation-adjusted change in FMR for two-bedroom apartment; 1980–1987 growth in employment in the county as proportion of 1980 employment; 1980–1987 increase in number employed in county; and 1980–1987 change in employment in the retail sector.

reduces homelessness. However, when high growth and high manufacturing occur together, more homelessness results.

Other new variables in Table 10-1 include the 1980–1987 inflation-adjusted change in the per person average annual payroll for people employed in a county (CHG AVG $); the inflation-adjusted change in maximum AFDC monthly benefit for a family of three; the change in wholesale trade, transportation/communications/utilities, and financial/insurance/real estate employment (CHG WHL, CHG TCU, and CHG FIRE); the proportion of 1980 rental units with rents below $150 (% LOW RENT-80); and the 1980 proportion of employed people in a city who hold precision production, crafts, or operator jobs (% CRAFT-80).

Other points of interest in Table 10-1 include the effects of 1989 fair market rents (the maximum rent HUD will subsidize) and of per capita spending for mental health (PC MH $-87) and alcohol and other drug abuse (PC AODA $-88). Since rent is a critical component of living costs, it is not surprising to see that higher rents are associated with more homelessness in low-manufacturing and high-growth cities. If both fair market rents and the cost of living variable are considered together, one or the other appears as a predictor in four of the five equations in Table 10-1, underscoring the link between high living costs and homelessness.

One might think that per capita spending for mental health (PC MH $-87) and for alcohol and other drug abuse (PC AODA-88) would tend to have the same effect on homelessness (that is, they should have the same sign). But this is never the case in our data set. Spending for alcohol and other drug abuse is always positively related to homelessness, whereas spending for mental health is always negatively related. The explanation appears to lie in the different populations being served. As we saw in Chapter 6, the number of seriously mentally ill persons in need of support and care has not increased during the 1980s. Therefore higher levels of funding should translate into improved conditions for this population, including lower levels of homelessness. The situation for drug abuse is quite different. In most states the need for drug abuse treatment has increased sharply during the latter half of the 1980s. Most of the increase in spending for alcohol and drug abuse has gone into drug treatment, and appears to be following growth in demand. The increase in drug abuse, particularly of crack cocaine, is thus likely to be the antecedent condition driving increases in both homelessness and public spending for treatment.

THE FOUR BEST VARIABLES

In stepwise regression, the procedure selects first the variables that account for the largest amount of variance. In the present analysis, the first four variables selected for each of the equations contribute 46 to 81 percent of the explanatory power of the full equation. In many instances a policy analyst would be happy to settle for this reduction in the amount of variance explained because the use of only four variables would greatly simplify the data collection work. Table 10-2 presents these first four variables, the R^2 change they account for, and the cumulative R^2s and AR^2s, for all cities and each subgroup of cities.

Table 10-2 The Four Best Variables for Each Analysis of 1989 Homelessness Rates

	Step	Variable	R^2 Change	Significance of R^2 Change	R^2	AR^2
All Cities	1	% ONE–80	.222	.000	.222	.216
	2	P.C. AODA $-88	.064	.000	.286	.276
	3	% SRV–87	.027	.020	.312	.298
	4	CHG WHL	.020	.043	.332	.313
High	1	% ONE–80	.095	.009	.095	.082
Manufacturing	2	% RTL–87	.083	.011	.178	.154
	3	GA $-89	.055	.031	.233	.199
	4	P.C. MH $-87	.077	.009	.310	.268
Low	1	$ RTL–87	.362	.000	.362	.354
Manufacturing	2	P.C. AODA $-88	.087	.001	.449	.434
	3	GROWTH 80–86	.059	.004	.509	.488
	4	FMR–2BR–89	.035	.022	.544	.518
High Growth	1	% ONE–80	.133	.002	.133	.120
	2	CHG VAC RATE	.063	.027	.197	.172
	3	UE–89	.056	.031	.253	.218
	4	E/P–89	.059	.023	.313	.269
Low Growth	1	% ONE–80	.281	.000	.281	.272
	2	% SRV–80	.065	.007	.346	.329
	3	CHG AVG $	.037	.038	.383	.358
	4	12 + YRS–80	.027	.071	.410	.378

Notes: % ONE–80 = 1980 % of one-person households; P.C. AODA $-88/P.C. MH $-87 = 1988/1987 per capita state spending for alcohol and other drug abuse/mental health services; % SRV–87, % RTL–87, % SRV–80 = proportion of county employment in services and retail for 1987, and services for 1980; CHG WHL = 1980–1987 increase in wholesale trade employment as % of 1980 wholesale employment; GA $-89 = 1989 GA payment level; GROWTH 80–86 = dummy variable for low-/high-growth cities; FMR–2BR–89 = 1989 FMR for two-bedroom apartment; CHG VAC RATE = 1980–1988 change in rental vacancy rate; UE–89 = 1989 unemployment rate; E/P–89 = 1989 employment-to-population ratio; CHG AVG $ = 1980–1987 inflation-adjusted change in average annual payroll per employed person; 12+ YRS–80 = 1980 % adult population with twelve or more years education. See Chapter 8 for full description.

The proportion of one-person households in 1980 is the most important single predictor variable in all analyses except low-manufacturing cities. Three other variables appear among the first four in two analyses: spending for alcohol and other drug abuse, and the proportion of employment in retail trade and in services.[3] In all, fourteen different variables are included in at least one of the "best four" analyses. Recent data appear to be the best predictors of 1989 homelessness rates. Half of the fourteen variables are from 1987–1989, four are change variables, and three are from 1980. Of the three from 1980, two (percentage of one-person households and percentage of adults with twelve or more years of education) are not available for later years. Later data, if available, might have proved to be more important than the 1980 variables.

Virtually all of the variables in Table 10-2 are readily available from the sources noted in Chapter 8. The single exception is payment levels for General Assistance, which were gathered for this research through a telephone survey. The 1989 values are given in Appendix A. The difficulty of obtaining this information probably means that the variable will be impractical for most policymakers to use if data are desired for years later than 1989.

ACCOUNTING FOR 1981–1989 CHANGES IN HOMELESSNESS RATES

The stepwise regression approach was also used to develop the best predictors of change in homelessness rates between 1981 and 1989. Table 10-3 presents the results.

The Full Models

Table 10-3 introduces three new variables: 1980–1989 change in median renter income; housing density expressed as the proportion of dwelling units in buildings with five or more units (% MULTIUNIT-80); and housing tenure (% OWN-80).

As in the analysis of 1989 rates, this approach offers a significant improvement in predictive power. In comparison with the best models in Chapter 9, the equations of Table 10-3 explain 4 to 18 more percentage points of the variance in 1981–1989 changes in homelessness rates. The best improvements come in the high-manufacturing and low-growth subgroups; the

---

[3]Sometimes the impact of variables entering the analysis early is attenuated when other variables are included. This effect can be seen in low-growth cities, where the proportion of employment in services in 1980 is the second variable selected (Table 10-2), but loses its significance in the presence of other variables (Table 10-1). Nevertheless, its role as an indicator—one of the four best variables—remains important.

Table 10-3 Accounting for the Most Variance in 1981-1989 Changes in Homelessness Rates

	All Cities	High Manufacturing	Low Manufacturing	High Growth	Low Growth
Later Variables					
VLI R/U-85	—	.362	—	—	−.160
P.C. INC-85	—	—	−.265	—	—
GA $-89	—	—	—	−.383	.298
P.C. AODA $-88	.338	—	.287	—	.544
P.C. MH $-87	—	−.288	—	—	−.273
UE-89	.158	.332	—	—	—
HILOMFG-87	—	—	—	—	−.313
% RTL-87	—	.307	−.381	—	.203
% SRV-87	.228	—	—	—	—
FMR-89	—	—	—	.259	—
COST/LIVING	.344	—	.229	—	.625
CITY POP-86	—	−.297	−.148	—	−.188
Change Variables					
CHG AVG $	.288	.304	—	—	.343
CHG VAC. RATE	—	−.208	—	—	—
GROWTH 80-86	—	.176	.105	—	—
CHG GA $	—	.338	—	—	—
CHG AFDC $	−.202	—	−.264	—	—
CHG UE	—	—	—	.216	—
CHG MFG	.219	—	—	.434	—
CHG TCU	—	—	—	−.199	—
CHG WHL	−1.54	−.231	—	—	−.201
CHG # EMP	−.094	—	—	—	—
CHG MED RTR INC.	−.195	—	—	—	−.364
Early Variables					
PC INC-79	—	—	—	.302	—
% MULTIUNIT-80	.199	—	.372	—	.290
% OWN	—	—	—	—	.462
% LOW RENT-80	.367	—	—	—	.290
% FH-80	−.302	—	—	−.580	—
% ONE-80	—	.557	—	.211	.217
% 12 + YRS-80	—	—	—	−.627	—
E/P-80	—	—	—	.261	—
UE-80	—	—	—	.857	—
% CRAFT-80	—	−.392	—	.404	—
% MFG-80	—	.248	—	—	—
% CNS-80	—	—	—	—	−.213
% RTL-80	−.218	—	—	−.326	—
% SRV-80	—	—	—	—	−.236
R^2	.565	.552	.691	.645	.726
AR^2	.519	.450	.654	.560	.650
Chapter 9- Best Models					
R^2	.498	.397	.686	.588	.605
AR^2	.428	.272	.614	.470	.502

Note: a coefficient is underlined if $p < .05$ for all analyses.

least improvement is in low-manufacturing cities, where 61 percent of the variance was already explained in Chapter 9.

One might expect the change in homelessness over the decade to respond to somewhat different influences from those that affect 1989 homelessness rates. In particular, one might expect changes in homelessness to be more closely related to conditions early in the decade and changes in conditions over the decade than to conditions in 1987–1989. This pattern is seen among high-growth cities, in which eight of the thirteen predictors are 1980 variables and three more are change variables. In the other analyses, however, conditions in the latter part of the 1980s are more influential.

Compared with the analyses of 1989 rates, these change analyses reveal fewer consistently strong influences. No variable appears in four or more equations; only eight of the thirty-eight appear in three equations (per capita chemical dependency spending; retail employment in 1987; cost of living; 1986 city population; change in average annual salary paid in the county; change in the proportion of wholesale trade employment; proportion of dwelling units in multiunit buildings; and proportion of one-person households). If both 1987–1989 and 1980 values of the same variable are tallied, the three-equation test is also met by employment sector and unemployment variables. These results reinforce the idea that many factors may contribute to the growth in homelessness. Further, the general context, represented here by the subgroup breaks, appears to make a considerable difference in which factors will most influence the growth of homeless populations.

The Four Best Variables

Table 10-4 presents the four variables that explain the biggest proportion of the variance in the equations given in Table 10-3. Fifteen different variables appear among the first four in one or more of these analyses. The proportion of units in multiunit buildings, per capita spending on alcohol and drug abuse, and employment in services and in retail trade occur in more than one analysis.

One would expect conditions at the beginning of the decade to play a greater role in predicting changes than in predicting 1989 levels of homelessness. In fact, seven of the fifteen "best variables" are for 1980 and three are change variables. (In contrast, the best variables predicting 1989 rates (Table 10-2) were more heavily oriented toward 1987–1989 variables.) In both high- and low-growth cities, three of the four best predictors are 1980 variables.

The four best predictors together account for between 56 percent of the total variance explained in the corresponding Table 10-3 model (high-manufacturing cities) and 86 percent of that variance (low-manufacturing cities). Again, most of the variables used would be readily accessible to policy analysts, with

Table 10-4 The Four Best Variables for Each Analysis of 1981-1989 Change in Rates

	Step	Variable	R^2 Change	Significance of R^2 Change	R^2	AR^2
All Cities	1	% MULTI-UNIT-80	.224	.000	.224	.218
	2	P.C. AODA $-88	.078	.000	.301	.292
	3	% SRV-87	.050	.001	.351	.338
	4	% RTL-80	.039	.003	.390	.373
High	1	CHG GA $	.097	.008	.097	.084
Manufacturing	2	% CRAFT-80	.084	.010	.181	.157
	3	CHG VAC RATE	.059	.026	.240	.252
	4	UE-89	.055	.027	.295	.252
Low	1	COST/LIVING	.362	.000	.362	.353
Manufacturing	2	% RTL-87	.139	.000	.501	.487
	3	GROWTH 80-86	.060	.003	.561	.543
	4	P.C. AODA $-88	.028	.033	.589	.565
High Growth	1	% ONE-80	.145	.001	.145	.132
	2	UE-80	.093	.007	.238	.215
	3	E/P-80	.123	.001	.362	.332
	4	% SRV-87	.032	.074	.393	.355
Low Growth	1	% MULTI-UNIT-80	.278	.000	.278	.269
	2	% SRV-80	.126	.000	.404	.388
	3	% RTL-80	.052	.009	.456	.434
	4	P.C. AODA $-88	.018	.121	.474	.445

Notes: MULTIUNIT-80 = 1980 % of dwelling units in buildings with five or more units; % ONE-80 = 1980 % of one-person households; P.C. AODA $-88 = 1988 per capita state spending for alcohol and other drug abuse services; % SRV-87, % RTL-80, % SRV-80 = proportion of county employment in services and retail for 1980, and services for 1987; % CRAFT-80 = 1980 proportion of employed persons with jobs in precision production, craft or operators; GA $-89 = 1989 GA payment level; GROWTH 80-86 = dummy variable for low-/high-growth cities; CHG VAC RATE = 1980-1988 change in rental vacancy rate; UE-89/80 = 1989/1980 unemployment rate; E/P-80 = 1980 employment-to-population ratio; COST/LIVING = ACCRA cost of living index. See Chapter 8 for full description of variables.

the exception of the change in General Assistance payments for individuals living independently. Both 1981 and 1989 GA levels were obtained for this study through a telephone survey, and are not available from any routine or systematic data base.

SUMMARY AND IMPLICATIONS

The analyses presented in this chapter make clear that a very significant level of prediction can be obtained for both 1989 homelessness rates and 1981–1989 changes in rates. For the all-cities analysis and for each group, the best predictive models offered significant gains over their counterparts in Chapter 9, in terms of the percentage of the variance explained in 1989 homelessness rates:

- All cities: 11.1 percentage points, to $AR^2 = .501$;
- High-manufacturing cities: 17.7 percentage points, to $AR^2 = .483$;
- Low-manufacturing cities: 9.5 percentage points, to $AR^2 = .639$;
- High-growth cities: 14.7 percentage points, to $AR^2 = .585$;
- Low-growth cities: 19.4 percentage points, to $AR^2 = .632$.

Prediction improvements were also substantial in the 1981–1989 change analyses:

- All cities: 9.1 percentage points, to $AR^2 = .519$;
- High-manufacturing cities: 17.8 percentage points, to $AR^2 = .450$;
- Low-manufacturing cities: 4.0 percentage points, to $AR^2 = .654$;
- High-growth cities: 9.0 percentage points, to $AR^2 = .560$;
- Low-growth cities: 14.8 percentage points, to $AR^2 = .650$.

This level of prediction is adequate for many policy applications. Since this research used available data sources whenever possible, its analyses can be replicated with the same sources, a good research assistant, and a good spreadsheet program. Many of the variables are computer accessible through the Census Bureau's publications, which include CD-ROM disks in DBASE format for the *County and City Data Book: 1988* and for the annual publications of *County Business Patterns*. The least available data are General Assistance policies and benefit levels, and the dependent variable itself, rates of homelessness. To the extent that 1990 Census data can supply the latter need, analysts should be able to use the research presented here to contribute to decisions about resource distribution, service needs, and other policy matters.

It must be remembered, of course, that this study covered only large cities (over 100,000 population). The same variables may have less predictive utility when applied to smaller cities or to nonurban environments (proportions of employment in the mining and agricultural sectors were not even included in the present data set). Nevertheless, the results of the present study provide a framework useful to analysts who undertake predictive work with different kinds of samples. The differences between the large cities examined here and jurisdictions of other types will be informative and important.

CHAPTER ELEVEN

Summary and Recommendations

■ Asking why homelessness grew so much in the 1980s, we began by hypothesizing that a change in the affordability of rental housing was responsible. Our model of homelessness posited affordability as the relationship between the price of housing and the incomes of households needing housing. Four factors were suggested that might influence the price of housing:

- Government policy focused specifically on housing for low-income households.
- Housing market structure.
- Federal tax policy.
- Federal fiscal and monetary policy (affecting interest rates and the national debt).

The model also depicted four factors potentially acting on household incomes:

- Social policy affecting public benefit programs.
- Social policy affecting services and supports for people with disabilities.
- Employment opportunities, including the structure of local labor markets, wages, and unemployment.
- Household resources, including the number of potential workers; their education and skills; their physical and mental health; their connections to family, friends, and neighborhood; their housing tenure (rent or own); and their financial capital.

After Chapter 2's brief review of the characteristics of the homeless population, Chapters 3 through 6 examined national changes in the model's hypothesized causal factors. Chapters 7 through 10 then explored the effects of these factors on the growth of homelessness during the 1980s in U.S. cities that had populations of 100,000 or more in 1986.

THE GROWTH OF HOMELESSNESS IN THE 1980s

Two estimates based on independently collected data support the widespread impression that homelessness in the United States grew during the 1980s. In 1984 the Department of Housing and Urban Development estimated that there were between 250,000 and 350,000 homeless people in the United States at any given time (HUD, 1984). A later study by the Urban Institute (Burt and Cohen, 1989a) suggested that by 1987 that number had grown to between 500,000 and 600,000. In all likelihood there were far fewer than 250,0000 homeless people in 1980; although no studies document a precise number for that year, all observers date the beginning of the substantial growth in homelessness from the 1981–1982 recession. Further, the number of shelter beds available throughout the country almost tripled between 1984 and 1988, rising from slightly under 100,000 to about 275,000, according to two studies conducted by the Department of Housing and Urban Development (1984, 1989), which used similar methodologies.

The present study provides independent documentation of the increase in shelter beds from 1981 to 1989 in cities over 100,000 (Chapter 7). In 1981 these cities had about 41,000 shelter beds available to the homeless; by 1989 that number stood at 117,000. These data on shelter beds were then used to create homelessness rates; in the 147 primary cities with populations over 100,000, we found, homeless rates per 10,000 city population rose from 6 in 1981 to almost 18 in 1989. In the thirty-five suburbs of these primary cities that themselves had populations of more than 100,000, homelessness rates went from 0.7 per 10,000 in 1981 to 4.6 per 10,000 in 1989.

Because these rates include only people who use shelters, the "real" rates of homelessness, could they be known, would be even higher. However, the rates reported here do give a reasonably accurate sense of the growth of the homeless population, and are quite useful for intercity comparisons. It should be remembered that these rates apply only to large urban areas (cities over 100,000). Rates for smaller urban areas and for nonurban areas would undoubtedly be lower.

CHARACTERISTICS OF THE HOMELESS POPULATION

The profile of the urban service-using homeless developed from the Urban Institute's 1987 study (Burt and Cohen, 1989a; 1989b) pointed toward several distinctive population characteristics. Homeless households are overwhelmingly composed of single males (73 percent), followed by family households (either married couples without children—2 percent—or one or both parents with at least one child—10 percent); and single women (9 percent). (The remainder were unrelated individuals without children in parties of two or more.) Virtually all were very poor before they became homeless, more than half had never married (including women with children), and more than a third had lived by themselves immediately before becoming homeless. Slightly less than half had no high school diploma or its equivalent, fewer than one in ten were currently working at a steady job, and the average length of time without a steady job for those who had ever worked was between three and four years. Nine percent had experienced institutionalizations for both mental illness and chemical dependency; another 10 percent had a history of mental hospitalization only; another 24 percent had received only chemical dependency inpatient treatment; and 57 percent (more than half) had never experienced either type of institutionalization.

Guided by the characteristics of the homeless population, this research looked at factors affecting poverty, and focused as much as possible on what happened during the 1980s to single, relatively less-educated males, and to people living alone. Among families, factors affecting poor female-headed households were the focus. In addition, we examined what happened to change the probability that people with personal problems such as mental illness or chemical dependency would become homeless.

CAUSES OF HOMELESSNESS:
CONCLUSIONS FROM REVIEW OF EXISTING LITERATURE

Mental Illness and Chemical Dependency

The proportion of the seriously mentally ill who are homeless appears to have increased at least 500 percent, perhaps as much as 900 percent, between 1980 and 1987; the increase in homelessness among alcohol abusers and alcoholics was probably about 500 percent during the same period (Chapter 6). Yet the prevalence of serious mental illness and alcohol dependency did not increase in the general population during the 1980s. Thus the growth in homelessness among these groups does not result from an increase in their overall size. No data are available to calculate parallel figures for drug abuse. However, it is probable that the increased abuse of crack cocaine affected homelessness, but only toward the end of the 1980s. This trend cannot therefore explain the increase in homelessness that began early in the decade.

One thing did change over the 1980s: the amount of resources available for the seriously mentally ill and chemically dependent was reduced. Access to SSI/SSDI was cut at the beginning of the decade, and the value of these benefits shrank for those who could get them. So did the value of General Assistance. In addition, many of the day labor jobs that sustained skid row populations in the past disappeared. These changes, coupled with reductions in the supply of appropriate and affordable housing (SROs, lodging houses), appear to have drastically undercut the ability of people with these severe problems to remain housed. State mental health systems also changed, raising their admissions criteria, keeping people for shorter stays, and sometimes releasing them before their mental condition and community living situation stabilized. Commitment laws also tightened, making it more difficult to hospitalize persons involuntarily unless they posed an immediate danger to themselves or others. At the same time, the practical consequence of decriminalizing public drunkenness was that even the city jail no longer offered shelter on a cold night.

During the 1950s, 1960s, and even the 1970s, many people with mental illness or chemical dependency conditions could and did maintain themselves in at least minimal housing. The many descriptions of life on America's skid rows suggest that even extraordinarily poor people, including alcoholics whom one might expect to spend all their money on drink, chose to get off the streets when they could afford to do so. And they appear to have been able to do so most of the time. There is no reason to think that the preferences of mentally ill and chemically dependent individuals have changed. Thus it appears that changes in resources and in housing options are the proximal causes of their increasing homelessness in the 1980s. If housing were available today that people supported by public benefits or day labor could afford, we can assume they would purchase it, as they did in the past. Whether or not they desire a middle-class lifestyle, or are able to maintain a steady job, they almost certainly would not "choose" the streets, given the option of a minimal roof. Their past behavior is the best guide to their preferences.

Changes Affecting Housing Affordability

There was not enough standard-quality housing in the existing rental stock in many metropolitan areas in the early 1980s to house all renter households, even if they had been able to pay the asking rent (Chapter 3). Because rents increased and renter household incomes declined at the same time, low-income renters had to commit increasing proportions of their incomes to housing costs as the decade progressed. Shifts in the types of households that made up the renter population accounted for some of the decline in real renter income. Other factors include lower real wages of low-skilled workers, and the lower real value of public benefits.

Virtually all poor renter households continued to be housed. Yet the reduction in their real income during the 1980s placed them under considerable pressure, with rent burdens that might leave them little to spend on other essentials. Further, even the poorest of poor renters had higher incomes than the average homeless household (Rossi, 1989).

Poor renters in the 1980s were more likely than those of the 1970s to be single-person households or households that included only one adult (usually, these were households headed by women). Both household types have less ability to weather a crisis than do husband-wife households. They are less able to support disabled or unemployed family members. Moreover, if some crisis pushes them into homelessness (e.g., losing a job, or eligibility for welfare), their marginal assets are less likely to be enough to get them back into the housing market. Thus their circumstances, combined with increasing housing costs, put them and their wider network of family and friends at higher risk of homelessness. As housing affordability decreased (real rent burdens increased) in the 1980s, so did the risk of homelessness.

The federal policies related to housing that probably had the strongest influence on changes in housing affordability were those related to the tax code, deficit spending, and inflation control. The sharp reduction in the budget authority of the Department of Housing and Urban Development appears to have had less impact, dramatic as that reduction may appear on paper. Further, while having too few rental units in the housing stock contributes to the "housing problem," its major component is inadequate income among would-be renters. To the extent that federal policies outside the housing arena reduced eligibility for, and benefits from, income support programs in a period of increasing unemployment and poverty, they did at least as much as direct low-income housing policy to decrease housing affordability.

Changes in Poverty, Inequality, and Employment Opportunity

The 1980s saw an increase in poverty and inequality, along with very high levels of unemployment during the first few years of the decade (Chapter 4). These patterns continued trends that for many households began in the 1970s. The increase in poverty arose primarily from reductions in the amounts people could earn by working, changes in means-tested benefit programs (fewer people got benefits, and many of those who did found their value reduced), population growth, reduced unemployment insurance coverage, and changes in federal tax policy.

Inequality also increased in the 1980s, following the trend of the 1970s, but with a difference. During the 1970s inequality increased largely because of gains in the incomes of higher-income people; during the 1980s, the incomes of lower-income people decreased as well. Thus the 1980s saw the further impoverishment of the already poor—a circumstance more likely to contribute to homelessness than the pattern of the 1970s.

While unemployment stood at historical highs in the early 1980s, unemployment insurance programs reduced their coverage in ways that made them least effective at reducing poverty just when the need was greatest. Employment increased during the later part of the decade, but did not fully replace the jobs lost earlier. The new jobs were, on the whole, more service-oriented rather than production-oriented, they paid less, and they offered less security and fewer benefits. In short, average wages and living standards of American workers declined while a two-tiered job structure developed in which the well-educated and highly skilled have considerably more favorable prospects than do the poorly educated and low-skilled—all developments that made many households more vulnerable to homelessness.

These changes affected most strongly the people with the highest risk of experiencing homelessness: minorities and low-skilled men, unrelated individuals, and among families, those headed by women. The characteristics of homeless adults and the characteristics of people in poverty are very similar.

Many popular discussions of homelessness disregard poverty as a root cause of the problem. Assertions of the similarities between homeless people and the general public are intended to arouse sympathy for the homeless and support for policies to relieve their condition. But this strategy may backfire as the average American confronts the facts about common characteristics of the homeless. Programs and policies that hope to make any difference in preventing homelessness must do something substantial about the poverty that underlies almost all homelessness.

Changes in Public Benefit Programs

Changes in the major federal and nonfederal safety-net programs during the 1980s may have contributed to the increase in homelessness among their potential recipients (Chapter 5). Benefits available through several of the programs (AFDC, SSI state supplemental payments, General Assistance) lost some of their purchasing power because they were not adjusted for inflation. Further, in several programs (AFDC, food stamps, SSI, federal rental assistance) eligibility, co-payments, and other program requirements changed to exclude many who had been eligible in 1980 or increase the financial burden on the household receiving the benefit. As noted before, most of these programs do not cover single adults, the largest subgroup of households among the homeless. This exclusion makes poor single adults particularly vulnerable to homelessness.[1]

Thus it is plausible to conclude that changes in these safety-net programs contributed to the increasing homelessness during the 1980s. The premise of this book is that changes in any combination of factors that affect housing affordability could increase homelessness, by increasing the cost of housing or

---

[1]The National Affordable Housing Act of 1990 changed the regulations governing federal housing subsidies to make nonelderly able-bodied single people eligible for Section 8 certificates and vouchers as of October 1, 1991.

by reducing any of the variety of resources that households use to purchase housing. The safety-net programs increase affordability by giving very poor households resources they would not otherwise have. A withdrawal or reduction of these resources such as occurred during the 1980s makes housing less affordable, assuming housing costs stayed the same or increased.

ANALYZING FACTORS THAT AFFECT HOMELESSNESS IN LARGE AMERICAN CITIES IN THE 1980S

The second half of this inquiry examined the impact of factors hypothesized to affect homelessness in a sample of large American cities. The original sample included the 182 U.S. cities with populations over 100,000. Most of the detailed analyses were performed on the 147 primary cities in the group, dropping the thirty-five suburbs that qualified on the basis of population alone. Homelessness rates were developed for 1981, 1983, 1986, and 1989, based on the number of shelter beds available in each city in those years (Chapter 7). Results indicated that homelessness based on shelter beds as an indicator almost tripled between 1981 and 1989 in every region of the country and in cities of all sizes and levels of prosperity.

A data set was developed to represent conditions in these cities in the 1979 to 1981 period, before the onset of highly visible homelessness, and conditions later in the decade, usually covering the years 1987 to 1989 (Chapter 8). Regression analysis (Chapter 9) was used to assess the relationships among the variables representing the hypothesized causal factors and homelessness rates (between-city comparisons for 1989), and between the factors and increases in homelessness between 1981 and 1989 (within-city changes).

As Chapter 9 discussed, the predictive model on which this research is based can explain a good deal of the between-city variance in 1989 homelessness rates and within-city changes in homelessness rates between 1981 and 1989. The most important variables in the model were found to be:

- the unemployment rate and the employment structure faced by city residents;
- the city's population change (growth, stagnation, or loss), which is also a reflection of its economic fortunes;
- the city's proportion of one-person households;
- the unavailability of General Assistance;
- the cost of living for city residents;
- the failure of public benefit payment levels to maintain their purchasing power.

Although poverty is implicated in every discussion of the causes of homelessness, a city's poverty rate rarely contributed to explaining between-city differences in homelessness rates. Another unexpected finding was that the payment level of public benefits had a positive association with homelessness; payment levels increase as a city's cost of living increases, and higher levels of both predict more homelessness.

The important predictive factors accounted for much more of the variance in cities with low rather than high proportions of manufacturing employment. Splitting the sample into cities with high and low population growth produced the best level of explanation for both subgroups. Analyses of these subgroups revealed that quite different urban conditions can lead to homelessness.

One pattern prevails in low-growth cities, and most especially in low-growth cities where manufacturing represents a small share of employment. The economy in these cities is quite depressed, and its effects on increased unemployment and poverty contribute to homelessness despite the relative availability of housing. However, cities with growing economies also have homelessness. In these burgeoning cities, the poorest segment of the population apparently does not participate in the general well-being. The demand for housing from prosperous residents, which may be coupled with urban revitalization and pressures on housing traditionally occupied by the poor, creates a squeeze on housing in which the poor are increasingly less able to compete successfully. This squeeze seems to increase their risk of homelessness.

Because the causes of homelessness are so varied, an equally broad range of remedial approaches might be pursued. It will be most effective, however, to tailor these efforts to the circumstances producing homelessness in a particular city. Obvious possibilities include raising benefit levels in relation to the cost of living, increasing housing subsidies, and bolstering the human capital (and hence the earning power) of those most vulnerable to homelessness.

Our analyses can point to associations between homelessness and various antecedent conditions, but it cannot always distinguish true causes from merely indicative associations. My own sense is that unemployment and the structure of a city's employment opportunities have a causal relation to homelessness. When a local economy loses a large number of jobs in any sector, and particularly when an economy that has included many high-paying jobs for people with relatively little formal education, such as manufacturing jobs, shifts toward low-paying service jobs, the risk of homelessness increases. I also believe that higher living costs and a squeeze on poor households increased homelessness levels later in the 1980s, and accelerated the growth of homelessness throughout the decade in high-growth and low-manufacturing cities.

In cities where this squeeze occurred, neither higher initial levels of public benefits nor increases in these benefits nor increased levels of public housing were adequate to offset its effects as the decade progressed. Higher benefit levels and greater growth in the real value of benefits were associated with higher rates and greater increases of homelessness, as were increases in public housing units available per capita (not shown). Thus compensatory mechanisms could not fully protect very poor people trying to maintain a viable position in the housing market. The positive association of public benefit levels and homelessness rates is probably due to their common relationship to the cost of living.

Certain housing variables were strongly associated with homelessness, including the shortage of affordable housing and tighter rental housing markets (lower vacancy rates). These effects were diminished when the model also included more antecedent variables reflecting components of affordability. Most analyses pointed to inadequate household income as the most important reason why housing became less affordable; in some cities the increasing cost of housing also contributed, independent of shifts in income.

Population growth patterns are highly predictive of homelessness levels, reflecting a city's economic environment and pressures on available housing. Low-growth cities have lost population because they have lost jobs, with resulting high unemployment and poverty rates; rental housing is available, but people cannot afford it. High-growth cities have gained jobs and population, but experience very tight rental housing markets and escalating living costs. Both conditions can push some people over the edge into homelessness.

The effect of the proportion of one-person households may reflect a true causal influence and also an association based on a common relationship with another cause. A large number of single-person households strains a city's housing resources simply because it takes more units to house the same number of people, and may lead to overcrowding in the remaining units. Greater competition for housing may lead to higher prices, rendering housing unavailable to the very poor. In addition, high rates of one-person households may indicate a relatively high proportion of people living alone who have disabilities such as mental illness or physical handicap, or who are isolated from any family or friends. These conditions may make them vulnerable to homelessness if faced with a crisis situation affecting either their income or their housing (such as displacement due to destruction or conversion of SROs (Lee, 1989)). Finally, high proportions of one-person households are most common in low-growth cities. The conditions leading to low growth or economic decline may account for part of the effect on homelessness of one-person households in these cities.

The unimportance of city poverty rates in predicting homelessness was initially puzzling, as discussed in some detail in Chapter 9. Poverty rates also failed to predict homelessness in other analyses that used HUD's 1984 estimates of homelessness in a sample of sixty cities (Elliott and Krivo, 1991; Quigley, 1989). I have concluded that poverty should be viewed as a factor making one vulnerable to homelessness, but that homelessness depends less on the proportion of a city's population that is poor than on the external conditions affecting poor people. Poverty reduces a household's ability to cope under heavy pressures, in much the same way that mental illness, chemical dependency or a physical handicap may reduce one's ability to cope. But it is the structural pressures of poor quality jobs, high living costs, pressure from the middle class, and tight housing markets that tip poor people into homelessness.

Prediction

Analyses of the predictive power of variables in our data set were reported in Chapter 10. A very significant level of prediction can be obtained for both 1989 homelessness rates and 1981–1989 changes in rates. In the all-cities analysis, the best predictive model explained 50.1 percent of the variance in 1989 homelessness rates and 51.9 percent of the variance in changes in homelessness between 1981 and 1989. The best predictive models for subgroups of cities increased the variance explained in 1989 homelessness rates beyond that attributable to the causal model in Chapter 9 by 10 to 19 percentage points. Prediction improvements were also substantial in the 1981–1989 change analysis, where the increased variance explained ranged from 4 to 18 percentage points. This level of prediction is good enough for many policy applications. Moreover, since our model relies almost entirely on readily available data sources, policymakers can use it to contribute to decisions about resource distribution, service needs, and other policy matters relevant to homelessness in urban areas.

IMPLICATIONS AND RECOMMENDATIONS

Although this research is exploratory, it suggests a wide variety of approaches that policymakers might use to stem the growth of homelessness, and to alleviate the condition for those who are already homeless. I divide the policy options into those pertaining to housing, to employment and income, and to people with disabilities.

Housing Production and Subsidies

Subsidize More Renters. Our findings indicate that housing subsidies for very poor people must increase if more homelessness is to be avoided. Homelessness is significantly higher in cities with severe rather than moderate shortages of affordable housing, and its increase over the decade in many cities is associated with decreases in the availability of rental housing, increases in the cost of living, and other evidence of a squeeze on poor households' ability to compete for housing. Subsidies should be aimed at the very poorest, not merely at "low-income" households. Further, for these households subsidies should be an entitlement. This means offering rent supports to households whose income, adjusted for family size, is below 35 percent of the area median, or even below 25 percent, rather than the 50, 60, or even 80 percent cutoff now governing much federal policy. The problem with less restrictive eligibility criteria is that a limited amount of resources is spread too thinly. Adequate relief is not delivered to these poorest households, which are far more likely than others to be paying excessive amounts of their incomes for rent, and to have other housing problems as well (Nelson, 1990).

Until rent subsidies become an entitlement for all people who need them, rather than being controlled by a legislated spending cap, all federal housing subsidy resources should be targeted to the very poorest households, contrary to recent policy changes that eased the income criteria for "priority" treatment. State and local housing subsidies, whether in the form of housing supplements to AFDC or General Assistance recipients or other tenant assistance programs, should also target the very poor. The support levels of these programs should be increased to reflect the true cost of housing in the locality where recipients live.

Provide More Units. Many cities lack an adequate supply of appropriate units, regardless of price (Milgram and Bury, 1987). No single federal policy can explain this lack, which reflects many aspects of the housing market. If all other things were equal, it would seem likely that federal withdrawal from the production of new or substantially rehabilitated low-cost units could have increased homelessness, because lower supply would have resulted in higher prices, and housing would have become less affordable to the poor. Although the absolute number of low-cost units has gone down in the 1980s, it is not clear that the number of affordable units has similarly declined, if one takes into account the increased number of units rendered low-cost through subsidies that reduce renter payments to 30 percent of income.

The number of units added through federal new construction/substantial rehabilitation programs began to decline in the late 1970s. This slowdown would take some years to affect the availability of low-cost rental units in any case. Too little is known about the simultaneous actions of other factors, including the proportion of households receiving subsidies, the rate of loss of low-priced units, and the rate of creation of low-priced units stimulated by federal policies, to draw firm conclusions about their effects.

Subsidies (certificates or vouchers) covered a higher proportion of poor households during the late 1980s than in earlier years. Yet because the number of poor households increased significantly after 1980, and the average incomes of the poorest of the poor shrank, the number of poor households that did not receive subsidies grew, and the rents they could afford declined. Between 1981 and 1987, moreover, 1.2 million units were lost from the low-cost stock. (Some of these "losses" occurred because the rent increased beyond $300, removing them from the low-cost category, but subsidies could still make them affordable.) In addition, the number of units available in the housing stock, independent of price, was inadequate to meet the need for standard-quality rental housing in the early 1980s.

At the same time, several mechanisms created by federal policy (reviewed in Chapter 3) led to significant additions to the affordable stock in the 1980s. It is not easy to determine the total number of additional units and their rents, and I know of no analysis that has calculated their net effect on the affordable stock. Given these uncertainties, it is perhaps premature to blame the crisis of homelessness on the single federal policy shift from creating new units to subsidizing existing ones. Nor is it fair to blame the apparently massive cut in HUD's housing subsidy budget, for as we saw, other simultaneous changes had the effect of increasing the overall proportion of poor people who received subsidies.

Nevertheless, more housing must be built, rehabilitated, or converted to low-income use in many cities. Since it is no longer possible to build or rehabilitate housing that poor people can afford, the new housing must be made affordable to very poor people through subsidies. In all likelihood this means subsidies for monthly rents as well as for construction. Federal or state subsidies should be offered to nonprofit developers, either directly or through tax policies.

Until housing subsidies become an entitlement, targeting poor recipient households is no less important here than with rental subsidies for existing housing. If we set aside only a few units for very poor people (below 35 percent of area median income) and allow occupancy by households with 60 or 80 percent of area median income, under present law we will not provide adequate assistance to people who are in direst need; such a tenant mix is a very inefficient way to help very poor people.

Reduce Housing Segregation and Discrimination. To a great extent residential segregation by income occurs because poor people must live where there is housing they can afford. In principle, rental subsidies could expand the areas they could afford, but higher-income communities often raise barriers to the construction of housing designed for low-income households. Housing segregation by race also remains strong, and evidence of active discrimination is clear. These patterns of residential segregation are not likely to change without active and concerted efforts by federal, state, and local governments, such as the offer of services or tax advantages (e. g., reduced responsibility for road maintenance, as in Connecticut), or litigation and mediation (e. g., the Mt. Laurel case in New Jersey). These efforts must be made.

Relieve Squeeze Situations. It is not surprising to discover that higher rates of homelessness are associated with circumstances of reduced economic opportunity. Studies conducted in Houston (The Resource Group, 1989) and rural Ohio (Toomey, personal communication, 1991), as well as the research presented in this book, suggest that homelessness may also increase in a city where more people are going to work, and jobs and average incomes are increasing. Part of this homelessness probably comes from an influx of people looking for jobs, whose economic resources are not sufficient to sustain them until they find work. Another influence, however, appears to be the greater pressure on housing, resulting in rising rents and housing costs, that comes with economic prosperity for higher-income households. Our society has generally taken a laissez-faire attitude toward the fate of poor people caught in the squeeze of tight housing markets and conditions of high income inequality; the result has been higher rates of homelessness. An entitlement to rental subsidy would cover all low-income people facing steep housing costs, whether arising from a squeeze situation or from income loss. Until the enactment of such an entitlement, however, resources must be made available to ease the growing financial burden on these households. Compensatory mechanisms must be developed to provide affordable housing to poor or nonworking people displaced by the increasing economic prosperity of others.

Employment and Income

Better Jobs, Education, and Training. The United States' shift from a manufacturing to a services economy and our loss of worldwide competitiveness have been widely noted, as have the effects of these changes on American living standards (see, for example, Burtless, 1990a, 1990b; Council on Competitiveness, 1987; Dertouzos, Lester, Solow, and the MIT Commission on Industrial Productivity, 1989; Friedman, 1988; Greider, 1988; Litan, Lawrence, and Schultze, 1988; National Research Council, 1986; President's Commission on Industrial Competitiveness, 1985). This may be the first empirical study, however, to link persistent homelessness to these changes. The analyses in this book consistently point to the effects of local economic structure and the relationship between manufacturing and service jobs, homelessness rates, and increases in those rates over the decade of the 1980s.

When the growth of homelessness was first recognized, it was assumed to be a short-term consequence of the recession of 1981–1982. Under conditions of economic recovery, job growth, and reduced unemployment after 1984, however, homelessness has persisted and grown. The results of my analysis indicate a gloomier view of the phenomenon of homelessness—that it is an indicator of the erosion of living standards caused by economic stagnation and productivity loss. Since it is unlikely that this country will reverse its economic situation soon, and it may not be able to do so at all, homelessness appears likely to be with us for a very long time.

Various writers have recommended immediate and long-term steps that should be taken to restore American productivity and competitiveness. For example, Dertouzos et al. (1989) outline six aspects of American industry that must change: outdated strategies, short time horizons, technological weaknesses in development and production, neglect of human resources, failures of cooperation, and government and industry at cross-purposes. If such measures boost productivity growth, they will also help prevent homelessness. In this domain the interests of the homeless and of a very large segment of working Americans are highly compatible.

Revitalizing the American economy depends, in part, on producing an educated and well-trained work force that can participate in cooperative productive endeavor and respond to changing demands. In the past, however, prevailing attitudes have been to expect little from the work force, to structure jobs to require few skills, and to discard workers with outmoded skills rather than retrain them. Some who are discarded end up homeless; many end up with poorer-paying jobs that force reductions in living standards. In this environment young men with little education and poor skills—a major component of the homeless population—lose out in every way. Unlike their fathers, they cannot get a factory job that pays enough to support a family. The jobs open to those without a high school education have no future, and do not pay enough to live on.

Our educational system has failed most extremely with those who need training the most, and who are most vulnerable to homelessness—very poor people and their children. As many others have urged, it is essential that we revitalize public education, especially for our poorest children; develop more sophisticated job training and apprenticeship programs, with greater coopera- tion between employers and educators; and encourage employers to invest more in the continuous education and training of workers.

Benefit Levels and Eligibility. In general, the payment levels of federal, state, and local public benefit programs have not kept pace with inflation during the 1980s. At the same time, eligibility rules have been tightened, so that many individuals and households lost their benefits. These changes have influenced homelessness, but an even more serious problem is the almost complete lack of program coverage for the type of people who make up most of the homeless— single people, and particularly single males. Rental subsidies will be available to poor able-bodied single people for the first time as of October 1991, thanks to a change in program rules mandated by the National Affordable Housing Act of 1990.

Benefit levels appear to have responded to perceived need, although not enough to offset the higher living costs and the squeeze on poor households. (As a result, our analyses showed higher benefit levels to be associated with higher rates of homelessness.) For public benefit programs to prevent homelessness, they must both reach the households most vulnerable to loss of housing, and provide enough support to let the recipient pay for housing at prevailing local prices. Very few public benefit programs meet both of these criteria. In fact, recipients in some states successfully sued for increases in the existing housing allowance, demanding a level sufficient to cover prevailing local housing costs.

If a housing subsidy for extremely needy households were a federal entitlement, as recommended above, then the payment level of state and local benefit programs might not need to be raised dramatically. But in the absence of a federal housing entitlement, state and local programs will continue to be the focus of efforts to obtain adequate housing assistance.

Eligibility rules also need to change if certain kinds of homelessness are to be prevented. Single persons are now most vulnerable to homelessness, and least covered by public benefit programs. Many states have no benefit programs open to single individuals, even if they are disabled. Other states restrict eligibility for singles to those with disabilities. Still others limit the number of months during any twelve-month period that a single person can receive assistance. If single homeless people are to be helped to leave the streets, and to avoid homelessness in the first place, an assistance program of last resort must be established in those jurisdictions that lack one, and existing General Assistance programs must expand their eligibility.

Policies for People with Disabilities

Housing plus Services. Many sources document the failures of public policy with regard to people with mental illness, chemical dependency, and physical disabilities. Their disproportionate presence among the homeless is a reflection of these policy failures. Indeed, the Conference for Security and Cooperation in Europe (meeting in November 1990) cited the homeless situation in the United States and the failure of public policy to resolve it as a human rights violation under the Helsinki accords.

The public must finally make good on its commitments to the seriously mentally ill by providing the resources for adequate support and care in the community. Adequate support includes housing, accompanied by services appropriate to the disability of the occupants, and provision for periodic hospitalization and medical care as needed. The Stewart B. McKinney Homeless Assistance legislation took a step in the right direction by establishing the Permanent Housing for the Handicapped Homeless program. The support available under this program, however, is far too little even to cover the people who are currently homeless, let alone the many others at high risk of becoming homeless. The Shelter Plus Care component of the National Affordable Housing Act of 1990 also authorizes appropriate housing options for this population, but it has not been funded at a level that will make any difference. If housing appropriate for people with disabilities does not exist in a community, it must be created. If it does exist, public policy must assure that it is not destroyed or converted to other uses unless equivalent or better housing is substituted to serve people with disabilities.

Income Supports. Eligibility for Supplemental Security Income (SSI) should be broadened and the qualification process relaxed so that more disabled people in extreme need can receive these benefits. Even at their maximum, however, SSI benefits provide an income that is only about 75 percent of poverty level, leaving SSI recipients with very limited resources to spend on housing. Many states do not supplement the federal portion of SSI with additional resources to apply to housing costs, and most of those that do offer supplements have not adjusted their payments to keep up with inflation. At a minimum, new federal legislation should require states to supplement SSI for recipients living independently, at least enough to allow them to maintain a stable residence at the SRO or boarding house level. Even better would be expansion of federal SSI benefits, which are indexed to inflation, to provide an additional housing allowance sufficient for recipients to pay for appropriate housing in the community.

Finally, treatment programs for very poor alcoholic and drug-dependent people need to be greatly expanded. Existing programs cannot begin to meet the demand presented by people who want to stop drinking or taking drugs and ask for treatment, let alone those who might be encouraged to do so if serious help were available. A "war on drugs" cannot succeed if it concentrates on punishment without providing adequate treatment, and without affecting the social conditions that make drug-taking and drug-dealing attractive. Not only do we need programs that help people kick their habits, we also desperately need supportive environments to help people resist returning to their addiction. Many small programs around the country are currently experimenting with creating these living spaces, which may be as simple and low-cost as group living in a house of their own for five or six men who have stopped drinking, have jobs, pay the rent, and form their own support group. All such efforts should be encouraged, and their example spread for other groups to follow.

*   *   *   *

Homelessness can be viewed from the perspective of the individuals who become homeless, or from the perspective of the social conditions that foster homelessness. Most research on homelessness throughout the 1980s focused on describing the homeless and their problems. The result is an emphasis on the personal pathologies and difficulties of the people who become homeless. Beyond the stopgap measures of providing emergency food and shelter, proposed solutions have focused on helping individuals leave homelessness, by completing their education, learning to manage money, or overcoming their alcoholism. But these solutions ignore the changing societal conditions that have pushed people with little money, perhaps coupled with some personal vulnerabilities, into homelessness. If we are to solve the problem of homelessness we must look further.

As we saw in Chapters 3 through 6, many important societal conditions that might increase the risk of homelessness have changed during the 1980s. These structural factors include the earning power of people with a high school education or less, the types of jobs available, unemployment, the number of poor people, the cost of rental housing, the availability of single-room-occupancy hotels and similar very inexpensive housing for the poor, the value of public benefits, and the eligibility of many households for public benefit programs. Each of these changes would affect housing affordability, either by driving up the cost of housing or by lowering the resources that poor households have to spend on housing. In Chapters 7 through 10 we explored the causal impact of these factors on homelessness rates and the growth of homelessness between 1981 and 1989 in U.S. cities with populations over 100,000. Each was found to be an important influence.

These results argue strongly for a deep and long-term view of solutions to homelessness. It is clear that personal conditions such as poverty, mental illness, alcoholism, physical handicap, and drug addiction increase a person's vulnerability to homelessness; hence a large proportion of homeless people exhibit these characteristics. But many people have had these vulnerabilities in past decades. Only the changes in structural factors can explain why the vulnerabilities led to a much larger homeless population during the 1980s than in earlier times.

To undo the effects of changing structural factors we will have to address the factors themselves, not the vulnerabilities of the people caught by changing times. We can take a short-term approach, raising benefit levels and expanding eligibility to cover those most vulnerable to homelessness. Such actions would prevent homelessness rather than ameliorate it, and are therefore preferable to building emergency shelters. They would not, however, change the underlying conditions, and the need for public support would be likely to continue indefinitely. A far better approach is to fulfill our commitments to support people, such as those with severe mental illness, who cannot be expected to support themselves, and also address simultaneously the employer and the employee requirements for increasing productivity, by reshaping the work environment and improving education and training. If we succeed at this much larger agenda, we will solve not only the problem of homelessness, but also the problem of declining living standards for a much broader spectrum of American workers.

References

Ahrentzen, Sherry. 1985. "Residential Fit and Mobility among Low-income, Female-Headed Family Households in the United States." In Willem Van Vliet and Fava Huttman, eds., *Housing Needs and Policy Approaches*. Durham, N.C.: Duke University Press.

American Chamber of Commerce Researchers Association. *Cost of Living Index*. Alexandria, Va.: ACCRA, quarterly for 1985–1987.

Apgar, William C., Jr. 1989. "Recent Trends in Rental Vacancies." Working Paper 89-3. Cambridge, Mass.: Joint Center for Housing Studies of Harvard University.

Apgar, William C., Jr., H. James Brown, Arthur A. Doud, and George A. Schink. 1985. "Assessment of the Likely Impacts of the President's Tax Proposals on Rental Housing Markets." Cambridge, Mass.: Joint Center for Housing Studies of Harvard University.

Apgar, William C., Jr., Denise DiPasquale, Nancy McArdle, and Jennifer Olson. 1989. "The State of the Nation's Housing. 1989." Cambridge, Mass.: Joint Center for Housing Studies of Harvard University.

Appleby, Lawrence, and Prakash Desai. 1987. "Residential Instability: A Perspective on System Imbalance." *American Journal of Orthopsychiatry* 57(4): 515–524.

Appleby, Lawrence, and Prakash Desai. 1985. "Documenting the Relationship between Homelessness and Psychiatric Hospitalization." *Hospital and Community Psychiatry* 36(5): 732–737.

Bachrach, Leona. 1982. "Young Adult Chronic Patients: An Analytical Review of the Literature." *Hospital and Community Psychiatry* 33(3): 189–197.

Bachrach, Leona. 1979. *Deinstitutionalization: An Analytical Review and Sociological Perspective*. Rockville, Md.: NIMH, (ADM)79-351.

Bahr, Howard M., and Theodore Caplow. 1973. *Old Men: Drunk and Sober*. New York: New York University Press.

Bane, Mary Jo, and Paul A. Jargowsky. 1988. "Urban Poverty Areas: Basic Questions Concerning Prevalence, Growth, and Dynamics." Cambridge, Mass.: Center for Health and Human Resources Policy Discussion Paper Series, John F. Kennedy School of Government, Harvard University.

Barrow, Susan, and Anne M. Lovell. 1982. "Evaluation of Project Reach Out, 1981–1982." New York: New York Psychiatric Institute.

Bassuk, Ellen, and H. Richard Lamb. 1986. "Homelessness and the Implementation of Deinstitutionalization." In Ellen L. Bassuk, ed., *The Mental Health Needs of Homeless Persons.* San Francisco: Jossey-Bass.

Baxter, Ellen, and Kim Hopper. 1984. "Shelter and Housing for the Homeless Mentally Ill." In H. Richard Lamb, ed., *The Homeless Mentally Ill: A Task Force Report of the American Psychiatric Association.* Washington, D.C.: American Psychiatric Association.

Beirne, Kenneth. 1989. "Who Are the Homeless and Why Are They on the Streets?" In *Rethinking Policy on Homelessness,* Washington, D.C.: Heritage Foundation.

Birch, Eugenie L. 1985. "The Unsheltered Woman: Definition and Needs." In Eugenie L. Birch, ed., *The Unsheltered Woman: Women and Housing in the 80s.* New Brunswick, N.J.: Center for Urban Policy Research, Rutgers University.

Blackburn, McKinley L., and David E. Bloom. 1987. "Earnings and Income Inequality in the United States." *Population and Development Review* 13(4): 575–609.

Blackburn, McKinley L., David E. Bloom, and Richard B. Freeman. 1990. "The Declining Economic Position of Less-skilled American Males." In Gary Burtless, ed., *A Future of Lousy Jobs?: The Changing Structure of U.S. Wages.* Washington, D.C.: Brookings Institution.

Bluestone, Barry. 1990. "Comment." In Gary Burtless, ed., *A Future of Lousy Jobs?: The Changing Structure of U.S. Wages.* Washington, D.C.: Brookings Institution, pp. 68–76.

Bluestone, Barry, and Bennett Harrison. 1988. "The Growth of Low-wage Employment: 1963–86." *American Economic Review* 78(5): 124–128.

Bluestone, Barry, and Bennett Harrison. 1982. *The Deindustrialization of America.* New York: Basic Books.

Bogue, Donald B. 1963. *Skid Row in American Cities.* Chicago: Community and Family Study Center, University of Chicago.

Brady, James. 1983. "Arson, Urban Economy, and Organized Crime: The Case of Boston." *Social Problems* 31(1): 1–27.

Burt, Martha R., and Barbara E. Cohen. 1990. "A Sociodemographic Profile of the Service-using Homeless: Findings from a National Survey." In Jamshid A. Momeni, ed., *Homelessness in the United States, Volume II: Data and Issues.* Westport, Conn.: Greenwood Press.

Burt, Martha R., and Barbara E. Cohen. 1989a. *America's Homeless: Numbers, Characteristics, and the Programs that Serve Them.* Washington, D.C.: Urban Institute Press.

Burt, Martha R., and Barbara E. Cohen. 1989b. "Differences among Homeless Single Women, Women with Children, and Single Men." *Social Problems* 36(5): 508–524.

Burt, Martha R., and Barbara E. Cohen. 1989c. "Who Is Helping the Homeless?: Local, State and Federal Responses." *Publius: The Journal of Federalism* 19(3): 111–128.

Burt, Martha R., and Barbara E. Cohen. 1988. *Feeding the Homeless: Does the Prepared Meals Provision Help?* Washington, D.C.: Urban Institute.

Burt, Martha R., and Karen J. Pittman. 1985. *Testing the Social Safety Net.* Washington, D.C.: Urban Institute Press.

Burtless, Gary, ed. 1990a. *A Future of Lousy Jobs?: The Changing Structure of U.S. Wages.* Washington, D.C.: Brookings Institution.

Burtless, Gary. 1990b. "Earnings Inequality over the Business and Demographic Cycles." In Gary Burtless, ed., *A Future of Lousy Jobs?: The Changing Structure of U.S. Wages.* Washington, D.C.: Brookings Institution.

Butler, J.S., and J. Raymond. 1987. *Knowledge Is Better than Money: The Effect of the Food Stamp Program on Nutrient Intake.* Madison, Wisc.: Institute for Research on Poverty.

Butler, Stuart M. 1989. "What Can Be Done to Reduce Homelessness?" In *Rethinking Policy on Homelessness,* Washington, D.C.: Heritage Foundation.

Chicago Department of Planning. 1985. "Housing Needs of Chicago's Single, Low Income Renters." Manuscript report. Cited in Rossi, 1989.

City of Boston, Emergency Shelter Commission. 1983. "The October Project: Seeing the Obvious Problem." Boston: City of Boston.

City of Boston. 1986. "Making Room: Comprehensive Policy for the Homeless." Boston: City of Boston.

Cohen, Barbara E., and Martha R. Burt. 1990. "Food Sources and Intake of Homeless Persons." In Jamshid A. Momeni, ed., *Homelessness in the United States, Volume II: Data and Issues.* Westport, Conn.: Greenwood Press.

Cohen, Barbara E., and Martha R. Burt. 1989. *Eliminating Hunger: Food Security Policy for the 1990s.* Washington, D.C.: Urban Institute.

Congressional Budget Office. 1988. *Current Housing Problems and Possible Federal Responses.* Washington, D.C.: U.S. Government Printing Office.

Cotton, Jeremiah. 1989. "Opening the Gap: The Decline in Black Economic Indicators in the 1980s." *Social Science Quarterly* 70(4): 803–819.

Council on Competitiveness. 1987. *America's Competitive Crisis: Confronting the New Reality.* Washington, D.C.: Council on Competitiveness.

Crouse, Joan M. 1986. *The Homeless Transient in the Great Depression: New York State, 1929–1941.* Albany: SUNY Press.

Danziger, Sheldon H., Robert H. Haveman, and Robert D. Plotnick. 1986. "Antipoverty Policy: Effects on the Poor and the Nonpoor." In Sheldon H. Danziger and Daniel H. Weinberg, eds., *Fighting Poverty: What Works and What Doesn't.* Cambridge, Mass.: Harvard University Press.

Denton, Nancy A., and Douglas S. Massey. 1989. "Residential Segregation of Blacks, Hispanics, and Asians by Socioeconomic Status and Generation." *Social Science Quarterly* 69: 797–817.

Department of Housing and Urban Development. 1989. *A Report on the 1988 National Survey of Shelters for the Homeless.* Washington, D.C.: Department of Housing and Urban Development, Office of Policy Development and Research.

Department of Housing and Urban Development. 1984. *A Report to the Secretary on the Homeless and Emergency Shelters.* Washington, D.C.: Department of Housing and Urban Development, Office of Policy Development and Research.

Dertouzos, Michael L., Richard K. Lester, Robert M. Solow, and the MIT Commission on Industrial Productivity. 1989. *Made in America: Regaining the Productive Edge.* Cambridge, Mass.: MIT Press.

Devaney, Barbara, and Robert Moffitt. 1990. "Assessing the Dietary Effects of the Food

Stamp Program. In C. Trippe, N. Heiser, and H. Beebout, eds., *Food Stamp Policy Issues: Results from Recent Research*. Alexandria, Va.: USDA, Food and Nutrition Service, January.

DiPasquale, Denise, and William Wheaton. 1989. "The Cost of Capital, Tax Reform and the Future of the Rental Housing Market." Cambridge, Mass.: Joint Center for Housing Studies of Harvard University.

Dolbeare, Cushing N. 1989. *Out of Reach: Why Ordinary People Can't Find Affordable Housing*. Washington, D.C.: Low Income Housing Information Service.

Dolbeare, Cushing N. 1988. "Why a Housing Entitlement Program?" Paper presented at Urban Institute Housing Seminar, Washington, D.C.: December.

Downs, Anthony. 1983. *Rental Housing in the 1980s*. Washington, D.C.: Brookings Institution.

Ehrenreich, Barbara. 1989. *Fear of Falling: The Inner Life of the Middle Class*. New York: Pantheon.

Elliott, Marta, and Lauren J. Krivo. 1991. "Structural Determinants of Homelessness in the United States." *Social Problems* 38(1) 113–131.

Ellwood, David T. 1988. *Poor Support: Poverty in the American Family*. New York: Basic Books.

Farr, Rodger K., Paul Koegel, and Audrey Burnam. 1986. *A Study of Homelessness and Mental Illness in the Skid Row Area of Los Angeles*. Los Angeles: Los Angeles County Department of Mental Health.

Fischer, Pamela J. 1987. "Substance Abuse in Contemporary Homeless Populations." In Deborah L. Dennis, ed., *Research Methodologies Concerning Homeless Persons with Serious Mental Illness and/or Substance Abuse Disorders*. Albany, N.Y.: Bureau of Survey and Evaluation Research, New York State Office of Mental Health.

Friedman, Benjamin M. 1988. *Day of Reckoning: The Consequences of American Economic Policy in the 1980s*. New York: Random House.

Galster, George C. 1987. "The Ecology of Racial Discrimination in Housing: An Exploratory Model." *Urban Affairs Quarterly* 23: 84–107.

General Accounting Office. 1988. *The Homeless Mentally Ill: Problems and Options in Estimating Numbers and Trends*. Washington, D.C.: USGPO, GAO/RCED-88-63.

General Accounting Office. 1987. *Homelessness: Implementation of Food and Shelter Programs under the McKinney Act*. Washington, D.C.: U.S. General Accounting Office, GAO/RCED-88-63.

General Accounting Office. 1985. *Changes in Rent Burdens and Housing Conditions of Lower Income Households*. Washington, D.C.: U.S. Government Printing Office, GAO/RCED-85-108.

Gilderbloom, John I. 1986. "Trends in the Affordability of Rental Housing." *Sociology and Social Research* 70: 301–302.

Gilderbloom, John I. 1985. "An Analysis of Intercity Rents." In Paul L. Niebanck, ed., *The Rent Control Debate*. Chapel Hill, N.C.: University of North Carolina Press.

Gilderbloom, John I., and Richard P. Appelbaum. 1988. *Rethinking Rental Housing*. Philadelphia: Temple University Press.

Goldman, Howard H. 1984. "Epidemiology." In John A. Talbott, ed., *The Chronic Mental Patient: Five Years Later*. Orlando, Fla.: Grune & Stratton, Inc.

Goplerud, Eric. 1987. "Homelessness in Fairfax County." Fairfax, Va.: George Mason University, Department of Sociology.

Gramlich, Edward M. 1976. "Impact of Minimum Wages on Other Wages, Employment, and Family Incomes." *Brookings Papers on Economic Activity* 2:409–451.

Greider, William. 1988. *Secrets of the Temple: How the Federal Reserve Runs the Country.* New York: Simon & Schuster.

Hamilton, Rabinowitz, and Alschuler, Inc. 1987. *The Changing Face of Misery: Los Angeles' Skid Row Area in Transition—Housing and Social Service Needs of Central City East.* Los Angeles: Community Redevelopment Agency.

Harrison, Bennett, and Barry Bluestone. 1988. *The Great U-Turn: Corporate Restructuring and the Polarizing of America.* New York, Basic Books.

Hartman, Chester. 1986. "The Housing Part of the Homelessness Problem." In Ellen L. Bassuk, ed., *The Mental Health Needs of Homeless Persons.* San Francisco: Jossey-Bass.

Hoch, Charles, and Robert A. Slayton. 1989. *New Homeless and Old: Community and the Skid Row Hotel.* Philadelphia: Temple University Press.

Hoch, Charles, and Diane Spicer. 1985. *SROs, an Endangered Species: Single-room Occupancy Hotels in Chicago.* Chicago: Community Shelter Organization and Jewish Council on Urban Affairs.

Hombs, Mary Ellen, and Mitch Snyder. 1982. *Homelessness in America: A Forced March to Nowhere.* Washington, D.C.: Community for Creative Non-Violence.

Hopper, Kim, and Jill Hamberg. 1986. "The Making of America's Homeless: From Skid Row to the New Poor, 1945–1984." In Rachel G. Bratt, Chester Hartman, and Ann Myerson, eds., *Critical Perspectives on Housing.* Philadelphia: Temple University Press.

Jackson, Kenneth M. 1987. "The Bowery: From Residential Street to Skid Row." In Rick Beard, ed., *On Being Homeless: Historical Perspectives.* New York: Museum of the City of New York.

Jargowsky, Paul, and Mary Jo Bane. 1990. "Urban Poverty: Basic Questions." Cambridge, Mass.: Center for Health and Human Resources Policy, John F. Kennedy School of Government, Harvard University.

Johnston, Lloyd D., Patrick M. O'Malley, and Jerald G. Bachman. 1989. *Drug Use, Drinking, Smoking: National Survey Results from High School, College, and Young Adult Populations, 1975–1988.* Rockville, Md.: DHHS/ADAMHA/NIDA, (ADM)89-1638.

Kanter, Arlene S. 1989. "Homeless but not Helpless: Legal Issues in the Care of the Mentally Ill." *Journal of Social Issues* 45(3): 91–104.

Klein, Bruce W., and Philip L. Rones. 1989. "A Profile of the Working Poor." *Monthly Labor Review,* 112(10): 3–13.

Kondratas, Anna. 1989. "What Can Be Done to Reduce Homelessness?" In *Rethinking Policy on Homelessness.* Washington, D.C.: Heritage Foundation.

Lamb, H. Richard. 1984. "Deinstitutionalization and the Homeless Mentally Ill." In H. Richard Lamb, ed., *The Homeless Mentally Ill: A Task Force Report of the American Psychiatric Association.* Washington, D.C.: American Psychiatric Association.

Lamb, H. Richard. 1981. "Young Adult Chronic Patients: The New Drifters." *Hospital and Community Psychiatry* 33: 465–468.

Lamb, H. Richard, and R. W. Grant. 1982. "The Mentally Ill in an Urban County Jail." *Archives of General Psychiatry* 39: 17–22.

Lee, Barrett A. 1989. "Stability and Change in an Urban Homeless Population." *Demography* 26(2): 323–334.

Lee, Barrett A. 1980. "The Disappearance of Skid Row: Some Ecological Evidence." *Urban Affairs Quarterly* 16(1): 81–107.

Leonard, Paul A., Cushing N. Dolbeare, and Edward B. Lazere. 1989. *A Place to Call Home: The Crisis in Housing for the Poor.* Washington, D.C.: Center on Budget and Policy Priorities/Low Income Housing Information Service.

Levine, Irene S., Ann D. Lezak, and Howard H. Goldman. 1986. "Community Support Systems for the Homeless Mentally Ill." In Ellen L. Bassuk, ed., *The Mental Health Needs of Homeless Persons.* San Francisco: Jossey-Bass.

Levy, Frank. 1988. "Incomes, Families and Living Standards." In Robert E. Litan, Robert Z. Lawrence, and Charles E. Schultze, eds. *American Living Standards: Threats and Challenges.* Washington, D.C.: Brookings Institution.

Levy, Frank. 1987. *Dollars and Dreams: The Changing American Income Distribution.* New York: Russell Sage Foundation.

Levy, Frank, and Richard C. Michel. 1991. *The Economic Future of American Families: Income and Wealth Trends.* Washington, D.C: Urban Institute Press.

Litan, Robert E., Robert Z. Lawrence, and Charles E. Schultze. 1988/1989. "Improving American Living Standards. *Brookings Review,* Winter 7(1): 27.

Litan, Robert E., Robert Z. Lawrence, and Charles E. Schultze, eds. 1988. *American Living Standards: Threats and Challenges.* Washington, D.C.: Brookings Institution.

Low Income Housing Information Service. 1985. *The Rental Housing Crisis Index.* Washington, D.C.: Low Income Housing Information Service.

Lurigio, Arthur J., and Dan A. Lewis. 1989. "Worlds that Fail: A Longitudinal Study of Urban Mental Patients." *Journal of Social Issues* 45(3): 79–90.

Marans, Robert W., and Mary Ellen Colten. 1985. "United States Rental Housing Practices Affecting Families with Children: Hard Times for Youth." In Willem Van Vliet and Fava Huttman, eds., *Housing Needs and Policy Approaches.* Durham, N.C.: Duke University Press.

Mare, Robert D., and Christopher Winship. 1991. "Socioeconomic Change and the Decline of Marriage for Blacks and Whites." In Christopher Jencks and Paul Peterson, eds., *The Urban Underclass.* Washington, D.C.: The Brookings Institution.

Massey, Douglas S. and Nancy A. Denton. 1989. "Residential Segregation of Mexicans, Puerto Ricans, and Cubans in Selected U.S. Metropolitan Areas." *Sociology and Social Research, 73:* 73–82.

Massey, Douglas S., and Nancy A. Denton. 1988. "The Dimensions of Residential Segregation." *Social Forces* 67: 281–315.

Massey, Douglas S., and Nancy A. Denton. 1987. "Trends in the Residential Segregation of Blacks, Hispanics and Asians: 1970–1980." *American Sociological Review* 52: 802–825.

Massey, Douglas S., and Mitchell L. Eggers. 1990. "The Ecology of Inequality:

Minorities and the Concentration of Poverty, 1970–1980." *American Journal of Sociology* 95(5): 1153–1188.

Maxwell, Nan L. 1989. "Demographic and Economic Determinants of United States Income Inequality." *Social Science Quarterly* 70(2): 245–264.

McLanahan, Sara S., Annemette Sorensen, and Dorothy Watson. 1989. "Sex Differences in Poverty, 1950–1980." *Signs: Journal of Women in Culture and Society* 15(1): 102–122.

Michel, Philip. 1983. "The SSI/SSDI Controversy: How and Why the Social Security Administration Has Reduced the Number of SSI/SSDI Beneficiaries." Ann Arbor, Mich.: State of Michigan, Interagency Task Force on Disability, April.

Michel, Richard C. 1990. "Economic Growth and Income Equality Since the 1982 Recession." Washington, D.C.: Urban Institute.

Milburn, Norweeta G. 1990. "Drug Abuse among Homeless People." In Jamshid A. Momeni, ed., *Homelessness in the United States: Volume II, Data and Issues.* Westport, Conn.: Greenwood Press.

Milgram, Grace. 1990. "Trends in Funding and Numbers of Households in HUD-Assisted Housing, Fiscal Years 1975–1989." Washington, D.C.: Congressional Research Service, CRS Report for Congress 90-266 E.

Milgram, Grace. 1989. "Urban Housing Assistance Programs in the United States." Washington, D.C.: Congressional Research Service, CRS Report for Congress 89-137 E.

Milgram, Grace, and Robert Bury. 1987. "Existing Housing Resources vs. Need." Washington, D.C.: Congressional Research Services, CRS Report for Congress 87-81-E.

Minarik, Joseph J. 1988. "Family Incomes." In Isabel V. Sawhill, ed., *Challenge to Leadership: Economic and Social Issues for the Next Decade.* Washington, D.C.: Urban Institute Press

Mincy, Ronald B. 1990. "Raising the Minimum Wage: Effects on Family Poverty." *Monthly Labor Review* 113(7): 18–25.

Minimum Wage Study Commission. 1981. *Report of the Minimum Wage Study Commission: Volume I.* Washington, D.C.: U.S. Government Printing Office.

Moon, Marilyn, and Isabel V. Sawhill. 1984. "Family Incomes: Gainers and Losers." In John L. Palmer and Isabel V. Sawhill, eds., *The Reagan Record.* Washington, D.C.: Urban Institute Press.

Morrissey, Joseph P., and Howard H. Goldman. 1984. "Cycles of Reform in the Care of the Chronically Mentally Ill." *Hospital and Community Psychiatry* 35: 785–793.

Mulkern, Virginia, and Rebecca Spence. 1984. "Illicit Drug Use among Homeless Persons: A Review of the Literature." Boston, Mass.: Human Services Research Institute.

Mutchler, Jan E., and Lauren J. Krivo. 1989. "Availability and Affordability: Household Adaptation to a Housing Squeeze." *Social Forces* 68(1): 241–261.

National Association of State Alcohol and Drug Abuse Directors. 1984, 1985, 1986, 1987, 1988. "State Alcohol and Drug Abuse Profiles, 1984–1988." Washington, D.C.: National Association of State Alcohol and Drug Abuse Directors.

National Association of State Mental Health Program Directors and NASMHPD Research Institute, Inc. 1990. *Funding Sources and Expenditures of State Mental Health Agencies: Revenue/Expenditure Study Results FY 1987.* Alexandria, Va.: NASMHPD and NASMHPD Research Institute, Inc.

National Institute on Alcohol Abuse and Alcoholism. 1987. *Sixth Special Report to the U.S. Congress on Alcohol and Health.* Rockville, Md.: USDHHS/NIAAA.

National Institute on Drug Abuse. 1990. Unpublished data from the DAWN System—"Dawn Drug-by-SMSA Quarter Totals for 60 Months Ending December 1989." Rockville, Md.: NIDA, Run date: April 20.

National Institute on Drug Abuse. 1989. *National Household Survey on Drug Abuse: Population Estimates, 1988.* Rockville, Md.: NIDA, (ADM)89-1636.

National Institute on Drug Abuse. 1987a. *Trends in Drug Abuse Related Hospital Emergency Room Episodes and Medical Examiner Cases for Selected Drugs: DAWN, 1976–1985.* Rockville, Md.: NIDA, Series H, Number 3 (ADM)87-1524.

National Institute on Drug Abuse. 1987b. *Cocaine-related Client Admissions, 1979–1984.* Rockville, Md.: NIDA, (ADM)87-1528.

National Research Council. 1983. *Toward a New Era in U.S. Manufacturing: The Need for a New Vision.* Washington, D.C.: National Academy Press.

Nelson, Kathryn. 1990. "Assisting Low Income Families: Policy Implications of Priority Housing Needs." Washington, D.C.: Department of Housing and Urban Development, Office of Policy Development and Research. Paper presented at the American Sociological Association Annual Meeting, August.

Neuhauser, L. 1988. *Method for Determining Welfare Food Allowances for Recipients of General Assistance.* Berkeley, Calif.: University of California at Berkeley, Doctoral Dissertation.

Newman, Katherine S. 1988. *Falling from Grace: The Experience of Downward Mobility in the American Middle Class.* New York: Free Press (Macmillan).

Newman, Sandra J., and Ann B. Schnare. 1988. *Subsidizing Shelter: The Relationship between Welfare and Housing Assistance.* Washington, D.C.: Urban Institute Press.

Pepper, Bert, M.C. Kirshner, and Harriet Ryglewicz. 1981. "The Young Adult Chronic Patient: Overview of a Population." *Hospital and Community Psychiatry* 32: 463–469.

Pepper, Bert, and Harriet Ryglewicz. 1984. "Young Adult Chronic Patients." In John A. Talbott, ed., *The Chronic Mental Patient: Five Years Later.* Orlando, Fla.: Grune & Stratton, Inc.

Peterson, Richard A., and Bruce Weigand. 1985. "Ordering Disorderly Work Careers on Skid Row." In Richard L. Simpson and Ida H. Simpson, eds., *Research in the Sociology of Work: Unemployment.* Greenwich, Conn.: JAI Press.

Piliavin, Irving, Michael R. Sosin, and Herb Westerfelt. 1987. "Tracking the Homeless." *Focus* 10(4): 20–25.

Piliavin, Irving, Herb Westerfelt, and Elsa Elliott. 1989. "Estimating Mental Illness among the Homeless: The Effects of Choice-based Sampling." *Social Problems* 36(5): 525–531.

President's Commission on Industrial Competitiveness. 1985. *Global Competition: The New Reality.* Washington, D.C.: U.S. Government Printing Office.

Quigley, John M. 1990. "Does Rent Control Cause Homelessness?: Taking the Claim Seriously." *Journal of Policy Analysis and Management* 9: 88–93.

The Resource Group. 1989. *Homelessness in Houston, Harris County and Gulf Coast United Way Service Delivery Areas: Report of Data Collection and Analysis*. Austin, Tex.: Resource Group.

Ricketts, Erol R., and Isabel V. Sawhill. 1988. "Defining and Measuring the Underclass." *Journal of Policy Analysis and Management* 7: 316–325.

Ridgely, M. Susan, Howard H. Goldman, and Mark Willenbring. 1990. "Barriers to Care for Persons with Dual Diagnoses: Organization and Financing Issues." *Schizophrenia Bulletin* 16(1): 123–132.

Rossi, Peter H. 1989. *Down and Out in America: The Origins of Homelessness*. Chicago: University of Chicago Press.

Rossi, Peter H., Gene A. Fisher, and Georgianna Willis. 1986. *The Condition of the Homeless in Chicago*. Amherst, Mass., and Chicago: Social and Demographic Research Institute and the National Opinion Research Center.

Roth, Dee, Jerry Bean, Nancy Lust, and Traian Saveanu. 1985. *Homelessness in Ohio: A Study of People in Need*. Columbus, Ohio: Ohio Department of Mental Health.

Schervish, Paul G. 1985. "Unemployment as a Transition Status: Micro Evidence for Structural Shifts in the Labor Market." In Richard L. Simpson and Ida H. Simpson, eds., *Research in the Sociology of Work: Unemployment*. Greenwich, Conn.: JAI Press.

Shapiro, Isaac, and Robert Greenstein. 1988. *Holes in the Safety Nets*. Washington, D.C.: Center on Budget and Policy Priorities.

Shern, David L., Richard C. Surles, and Jonas Waizer. 1989. "Designing Community Treatment Systems for the Most Seriously Mentally Ill: A State Administrative Perspective." *Journal of Social Issues* 45(3): 105–118.

Smith, Lawrence B., Kenneth T. Rosen, Anil Markandya, and Pierre-Antoine Ullmo. 1984. "The Demand for Housing, Household Headship Rates, and Household Formation: An International Analysis." *Urban Studies* 21: 407–414.

Smith, Neil, Betsy Duncan and Laura Reid. 1989. "From Disinvestment to Reinvestment: Tax Arrears and Turning Points in the East Village." *Housing Studies* 4(4): 238–252.

Smith, Neil, and Peter Williams. 1986. *Gentrification of the City*. Boston: Unwin, Hyman.

Smith, Ralph E., and Bruce Vavrichek. 1987. "The Minimum Wage: Its Relation to Incomes and Poverty." *Monthly Labor Review* 110(6): 24–30.

Snow, David A., Susan G. Baker, and Leon Anderson. 1989. "Criminality and Homeless Men: An Empirical Assessment." *Social Problems* 36(5): 532–549.

Sosin, Michael R., Paul Colson, and Susan Grossman. 1988. *Homelessness in Chicago: Poverty and Pathology, Social Institutions and Social Change*. Chicago: Chicago Community Trust.

Stanback, Thomas M., Jr., and Thierry Noyelle. 1982. *Cities in Transition*. Totowa, N.J.: Allanheld, Osmun.

Stark, Louisa. 1987. "A Century of Alcohol and Homelessness: Demographics and Stereotypes." *Alcohol Health and Research World* 11(3): 813.

Steering Committee on the Chronically Mentally Ill. 1980. *Toward a National Plan for the Chronically Mentally Ill*. Washington, D.C.: U.S. Department of Health and Human Services, Publication (ADM) 81-1077.

Stein, Leonard I., and Mary Ann Test. 1980. "Alternatives to Mental Hospital Treatment

I: Conceptual Model, Treatment Program, and Clinical Evaluation. *Archives of General Psychiatry* 37: 392–397.

Sternlieb, George, and James W. Hughes. 1985. "The Market Structure of the Rental Sector." In Paul L. Niebanck, ed., *The Rent Control Debate*. Chapel Hill, N.C.: University of North Carolina Press.

Stone, Michael E. 1983. "Housing and the Economic Crisis: An Analysis and an Emergency Program." In Chester Hartman, ed., *America's Housing Crisis: What Is to Be Done?* Boston: Routledge & Kegan Paul.

Struyk, Raymond J., Margery A. Turner, and Makiko Ueno. 1988. *Future U.S. Housing Policy: Meeting the Demographic Challenge*. Washington, D.C.: Urban Institute Press.

Sullivan, Patricia A., and Shirley P. Damrosch. 1987. "Homeless Women and Children." In Richard D. Bingham, Roy E. Green, and Sammis B. White, eds., *The Homeless in Contemporary Society*. Beverly Hills, Calif.: Sage Publications.

Suro, Roberto. 1991. "Where Have All the Jobs Gone? Follow the Crab Grass." *New York Times*, Section E, p. 5, Sunday, March 2.

Tessler, Richard C., and Deborah L. Dennis. 1989. *A Synthesis of NIMH-funded Research Concerning Persons Who Are Homeless and Mentally Ill*. Amherst, Mass.: Social and Demographic Research Institute.

Tessler, Richard C., and Howard H. Goldman. 1982. *The Chronically Mentally Ill: Assessing Community Support Programs*. Cambridge, Mass.: Ballinger.

Toomey, Beverly. 1990. The Ohio State University, College of Social Work. Principal Investigator, study of rural homelessness in Ohio. Personal communication, November.

Turner, Margery, Raymond J. Struyk, and John Yinger. 1990. "Access Denied, Access Constrained: Housing Discrimination in Urban America." Washington, D.C.: Urban Institute.

U.S. Bureau of the Census. 1989. *County Business Patterns: 1987*. Washington, D.C.: USGPO.

U. S. Bureau of the Census. 1989. *Money Income and Poverty Status in the United States: 1988*. Bureau of the Census, Current Population Reports, Series P-60, No. 166.

U. S. Bureau of the Census. 1988. *County and City Data Book: 1988*. Washington, D.C.: USGPO.

U.S. Bureau of the Census. 1988. *Local Government Finances in Major County Areas: 1985–1986* (GF-86-6). Washington, D.C.: USGPO.

U. S. Bureau of the Census. 1982. *Census of Population* (PC80-1-C). Washington, D.C.: USGPO.

U. S. Bureau of the Census. 1982. *Census of Housing* (HC80-2-58/380). Washington, D.C.: USGPO.

U.S. Bureau of the Census. 1982. *County Business Patterns: 1980*. Washington, D.C.: USGPO.

U.S. Department of Agriculture, Food and Nutrition Service, Office of Analysis and Evaluation. 1990. *Characteristics of Food Stamp Households: Summer 1987*. Alexandria, Va.: FNS/OAE.

U.S. Department of Health and Human Services and U.S. Department of Agriculture.

1986. *Nutrition Monitoring in the United States: A Report from the Joint Nutrition Monitoring Evaluation Committee*. Washington, D.C.: USDHHS.

U.S. Department of Health and Human Services, Steering Committee on the Chronically Mentally Ill. 1980. *Toward a National Plan for the Chronically Mentally Ill*. Washington, D.C.: USDHHS.

U.S. House of Representatives, Committee on Ways and Means. 1990. *Overview of Entitlement Programs: The 1990 Green Book*. Washington, D.C.: USGPO.

U.S. House of Representatives, Committee on Ways and Means. 1989. *Background Material and Data on Programs within the Jurisdiction of the Committee on Ways and Means*. Washington, D.C.: USGPO.

Urban Systems Research and Engineering, Inc. 1983. *1982 Characteristics of General Assistance Programs*. Washington, D.C.: Urban Systems R&E, Inc.

Vernez, Georges, M. Audrey Burnam, Elizabeth A. McGlynn, Sally Trude, and Brian Mittman. 1988. *Review of California's Program for the Homeless Mentally Disabled*. Santa Monica, Calif.: Rand Corporation.

Warner, Richard. 1989. "Deinstitutionalization: How Did We Get Where We Are?" *Journal of Social Issues* 45(3): 17–30.

Weicha, Jean L., and Ruth Palombo. 1989. "Multiple Program Participation: Comparisons of Nutrition and Food Assistance Program Benefits with Food Cost in Boston, Massachusetts." *American Journal of Public Health* 79(5):591–594.

Weicher, John C., Kevin E. Villani, and Elizabeth A. Roistacher, eds. 1981. *Rental Housing: Is There a Crisis?* Washington, D.C.: Urban Institute.

Weigand, R. Bruce. 1990. "Sweat and Blood: Sources of Income on a Southern Skid Row." In Jamshid A. Momeni, ed., *Homelessness in the United States: Volume II, Data and Issues*. Westport, Conn.: Greenwood Press.

Weigand, Bruce. 1985. "Counting the Homeless: Nashville, Tennessee." *American Demographics*, December.

Weitzman, Beth C. 1989. "Pregnancy and Childbirth: Risk Factors for Homelessness?" *Family Planning Perspectives* 21(4): 175–198.

Wienk, Ron, Cliff Reid, John Simonson, and Fred Eggers. 1979. *Measuring Racial Discrimination in American Housing Markets: The Housing Market Practices Survey*. Washington, D.C.: U.S. Department of Housing and Urban Development.

Wilson, William Julius. 1987. *The Truly Disadvantaged: The Inner City, the Underclass, and Public Policy*. Chicago: University of Chicago Press.

Wright, James D., Janet W. Knight, Eleanor Weber-Burdin, and Julie Lam. 1987. "Ailments and Alcohol: Health Status among the Drinking Homeless." *Alcohol Health and Research World* 11(3): 22–27.

Wright, James D., and Julie A. Lam. 1987. "Homelessness and the Low-Income Housing Supply." *Social Policy* 17:48–53.

Wright, James D., and Eleanor Weber. 1987. *Homelessness and Health*. New York: McGraw-Hill.

Appendix A Cities Over 100,000 in 1986

City	State	Suburb[a]	1986 Population	1980 Population	1989 Homeless Rate	1989 Unemployment Rate	1989 GA Payment	1989 GA Type[b]
Anchorage	AK	0	235	174	22.21	5.1	120	2
Birmingham	AL	0	278	284	35.17	7.9	0	0
Mobile	AL	0	203	200	6.15	8.9	0	0
Montgomery	AL	0	194	178	5.66	6.4	0	0
Huntsville	AL	0	163	143	25.46	4.9	0	0
Little Rock	AR	0	181	159	25.96	5.8	0	0
Phoenix	AZ	0	894	790	15.31	4.4	173	1
Tucson	AZ	0	359	331	27.20	4.5	173	1
Mesa	AZ	1	251	152	2.43	4.0	173	1
Tempe	AZ	1	136	107	3.66	3.6	173	1
Glendale	AZ	1	126	97	1.11	4.3	173	1
Scottsdale	AZ	1	111	89	.00	3.1	173	1
Los Angeles	CA	0	3259	2969	13.18	5.2	312	2
San Diego	CA	0	1015	876	8.85	4.0	291	2
San Francisco	CA	0	749	679	36.89	4.1	341	2
San Jose	CA	0	712	629	12.51	3.2	341	2
Long Beach	CA	1	396	361	5.48	4.5	312	2
Oakland	CA	0	357	339	11.68	5.9	320	2
Sacramento	CA	0	324	276	21.79	5.6	281	2
Fresno	CA	0	285	217	19.71	8.8	341	2
Anaheim	CA	1	241	219	2.24	3.3	321	2
Santa Ana	CA	0	237	204	13.35	3.8	321	2
Riverside	CA	0	197	171	6.71	6.6	253	2
Huntington Beach	CA	1	184	171	.27	2.9	321	2
Stockton	CA	0	183	150	21.04	9.4	233	2
Glendale	CA	1	154	139	1.78	3.1	312	2
Fremont	CA	1	154	132	7.88	3.6	320	2

City	State							
Bakersfield	CA	0	150	106	6.98	7.0	341	2
San Bernardino	CA	0	139	119	10.03	6.0	222	2
Torrance	CA	1	136	130	.00	2.7	312	2
Garden Grove	CA	1	135	123	2.08	3.4	321	2
Modesto	CA	0	133	107	32.04	9.7	310	2
Pasadena	CA	1	130	118	8.24	3.7	312	2
Oxnard	CA	0	127	108	32.84	7.5	326	2
Chula Vista	CA	1	119	84	4.21	2.9	291	2
Pomona	CA	1	116	93	11.03	5.8	312	2
Ontario	CA	1	114	89	.00	4.3	222	2
Sunnyvale	CA	1	112	107	8.92	2.9	341	2
Fullerton	CA	1	109	102	2.30	3.0	321	2
Concord	CA	1	106	104	15.75	3.7	284	2
Berkeley	CA	1	104	103	12.77	4.2	320	2
Inglewood	CA	1	103	94	19.80	5.2	312	2
Hayward	CA	1	102	94	16.06	4.4	320	2
Orange	CA	1	101	91	8.54	2.7	321	2
Denver	CO	0	505	493	29.68	6.2	0	0
Colorado Springs	CO	0	273	215	17.35	6.7	0	0
Aurora	CO	1	218	159	1.42	5.0	0	0
Lakewood	CO	1	122	114	9.58	4.7	0	0
Pueblo	CO	0	101	102	9.19	8.2	0	0
Bridgeport	CT	0	142	143	10.43	7.2	426	2
Hartford	CT	0	138	136	39.64	6.8	426	2
New Haven	CT	0	123	126	17.01	5.0	426	2
Waterbury	CT	0	102	103	21.80	5.6	426	2
Stamford	CT	0	101	102	18.80	3.0	426	2
Washington	DC	0	626	638	56.89	5.0	256	1
Jacksonville	FL	0	610	541	12.05	5.9	0	0
Miami	FL	0	374	347	24.44	7.9	0	0
Tampa	FL	0	273	272	25.87	5.4	0	0

Appendix A Continued

City	State	Suburb[a]	1986 Population	1980 Population	1989 Homeless Rate	1989 Unemployment Rate	1989 GA Payment	1989 GA Type[b]
St. Petersburg	FL	0	239	239	17.13	5.4	0	0
Hialeah	FL	1	162	145	.00	7.7	0	0
Ft. Lauderdale	FL	0	149	153	17.09	5.1	0	0
Orlando	FL	1	146	128	7.75	5.2	0	0
Hollywood	FL	0	121	121	.00	5.4	0	0
Tallahassee	FL	0	119	82	5.02	5.0	0	0
Atlanta	GA	0	422	425	65.44	7.5	240	1
Columbus	GA	0	180	169	19.48	5.6	0	0
Savannah	GA	0	147	142	20.57	5.7	0	0
Macon	GA	0	118	117	7.09	5.8	0	0
Honolulu	HI	0	372	365	17.16	2.2	357	1
Des Moines	IA	0	192	191	38.37	4.2	0	0
Cedar Rapids	IA	0	108	110	11.17	3.6	0	0
Boise City	ID	0	108	102	23.99	3.4	0	0
Chicago	IL	0	3010	3005	10.09	7.3	165	2
Rockford	IL	0	136	140	10.31	8.2	0	0
Peoria	IL	0	110	124	27.75	6.5	150	2
Springfield	IL	0	100	100	7.08	5.7	209	2
Indianapolis	IN	0	720	701	9.42	4.4	0	0
Ft. Wayne	IN	0	173	172	9.72	4.9	0	0
Gary	IN	0	137	152	7.02	8.9	0	0
Evansville	IN	0	129	130	13.13	5.2	0	0
South Bend	IN	0	107	110	17.26	5.2	0	0
Wichita	KS	0	289	280	6.72	4.6	198	2
Kansas City	KS	0	162	161	8.82	7.0	198	2
Topeka	KS	0	119	119	18.38	4.3	198	2
Louisville	KY	0	286	299	36.86	6.2	0	0

Lexington-Fayette	KY	0	213	204	8.27	3.3	0	0
New Orleans	LA	0	555	558	13.40	7.6	0	0
Baton Rouge	LA	0	241	220	6.43	6.6	0	0
Shreveport	LA	0	220	206	14.07	8.2	0	0
Boston	MA	0	574	563	46.69	3.9	344	1
Worcester	MA	0	158	162	21.55	4.5	344	1
Springfield	MA	0	149	152	17.80	5.3	344	1
Baltimore	MD	0	753	787	19.01	6.3	197	1
Detroit	MI	0	1086	1203	12.24	10.8	234	2
Grand Rapids	MI	1	187	182	31.47	6.7	234	2
Warren	MI	0	150	161	1.34	6.6	234	2
Flint	MI	0	146	160	16.14	14.1	234	2
Lansing	MI	1	129	130	10.16	6.9	234	2
Sterling Hgts	MI	0	112	109	.36	5.4	234	2
Ann Arbor	MI	1	108	108	9.74	2.5	234	2
Livonia	MI	0	101	105	.00	4.0	234	2
Minneapolis	MN	0	357	371	32.84	4.0	205	2
St. Paul	MN	0	264	270	14.98	4.2	203	2
Kansas City	MO	0	441	448	23.17	6.0	80	1
St. Louis	MO	0	426	453	30.68	8.1	80	1
Springfield	MO	0	139	133	20.24	4.5	80	1
Independence	MO	1	113	112	6.99	4.7	80	1
Jackson	MS	0	208	203	6.00	5.3	0	0
Charlotte	NC	0	352	315	15.71	3.0	0	0
Raleigh	NC	0	180	150	15.13	2.7	0	0
Greensboro	NC	0	177	156	11.04	3.6	0	0
Winston-Salem	NC	0	148	132	20.66	4.3	0	0
Durham	NC	0	114	101	14.93	3.2	0	0
Lincoln	NB	0	185	172	6.39	2.5	240	2
Omaha	NB	0	349	314	10.48	3.7	0	0
Newark	NJ	0	316	329	14.61	8.5	210	2

Appendix A Continued

City	State	Suburb[a]	1986 Population	1980 Population	1989 Homeless Rate	1989 Unemployment Rate	1989 GA Payment	1989 GA Type[b]
Jersey City	NJ	0	219	224	9.11	7.2	210	2
Paterson	NJ	0	139	138	9.85	8.0	210	2
Elizabeth	NJ	0	107	106	4.69	6.5	210	2
Albuquerque	NM	0	367	332	12.84	4.9	156	1
Las Vegas	NV	0	192	165	26.21	5.2	269	1
Reno	NV	0	110	101	43.10	5.2	205	2
New York	NY	0	7263	7072	40.62	5.8	334	2
Buffalo	NY	0	325	358	14.53	8.2	288	2
Rochester	NY	0	236	242	16.02	5.8	376	2
Yonkers	NY	0	186	195	35.15	4.8	390	2
Syracuse	NY	0	161	170	15.86	4.8	322	2
Columbus	OH	0	566	565	15.46	5.0	142	2
Cleveland	OH	0	536	574	10.69	7.6	148	2
Cincinnati	OH	0	370	385	14.52	5.6	142	2
Toledo	OH	0	341	355	11.21	6.8	144	2
Akron	OH	0	222	237	11.26	6.8	161	2
Dayton	OH	0	179	194	27.83	7.7	125	2
Youngstown	OH	0	105	116	15.28	8.7	148	2
Oklahoma City	OK	0	446	404	19.37	4.8	0	0
Tulsa	OK	0	374	361	12.09	5.5	0	0
Portland	OR	0	388	368	26.37	5.8	251	1
Eugene	OR	0	105	106	46.67	4.6	251	1
Philadelphia	PA	0	1643	1688	32.26	5.1	205	1
Pittsburgh	PA	0	387	424	8.77	4.4	205	1

Erie	PA	0	115	119	20.82	5.7	205	1
Allentown	PA	0	104	104	17.25	5.1	205	1
Providence	RI	0	157	157	17.68	4.4	260	1
Memphis	TN	0	653	646	9.75	4.9	0	0
Nashville	TN	0	474	456	16.28	3.6	0	0
Knoxville	TN	0	173	175	18.65	5.2	0	0
Chattanooga	TN	0	162	170	16.40	5.1	0	0
Houston	TX	0	1729	1595	8.73	6.3	0	0
Dallas	TX	0	1004	905	18.28	6.4	0	0
San Antonio	TX	0	914	786	7.40	7.9	0	0
El Paso	TX	0	492	425	12.22	10.1	0	0
Austin	TX	0	467	346	5.89	5.6	0	0
Ft. Worth	TX	0	430	385	21.18	6.9	0	0
Corpus Christi	TX	0	264	232	13.38	8.0	0	0
Arlington	TX	1	250	160	1.96	4.6	0	0
Lubbock	TX	0	186	174	5.74	5.0	0	0
Garland	TX	1	177	139	.00	4.2	0	0
Amarillo	TX	0	166	149	14.89	5.5	0	0
Irving	TX	1	129	110	.00	4.4	0	0
Beaumont	TX	0	120	118	6.51	7.7	0	0
Pasadena	TX	1	118	113	.00	6.6	0	0
Laredo	TX	0	117	91	9.14	12.6	0	0
Abilene	TX	1	112	98	6.94	7.0	0	0
Plano	TX	0	111	72	.00	4.0	0	0
Waco	TX	0	105	101	7.60	6.4	0	0
Brownsville	TX	0	102	85	9.79	11.4	0	0
Odessa	TX	0	101	90	9.29	7.6	0	0
Salt Lake City	UT	0	158	163	33.77	4.8	224	2
Virginia Beach	VA	0	333	262	7.50	3.8	157	1

Appendix A Continued

City	State	Suburb[a]	1986 Population	1980 Population	1989 Homeless Rate	1989 Unemployment Rate	1989 GA Payment	1989 GA Type[b]
Norfolk	VA	0	275	267	12.08	5.3	132	1
Richmond	VA	0	218	219	14.65	5.0	157	1
Newport News	VA	0	162	145	8.29	5.1	122	1
Chesapeake	VA	0	134	114	.60	4.1	104	1
Hampton	VA	0	126	123	1.35	5.4	146	1
Portsmouth	VA	0	111	105	1.89	6.6	122	1
Alexandria	VA	0	108	103	23.84	2.3	157	1
Roanoke	VA	0	102	100	24.34	4.5	145	1
Seattle	WA	0	486	494	40.27	5.0	320	1
Spokane	WA	0	173	171	20.71	6.7	320	1
Tacoma	WA	0	159	159	29.07	6.9	320	1
Milwaukee	WI	0	605	636	8.71	5.0	195	2
Madison	WI	0	176	171	17.40	2.8	240	2

[a]0 = primary city; 1 = suburb
[b]0 = no GA; 1 = for disabled and families only; 2 = employables eligible.

244

Appendix B Descriptive Statistics for Variables in the Data Sets

	Primary Cities (N = 147)				Suburbs (N = 35)			
	Mean	S.D.	Minimum	Maximum	Mean	S.D.	Minimum	Maximum
Housing Variables								
% Owner-occupied, 1980	53.2	10.4	21.0	73.0	60.8	12.7	34.7	92.0
% 5+ Units, 1980	24.9	10.4	7.0	65.0	26.1	10.1	6.0	45.0
% Unit Change 1970–80	25.1	35.2	−15.0	335.0	64.8	69.9	0.0	294.0
% Unit Change 1980–86	10.5	10.8	0.0	51.0	24.1	24.0	0.0	78.0
1980 Rental Vacancy Rate	9.1	3.7	2.0	17.9	9.5	3.7	4.9	17.9
1988 Rental Vacancy Rate	7.6	2.7	2.3	20.8	6.7	4.9	2.1	22.3
% Units LT $150, 1980	17.2	7.5	1.3	37.3	5.0	3.7	0.9	16.1
1980 FMR 2-BR	$ 486	$ 107	$ 342	$ 848	$ 623	$ 151	$ 388	$ 848
1980 FMR 1-BR	$ 413	$ 91	$ 281	$ 716	$ 531	$ 127	$ 330	$ 716
1989 FMR 2-BR	$ 289	$ 46	$ 202	$ 475	$ 336	$ 32	$ 266	$ 427
1989 FMR 1-BR	$ 245	$ 39	$ 171	$ 404	$ 285	$ 28	$ 225	$ 362
1980 Public Housing Units (per 100 people)	1.0	0.8	0.0	4.0	0.1	0.3	0.0	1.2
1980 Section 8 Units (per 100 people)	0.4	0.4	0.0	2.8	0.3	0.3	0.0	1.4
1989 Public Housing Units (per 100 people)	1.1	0.8	0.0	4.3	0.5	1.8	0.0	10.6
1989 Section 8 Units (per 100 people)	0.8	0.6	0.1	5.3	0.5	0.4	0.0	1.5
VLI Renters/Units, 1985	112.5	71.2	12.6	267.7	184.4	88.3	57.6	267.7
Population Variables								
1980 City Population	366,000	688,000	82,000	7,072,000	126,000	51,000	72,000	361,000
1980 County Population	668,000	971,000	99,000	7,447,000	2,360,000	2,412,000	145,000	7,447,000
1986 City Population	382,000	710,000	100,000	7,263,000	146,000	60,850	101,000	396,000
1986 County Population	712,000	1,035,000	102,000	8,296,000	2,657,000	2,676,000	211,000	8,296,000
1970–80 % Pop. Change	8.2	29.8	−27.2	262.5	43.5	68.6	−12.0	300.0
1980–86 % Pop. Change	5.3	10.7	−11.0	47.0	16.3	17.4	−7.0	65.0
% Black, 1980	21.6	16.5	0.1	70.8	5.3	10.6	0.1	57.3
% Hispanic, 1980	9.6	15.1	0.0	93.0	12.8	13.1	1.0	74.0
% Female-headed, 1980	13.7	3.8	8.0	28.0	9.8	2.2	7.0	19.0
% One-person, 1980	27.6	5.1	13.0	41.0	21.7	6.8	10.0	40.0
Persons/Household, 1980	2.7	0.2	2.1	3.8	2.8	0.3	2.3	3.2

Appendix B Continued

	Primary Cities (N = 147)				Suburbs (N = 35)			
	Mean	S.D.	Minimum	Maximum	Mean	S.D.	Minimum	Maximum
% 65+, 1980	11.2	2.8	5.0	26.0	10.0	3.0	5.0	20.0
Poverty and Income Variables								
% in Poverty, 1980	15.8	5.1	7.0	35.0	8.2	4.2	2.0	21.0
P.C. Income, 1979	$ 7,100	$ 1,200	$ 3,900	$12,200	$ 8,500	$ 1,200	$ 5,800	$10,400
P.C. Income, 1985	$10,500	$ 1,900	$ 5,300	$19,800	$12,600	$ 2,000	$ 8,300	$16,800
Med. Renter Inc., 1980	$11,400	$ 2,800	$ 7,600	$17,400	$13,000	$ 1,500	$10,300	$16,800
Med. Renter Inc. 1989	$20,200	$ 3,400	$11,900	$33,800	$23,600	$ 3,500	$18,600	$31,500
Mean Hshld. Income, 1980	$20,950	$ 2,826	$15,046	$38,337	—	—	—	—
SD Hshld. Income, 1980	$16,585	$ 1,749	$14,124	$28,485	—	—	—	—
Inequality, 1980	.80	.05	.71	.98	—	—	—	—
% Blacks in 40%+ Poverty Areas, 1980	18.1	15.2	0.0	49.5	—	—	—	—
Cost of Living, 1985–86	104.7	10.3	91.2	152.3	—	—	—	—
Education and Employment Variables								
% 12+ Yrs Educ., 1980	66.2	9.6	39.0	91.0	76.8	8.6	50.0	90.0
% 16+ Yrs Educ., 1980	17.7	7.1	6.0	56.0	20.2	9.0	8.0	52.0
% Professional, 1980	16.4	3.8	8.5	39.3	16.6	5.3	6.9	37.9
% Craft, 1980	19.8	5.5	7.6	36.9	20.6	5.6	8.3	34.6
Unemployment Rate, 1980	7.1	2.8	2.0	19.0	5.1	1.8	2.0	10.0
Unemployment Rate, 1989	5.9	2.0	2.0	14.0	4.3	1.2	3.0	8.0
Employment-to-Population Ratio, 1980	57.0	5.6	41.0	70.0	64.4	6.1	50.0	75.0
Employment-to-Population Ratio, 1989	64.7	8.9	41.5	85.5	72.7	9.6	51.9	89.4
% of 1980 Employment that is:								
Construction	6.6	2.9	0.6	18.9	6.9	2.6	2.8	13.9
Manufacturing	24.3	10.2	3.6	49.1	26.0	8.5	13.2	47.5
TCU	6.8	2.7	0.1	16.3	5.1	1.9	1.0	11.1
Wholesale	7.2	2.2	1.6	12.1	6.5	1.7	2.6	9.8
Retail	20.7	4.3	12.2	37.5	20.6	4.4	10.6	28.6
FIRE	7.4	2.7	1.7	17.1	7.1	2.0	>0.05	9.5
Services	24.7	5.5	14.3	53.1	22.5	4.8	5.8	28.2

% of 1987 Employment that is:								
Construction	6.1	2.5	2.1	20.0	6.3	2.1	2.7	11.1
Manufacturing	19.1	8.2	2.6	42.3	22.1	7.8	10.3	41.8
TCU	6.5	2.3	2.6	15.1	5.5	2.1	1.4	10.4
Wholesale	7.0	1.9	2.3	14.2	7.1	1.7	3.2	9.7
Retail	21.9	4.3	12.2	36.1	21.1	3.1	15.7	27.0
FIRE	8.1	2.9	2.9	18.7	8.3	2.4	3.4	13.8
Services	30.0	5.3	20.0	59.7	27.4	4.4	7.7	31.0
Benefits Variables								
1980 AFDC max, 3 pers.	$ 289	$ 119	$ 96	$ 475	$ 354	$ 145	$ 116	$ 164
1989 AFDC max, 3 pers.	$ 376	$ 158	$ 118	$ 809	$ 490	$ 197	$ 184	$ 663
1980 SSI State Supp.	$ 32	$ 55	$ 0	$ 235	$ 90	$ 79	$ 0	$ 164
1989 SSI State Supp.	$ 51	$ 97	$ 0	$ 384	$ 123	$ 116	$ 0	$ 234
1980 GA, single person	$ 100	$ 91	$ 0	$ 297	$ 137	$ 97	$ 0	$ 240
1989 GA, single person	$ 141	$ 136	$ 0	$ 426	$ 201	$ 134	$ 0	$ 341
1979 UE-% Covered	37.6	11.4	24.0	80.0	37.2	10.3	24.0	53.0
1986 UE-% Covered	31.3	10.1	2.0	65.7	34.8	10.5	18.3	45.5
1981 P.C. MH $	$ 26	$ 12	9	$ 73	$ 26	$ 8	$ 11	$ 36
1987 P.C. MH $	$ 25	$ 12	9	$ 72	$ 21	$ 8	$ 12	$ 45
1984 P.C. Alch/Drug $	$ 7	6	2	$ 51	$ 9	3	2	11
1988 P.C. Alch/Drug $	8	8	0	53	8	3	2	10
Other Variables								
P.C. County Revs, FY86:								
Total	$1,964	$ 706	$ 687	$6,390	$2,158	$ 413	$1,420	$2,790
from Property Taxes	$ 463	$ 199	$ 79	$1,322	$ 466	$ 137	$ 120	$ 761
FY86 County Expend. for:								
Public Welfare	$ 81	$ 112	>0.05	$ 843	$ 101	$ 91	1	$ 230
Education	$ 592	$ 125	366	$1,155	$ 612	$ 81	468	$ 857
Housing/Cmty Devel.	$ 55	$ 43	1	$ 291	$ 58	$ 37	5	$ 166
Average January Temp.	36.8	12.5	11.0	73.0	47.9	11.4	20.0	66.0
Average July Temp.	76.8	5.6	58.0	92.0	75.9	8.5	62.0	92.0
1984 P.C. Alch Adms.	0.7	0.7	0.0	2.6	1.6	1.1	0.0	2.6
1988 P.C. Alch Adms.	0.8	0.7	0.0	2.5	1.6	1.0	0.1	2.5
1984 P.C. Drug Adms.	0.2	0.3	0.0	1.0	0.6	0.5	0.0	1.0
1988 P.C. Drug Adms.	0.4	0.4	0.0	1.5	0.9	0.7	0.1	1.5
1984-88 Incr. Alch Adms.	0.1	0.2	-0.6	0.8	0.0	0.1	-0.1	0.2
1988 P.C. Alch Adms.	0.8	0.7	0.0	2.5	1.6	1.0	0.1	2.5

Appendix C, Table 1 Zero-Order Correlations for Variables in the Analysis of 1989 Homelessness Rates

	VLI RENTERS/ UNITS	VACANCY RATE	PCT. POVERTY	PER CAP. INCOME	GA$	GA TYPE	PCT. ONE	PCT. FH	PCT. 12 YRS+
VLI R/U	—								
VAC.RATE-88	−.212	—							
%-POV-80	−.017	.055	—						
PCINC-85	−.007	−.137	−.679	—					
GA%-89	.640	−.546	−.072	.071	—				
GA TYPE-89	.594	−.523	−.070	.016	.834	—			
% ONE-80	.139	−.361	.040	.294	.283	.226	—		
% FH-80	.040	−.217	.783	−.520	.091	.106	.084	—	
% 12 + YRS-80	−.027	−.028	−.744	.705	.029	.009	.121	−.759	—
E/P-89	.018	.038	−.545	.552	−.040	−.039	.050	−.537	.573
UE-80	.136	.250	.520	−.600	−.080	.027	−.237	.425	−.552
% MFG-87	−.003	−.232	−.011	−.139	.142	.209	−.014	.195	−.224
% CNS-87	.030	.303	−.150	.047	−.192	−.190	−.424	−.192	.169
% RTL-87	−.124	.377	−.083	−.143	−.226	−.202	−.488	−.358	.188
% SRV-87	.167	−.104	.008	.227	.126	.018	.387	.011	.183
CHA # EMP	.156	.061	−.087	.191	.041	.023	.029	−.152	.173
CHA % EMP	.158	.197	−.184	.187	−.089	−.083	−.224	−.342	.351
COL	.476	−.382	−.012	.282	.512	.400	.177	.118	.037
HILOMFG-87	.066	−.237	.065	−.187	.160	.222	.021	.223	−.270
GROW80-86	.055	.433	−.185	.174	−.247	−.227	−.367	−.388	.300

An underlined coefficient is significant at p <.01, two-tailed.

Notes: HLRATE = 1989 Homelessness rate per 10,000 city population; VLI RENTERS/UNIT = degree of shortage of affordable housing; VACANCY RATE = 1988 rental vacancy rate; PCT. POVERTY = 1980 percent of individuals below poverty line; PERCAP INCOME = 1985 per capita income; GA $ = 1989 maximum benefit for single individual living independently; GATYPE = none/disabled only/also employables; PCT. ONE = percent of one person households in 1980; PCT. FH = percent of households that are female headed in 1980. PCT. 12 YRS+ = percent of population 25 or older who have 12 or more years of education in 1980;

EMPL/ POPULA	PCT UE	PCT. MFG	PCT. CNS	PCT. RTL	PCT. SRV	CHA# EMP	CHA% EMP	COST/ LIVING	HILO MFG7	GROW 80-86
—										
−.532	—									
−.108	.092	—								
.168	.073	−.380	—							
.011	.152	−.403	.397	—						
.058	−.194	−.529	−.132	−.121	—					
.329	−.147	−.157	.074	−.094	.076					
.659	−.211	−.293	.450	.332	.056	.028	—			
.021	−.077	−.122	−.071	−.321	.273	.253	−.006	—		
−.145	.145	−.818	−.339	−.340	−.398	−.215	−.281	−.062	—	
.255	−.093	−.285	.407	.274	.032	.289	.543	−.078	−.323	—

EMPL/POPULA = ratio of employed to population 16 and older, 1989; PCT. UE = percent unemployed, 1989; PCT. MFG, PCT. CNS, PCT. RTL, PCT. SRV = proportion of employment in county that is in the manufacturing/construction/retail/services sector; CHA# EMP, CHA% EMP = 1980–1989 change in people employed in the city, expressed as a number, and as a percent of 1980 employment; COST/LIVING = cost of living; HILOMFG-87 = dummy variable for splitting sample on percent manufacturing ($\leq$17% = 0, >17% = 1); GROW 80-86 = dummy variable for splitting sample on 1980–1986 city population growth (<3% = 0, $\geq$3% = 1).

Appendix C, Table 2 Zero-Order Correlations for Variables in the Analysis of 1981-1989 Change in Homelessness

	VLI RENTERS/ UNITS	VACANCY RATE	PCT. POVERTY	PER CAP. INCOME	GA$	GA TYPE	PCT. ONE	PCT. FH	PCT. 12 YRS+
VLI R/U	—								
VAC.RATE-80	−.211								
% POV-80	−.017	−.175							
PCINC-79	.063	.083	−.744						
GA$-81	.510	−.254	−.105	.121					
GA TYPE	.594	−.179	−.070	.058	.821				
% ONE-80	.139	−.055	.040	.271	.283	.226			
% FH-80	.040	−.192	.783	−.613	.030	.106	.084		
% 12+ YRS-80	−.028	.153	−.744	.768	.095	.001	.121	−.759	
E/P-80	−.038	.004	−.635	.678	−.077	−.128	−.021	−.631	.599
UE-80	.178	.071	.439	−.468	.246	.357	.036	.638	−.481
% MFG-80	.007	−.171	.062	−.250	.097	.218	−.009	.297	−.332
% CNS-80	−.178	.216	−.209	.222	−.229	−.299	−.352	−.402	.344
% RTL-80	−.023	.175	−.086	−.005	−.153	−.144	−.415	−.369	.241
% SRV-80	.208	.060	−.052	.231	.155	.082	.363	−.021	.215
COST/LIVING	.476	−.194	−.012	.297	.404	.400	.177	.118	.037
CITY POP-80	.101	−.126	.118	.047	.184	.134	.174	.136	−.089
# EMP-80	.106	−.123	.084	.090	.179	.125	.186	.098	−.054
POPCHG70-80	−.007	.308	−.256	.290	−.140	−.097	−.447	.384	.373
CHG VACRATE	−.055	−.429	.171	−.171	−.306	−.368	−.310	−.072	−.131
CHG PCINC	−.176	−.224	.048	−.024	−.182	−.101	.108	.144	−.039
CHG GA $	.276	−.015	.059	−.063	−.216	.066	.014	.119	−.122
CHG E/P	.056	−.002	−.195	.121	.038	.055	.085	−.188	.263
CHG UE	−.100	−.045	−.087	.143	−.330	−.408	−.246	−.409	.111
CHG MFG	.103	.073	−.250	.146	−.036	−.032	−.143	−.286	.380
CHG CNS	.009	−.070	.095	−.119	−.091	−.061	−.061	.130	−.074
CHG RTL	.021	.042	−.182	.045	−.088	.060	−.262	−.159	.207
CHG SRV	.050	.037	−.107	.101	−.130	−.110	−.266	−.160	−.195
CHG # EMP	.156	.011	−.087	.178	.048	.023	.029	−.152	.173
CHG % EMP	.158	.109	−.184	.122	−.116	−.083	−.224	−.342	.351
POP CHG 80-86	.150	.160	−.119	.133	−.200	−.187	−.406	−.360	.298
HILOMFG-87	.066	−.109	.065	−.208	.116	.222	.021	.223	−.270
GROW80-86	.055	.096	−.185	.179	−.236	−.227	−.367	−.388	.300

An underlined coefficient is significant at p < .01, two-tailed.

Notes: VLI R/U-85 = ratio of very-low-income renters to units they can afford, 1985; VAC RATE-80 = 1980 rental vacancy rate; % POV-80 = % individuals below poverty line, 1980; P.C. INC-79 = per capita income, 1979; GA $-81 = maximum GA payment for one person living independently, 1981; GA TYPE = none/disabled only/also employables; % ONE-80 = % one-person households, 1980; % FH-80 = % female-headed households, 1980; % 12+ YRS-80 = % with 12 + yrs. education, 1980; E/P-80 = employment/population ratio, 1980; UE-80 = unemployment rate, 1980; % MFG-80 = % of employment in manufacturing, 1980; % CNS-80 = % of employment in construction, 1980; % RTL-80 = % of employment in retail, 1980; % SRV-80 = % of employment in services, 1980; COST/LIVING = cost of living; CITY POP-80 = 1980 city population; # EMP-80 = number of people employed in the county, 1980; POP

EMPL/POPULA	PCT UE	PCT. MFG	PCT. CNS	PCT. RTL	PCT. SRV	COST/LIVING	CITY POP-80	# EMP-80	CITY POP	CHG VAC
−.739										
−.201	.378									
.248	−.340	−.523								
−.017	−.140	−.509	.440							
.029	−.095	−.543	−.051	.024						
.078	.034	−.078	−.082	−.224	.249					
−.062	−.077	.036	−.153	−.269	.145	.368				
−.005	.029	−.047	−.140	−.272	.146	.372	.996			
−.305	−.221	−.384	.486	.375	.015	.125	−.103	−.091		
.134	−.372	−.140	.239	.217	−.168	−.226	−.058	−.052	−.070	
−.024	−.185	.106	−.158	−.107	.027	.010	.001	−.002	−.193	.094
−.035	−.027	.142	−.151	−.076	.055	.227	−.086	−.083	−.004	−.076
.050	.042	−.101	.076	.228	.161	−.039	−.089	−.087	.068	−.066
.486	−.717	−.335	.345	.251	−.108	−.107	−.086	−.053	.225	.623
.154	−.236	−.302	.311	.341	.173	−.032	−.126	−.118	.346	.051
−.120	.017	−.018	−.232	.063	−.010	−.043	−.046	−.052	.055	.044
.044	−.189	−.158	.336	.255	.020	.012	−.147	−.144	.347	−.003
.124	−.183	−.167	.336	.368	−.100	.086	−.130	−.122	.376	.139
.151	−.151	−.183	.120	.025	.108	.253	.651	.680	.145	.050
.171	.240	−.397	.369	.514	.152	−.001	−.097	−.088	.462	.110
.314	−.378	−.489	.480	.493	.045	.048	−.053	−.037	.629	.229
−.147	.319	.773	−.444	−.373	−.393	−.062	−.082	−.092	−.249	.149
−.247	−.392	−.393	.451	.359	.024	−.078	−.065	−.041	.503	.340

CHG 70-80 = 1970-1980 change in city population; CHG VAC. RATE = 1980-1988 change in rental vacancy rate; CHG P.C. INC = 1979-1985 change in per capita income; CHG GA $ = 1981-1989 change in GA $; CHG E/P = 1980-1989 change in E/P; CHG UE = 1980-1989 change in UE; CHG MFG = 1980-1987 change in MFG as percent of 1980 MFG; CHG CNS = 1980-1987 change in CNS as percent of 1980 CNS; CHG RTL = 1980-1987 change in RTL as percent of 1980 RTL; CHG SRV = 1980-1987 change in SRV as percent of 1980 SRV; CHG # EMP = change in the number of people employed in the city between 1980 and 1989; CHG % EMP = change in employment between 1980 and 1989, as a percent of 1980 employment; POP CHG 80-86 = 1980-1986 change in city population; HILOMFG-87=dummy variable for splitting sample on percent manufacturing (<17% = 0, >17% = 1); GROW 80-86 = dummy variable for splitting sample on 1980-1986 city population growth (<3% = 0, ≥3% = 1).

Appendix C, Table 2 Continued

	CHG PCINC	CHG GA $	CHG E/P	CHG UE	CHG MFG	CHG CNS	CHG RTL	CHG SRV	CHG # EMP
CHG PCINC	—								
CHG GA $	.302								
CHG E/P	.264	−.023							
CHG UE	−.083	−.038	−.213						
CHG MFG	.276	.043	.485	.013					
CHG CNS	.178	.081	.172	.063	.272				
CHG RTL	.399	.204	.465	−.046	.693	.228			
CHG SRV	.399	.106	.484	.047	.681	.276	.789		
CHG # EMP	.063	−.011	.313	.057	.241	−.002	.191	.263	
CHG % EMP	.195	.046	.739	.110	.731	.186	.662	.736	.428
POP CHG 80–86	−.006	.071	−.019	.438	.528	.048	.441	.542	.284
HILOMFG–87	.022	.091	−.071	−.262	−.078	.069	−.176	−.150	−.215
GROW80–86	.016	−.033	.049	.395	.447	.125	.318	.375	.289

An underlined coefficient is significant at p < .01, two-tailed.
Note: VLI R/U-85 = ratio of very-low-income renters to units they can afford, 1985; VAC RATE-80 = 1980 rental vacancy rate; % POV-80 = % individuals below poverty line, 1980; P.C. INC-79 = per capita income, 1979; GA $-81 = maximum GA payment for one person living independently, 1981; GA TYPE = none/disabled only/also employables; % ONE-80 = % one-person households, 1980; % FH-80 = % female-headed households, 1980; % 12+ YRS-80 = % with 12 + yrs. education, 1980; E/P-80 = employment/population ratio, 1980; UE-80 = unemployment rate, 1980; % MFG-80 = % of employment in manufacturing, 1980; % CNS-80 = % of employment in construction, 1980; % RTL-80 = % of employment in retail, 1980; % SRV-80 = % of employment in services, 1980; COST/LIVING = cost of living; CITY POP-80 = 1980 city population; # EMP-80 = number of people employed in the county, 1980; POP

CHG %	POP CG	HILO	GROW
EMP	80-86	MFG-87	80-86

.650
-.281 -.343
.544   .759   -.323   —

CHG 70-80 = 1970-1980 change in city population; CHG VAC. RATE = 1980-1988 change in rental vacancy rate; CHG P.C. INC = 1979-1985 change in per capita income; CHG GA $ = 1981-1989 change in GA $; CHG E/P = 1980-1989 change in E/P; CHG UE = 1980-1989 change in UE; CHG MFG = 1980-1987 change in MFG as percent of 1980 MFG; CHG CNS = 1980-1987 change in CNS as percent of 1980 CNS; CHG RTL = 1980-1987 change in RTL as percent of 1980 RTL; CHG SRV = 1980-1987 change in SRV as percent of 1980 SRV; CHG # EMP = change in the number of people employed in the city between 1980 and 1989; CHG % EMP = change in employment between 1980 and 1989, as a percent of 1980 employment; POP CHG 80-86 = 1980-1986 change in city population; HILOMFG-87 = dummy variable for splitting sample on percent manufacturing (<17% = 0, >17% = 1); GROW 80-86 = dummy variable for splitting sample on 1980-1986 city population growth (<3% = 0, ≥3% = 1).

Index

Boldface numbers refer to tables and figures.